Religion and Medicine: The Moral Control of Nervous Disorders

Elwood Worcester, Samuel McComb, Isador H. Coriat, Moffat, Yard and Company

Copyright © BiblioLife, LLC

This book represents a historical reproduction of a work originally published before 1923 that is part of a unique project which provides opportunities for readers, educators and researchers by bringing hard-to-find original publications back into print at reasonable prices. Because this and other works are culturally important, we have made them available as part of our commitment to protecting, preserving and promoting the world's literature. These books are in the "public domain" and were digitized and made available in cooperation with libraries, archives, and open source initiatives around the world dedicated to this important mission.

We believe that when we undertake the difficult task of re-creating these works as attractive, readable and affordable books, we further the goal of sharing these works with a global audience, and preserving a vanishing wealth of human knowledge.

Many historical books were originally published in small fonts, which can make them very difficult to read. Accordingly, in order to improve the reading experience of these books, we have created "enlarged print" versions of our books. Because of font size variation in the original books, some of these may not technically qualify as "large print" books, as that term is generally defined; however, we believe these versions provide an overall improved reading experience for many.

Religion and Medicine

THE MORAL CONTROL OF NERVOUS DISORDERS

BY

ELWOOD WORCESTER, D.D., Ph.D.

SAMUEL McCOMB, M.A., D.D.
Emmanuel Church, Boston

ISADOR H. CORIAT, M.D.

NEW YORK
MOFFAT, YARD & COMPANY
1908

Copyright 1908, by
MOFFAT, YARD & COMPAN
NEW YORK

CONTENTS

CHAPTER		PAGE
	Foreword	vii
I.	Introduction	1
II.	The Subconscious Mind	14
III.	Suggestion	43
IV.	Auto-Suggestion	93
V.	The Functional Neuroses	108
VI.	The Causes of Nervousness (Heredity)	125
VII.	The Causes of Nervousness (Environment)	133
VIII.	The Nervous System in Health and Disease	179
IX.	The Diseases of the Subconscious	199
X.	The Nature of Hypnotism	218
XI.	The Therapeutic Value of Hypnotism	234
XII.	Psychic and Motor Re-education	247
XIII.	The General Principles of Psychotherapy	260
XIV.	Fear and Worry	266
XV.	Abnormal Fears	281
XVI.	Faith and its Therapeutic Power	289
XVII.	Prayer and its Therapeutic Value	302
XVIII.	Suicide and its Prevention	320
XIX.	The Healing Wonders of Christ	338
XX.	The Outlook of the Church	369
Appendix I.	Some Physical Disorders having Mental Origin. By J. Warren Achorn, M.D.	389
Appendix II.	Experiments in Auto-Suggestion	412
Index		417

FOREWORD

THIS book is the joint work of three friends, each of whom is responsible for his own contribution.

Introduction and Chapters II, III, V, VI, VII, XX, are written by Dr. Worcester.

Chapters IV, XIV, XV, XVI, XVIII, are written by Dr. McComb.

Chapters VIII, IX, X, XI, XII, XIII, are written by Dr. Coriat.

Chapters XVII and XIX are written jointly by Dr. Worcester and Dr. McComb.

RELIGION AND MEDICINE

CHAPTER I

INTRODUCTION

THE object of this book is to describe in plain terms the work in behalf of nervous sufferers which has been undertaken in Emmanuel Church, Boston. So much has been written on the subject of our movement, in many instances by persons slightly acquainted with it, that we feel it due to the public and to ourselves to state what we are doing and to discuss the religious and scientific principles on which we are building. If a temporary digression may be pardoned, our Class for the Treatment of Nervous Disorders is not the first effort we have made for the relief of the sick. Nearly three years ago the Emmanuel Church Tuberculosis Class began its beneficent mission under the medical direction of Dr. Joseph H. Pratt. The question we attempted to answer in founding this class was, can the poorest consumptives be cured in the slums of a great city without removing them from their homes? The treatment consisted of the approved modern method of combating consumption, *plus* discipline, friendship, encouragement, and hope, in short, a combination of physical and moral elements, and we are satisfied that the personality of Dr. Pratt is largely responsible for the fact that while our work has been carried on under the most unfavorable environment, our records will bear comparison with those of the best sanatoria.

The success of our Tuberculosis Class, which is now generally recognized and which has led to the formation of many similar classes, convinced us that the Church has an important mission to discharge to the sick, and that the physician and the clergyman can work together to the benefit of the community. Accordingly, in the autumn of 1906 we determined to begin a similar work among the nervously and morally diseased. As a preliminary step we consulted several of the leading neurologists of New England to ascertain, first, whether such a project, undertaken with proper safeguards, would meet with their approval, and secondly, whether they would be willing to co-operate with us in it. A favorable response being given to these questions, our work began on a very stormy evening in November, when Dr. James J. Putnam presided at the preliminary meeting and gave the first address. Thus from the beginning our work has been closely associated with very able physicians and we have done nothing without their co-operation and advice. Had this assistance been withheld, we should not have proceeded further.

As we are attempting to establish no new dogma, and as our motives are entirely disinterested, our single desire is to give each patient the best opportunity of life and health which our means allow. We believe in the power of the mind over the body, and we believe also in medicine, in good habits, and in a wholesome, well-regulated life. In the treatment of functional nervous disorders we make free use of moral and psychical agencies, but we do not believe in overtaxing these valuable aids by expecting the mind to attain results which can be effected more

INTRODUCTION

easily through physical instrumentalities. Accordingly we have gladly availed ourselves of the services of the skilled medical and surgical specialists who have offered to co-operate with us, and we believe that our freedom in this respect and the combination of good psychical and physical methods have had much to do with our success. If a bad headache is caused by eye-strain, or a generally enfeebled condition is obviously the result of a digestive disturbance, a pair of glasses or a belt is frequently far more effective than suggestion. Most religious workers in this field have made the mistake of supposing that God can cure in only one way and that the employment of physical means indicates a lack of faith. This is absurd. God cures by many means. He uses the sunlight, healing and nourishing substances, water and air. The knitting of a broken bone, or the furrowing out of new blood courses in a diseased limb, is just as truly His work as the restoration of a wounded spirit. There is no peculiar piety involved in the use of suggestion. We have seen the consumptive nursed back to life, by rest, fresh air, abundant food and kindness, and we have seen more spectacular recovery from other diseases through confident expectation and the spoken word, but we have never felt that the one was necessarily more the act of God than the other. The fact remains that consumption can be cured in no other way, and that those who take a different view of the subject do not cure consumptives; they kill them by robbing them of their last chance of life; the same is true of other diseases.

For this reason we have confined our practice to that large group of maladies which are known to-day as functional nervous disorders. Although a sound psychical and moral method is a valuable adjunct in every branch of medicine, yet viewed as an independent remedial agent the legitimate sphere of psychotherapy is strictly limited. It is in the field of the functional neuroses that all its real victories have been won. Here again our conception of our mission differs decidedly from that of our predecessors. In answer to their taunt: "If you believe in God's power to cure disease, how dare you place any limit to that power?" we are content to reply: "We believe God has power to cure all disease, but we do not believe God cures all disease by the same means. At all events an authentic instance of recovery from organic disease through psychical means is what we are waiting for. While we do not believe that any man knows all that is to be known on this subject, or that we are in a position to affirm dogmatically what the mind can or cannot accomplish, yet we are surely safe in accepting as to this the overwhelming weight of scientific opinion, and in confining our practice to a field in which it is known to be efficacious. By so doing we avoid the one valid objection which has ever been urged against psychotherapeutics, namely, its employment in diseases which obviously require physical interference, with the result that many patients have died through sheer neglect.

Apart from this, it is in the domain of functional nervous disorders that such service as we are able to render is most needed, not merely because this branch of medicine is least developed in America and adequate treatment is difficult to obtain, especially by the poor, but because disorders of this nature are peculiarly associated with the moral life. An attack of typhoid fever may spring from no moral cause and it may have no perceptible influence upon character, but neurasthenia, hysteria, psychasthenia, hypochondria, alcoholism, etc., are affections of the personality. They spring from moral causes and they produce moral effects. In this domain the beneficent action of drugs and medicines is extremely limited, and the personality of the physician is everything. Other agencies such as electricity, baths, etc., probably owe much of their value to their suggestional effect, and so long as the training of our physicians is strictly material, such patients will continue to be their despair, for the reason that moral maladies require moral treatment.

Another important characteristic of our work is the pains taken in the diagnosis of disease and in the preservation of records, without which no treatment can be regarded as scientific or even safe. In nervous disorders this is the more necessary because so-called nervous affections are not infrequently indications or precursors of serious organic disease, failure to discover which is not merely loss of time and effort, it is frequently a gross wrong to the patient, and the exposure of oneself to merited criticism and contempt. We believe with Dr. Barker that the modern refinements of diagnosis should be exhausted in the study of all doubtful cases before the treatment is begun, and thanks to our facility of consultation we leave no stone unturned in this respect, and we admit no patient to the class until we are assured on good medical authority that he or she is likely to be benefited by the treatment. Our system of record is that of the

Massachusetts General Hospital supplemented by notes on the moral and spiritual advice given and on the effect of this advice. In this way we are collecting a mass of valuable material which will be used in a subsequent work.

We have dwelt on the scientific side of our work partly with the purpose of recommending it to honorable physicians, with whom we are always ready to co-operate, and partly to differentiate it as sharply as possible from cults and methods which we regard as unsound and irrational. The Christian character of our undertaking is to our mind guaranteed chiefly by the fact that it is absolutely disinterested. Our single desire is to help those it is given us to help. Our class is supported by the voluntary offerings received at its meetings, but that is all. We neither ask nor accept any reward for our services. As to the propriety of the Church engaging in such work, we venture to say that the time is come when the Church must enter more deeply into the personal lives of the people and make a freer use of the means modern science and the Gospel of Christ place at her disposal if she is to continue even to hold her own. It is evident that people to-day desire spiritual help and sustenance which they are not receiving, but which the Church as the representative of Christ is able to give them. If the Church, closing her eyes to the example of her Lord and deaf to His commands, withholds from the people the gifts committed to her by Jesus, she must expect to find herself forsaken for strange cults which with all their absurdities aim at supplying present strength for present needs. The teachings of modern psychology and physiology as to the essential unity of human nature and the mutual relations of mind and body have sunk so deep into the popular conscience that the Church can no longer address men as disembodied spirits, and no scheme of salvation causes the heart to beat with hope which does not include the whole man and which does not begin now. What will be the outcome of this movement no man can say. We feel that we have done something in attempting to separate truth from error and in applying that truth with good result to the lives of several thousand persons. What we have done, other men and other churches can do as well or better; and it is with the earnest hope that other qualified persons may be induced to help us and to relieve us of the pressure of patients from distant cities that we issue this tentative and imperfect statement.

We are living to-day in the midst of a great religious movement, which is the more interesting because it is spontaneous. Here and there one catches echoes of it from the pulpits of orthodox churches, but for the most part it has arisen outside the churches. Wherever one goes one finds certain groups of persons talking, reading, thinking of the spiritual life. Much of this talk and of this literature may strike the intelligent critic as bizarre and fantastic, but at all events it is idealistic and optimistic. Thousands of men and women to-day are seriously seeking for a better life, and many believe that they have found it. They have a feeling that there is more in religion than they have recognized or received in the past. There is a marked tendency to dispense with the tedious processes of criticism and dogma and to return to the Christ of the Gospels and to accept His words in a more literal sense. One marked characteristic of this movement is a renewed belief in prayer; another most curious aspect of it is the confident expectation that religious and spiritual states can affect health and that physical blessings will follow spiritual exercises. In short we see a decided reaction from the scientific materialism and the rational criticism in which we have grown up. If the nineteenth century was materialistic and critical, the first half of the twentieth century promises to be mystical and spiritual. Already we are conscious of a general revolt in the name of the soul. We feel the stirrings of a cold morning breeze, harbinger of a new day. Far-sighted writers like Renan and Paulsen anticipated this change. They realized that there is nothing in the mere exploration of Nature in which the human spirit can find its permanent rest. They knew too well the ever-refining processes of criticism to believe that in themselves they can afford the materials for a popular religion. Accordingly they spoke often of "the religion of the future," and Renan with his usual intuition declared that if it were already in our midst few of us would know it.

This prediction has proved true. The new religious movement has spoken a language so foreign to cultivated ears, its interpretation of the Bible is so false, it is so obviously committed to errors, illusions, and aberrations of every sort, that the intelligent have been disposed to shrug their shoulders in contempt and to ignore it. And yet they have not been able to ignore it altogether. Every once in awhile this curious superstition proves its existence with unexpected power. We see a hard-headed business man totally devoid of religious sentiment undergo a new kind of conversion which leaves him as devout and ardent as a Christian of the first century. An ailing wife or daughter whom no physician has been able to help, through some mysterious means is restored to health and happiness. The victim of an enslaving habit, apparently with very little effort, and without physical means, sufferings, or relapse, finds himself free. We enter a home where the new belief reigns and we find there a peace to which we are strangers.

Let us then remember Darwin's advice and distinguish sharply between facts and the hypotheses which are put forward to account for facts. The humblest attested fact remains, and may cause us to reconstruct our views of the universe, while it is the fate of all dogmas to fail and to be rejected one after another. What if the present movement makes its appearance largely under the form of error and illusion? It is in this form that most new thoughts and all our older sciences have presented themselves in this world. The important thing is that there is life in this thought, it is able to create faith. It is pressing onward by its own power. It is not a doctrine of the schools, it is one of those obscure movements of the human spirit which fashion their own message and means of communication and which grow by their own vitality. And yet sometimes when a seething chemical compound is over the fire the infusion of a few drops of the right fluid at the right time will cause a precipitation, and will clarify the whole mass. It is thus we venture to regard the position we have taken at Emmanuel Church. We have approached this subject with earnest faith, but with faith tempered by sobriety of thought and by respect for science truly so called. Religious movements can be guided only by believers. As Renan says rather too flippantly, they are like women who can be induced to do anything if one takes them the right way, but they yield nothing to force.

The doctrines of Christian Science, for example, have been denounced, ridiculed, exploited times without number, apparently with as much effect as throwing pebbles at the sea checks the rising of the tide. Preachers, physicians, editors of powerful journals, philosophers, humorists, unite in pouring contempt upon this despicable superstition, very much as Juvenal, Tacitus, and Celsus mocked at nascent Christianity, but in spite of them it lives. While most other religious bodies are declining or barely holding their own, it grows by leaps and bounds. All over this country solid and enduring temples are reared by grateful hands and consecrated to the ideal and name of Mrs. Eddy. And this strange phenomenon has occurred in the full light of day, at the end of the nineteenth and at the beginning of the twentieth century, and these extraordinary doctrines have propagated themselves not in obscure corners of the earth, among an illiterate and a fanatical populace, but in the chief centers of American civilization. Such facts may well cause the philosophical student of religion to reflect. The more absurd the Christian Science dogma is made to appear, the more difficult it becomes to account for men's faith in it. Unless we are prepared to confess ourselves utterly at a loss to explain this infatuation, we must be able to pass beneath the vulgar and repulsive exterior of Christian Science and to find a truth in it, a gift for men, a spiritual power answering to men's needs which the churches at present do not possess. Nor is this difficult to those who know that the metaphysical basis of a religion expressed by its dogmas is the last part to be accepted and embraced by its people. The metaphysical basis of Buddhism is complete negation, a denial of God, of prayer, of the soul, of immortality, in short, of all the elements which elsewhere constitute religion. That did not stand in the way of the adoring multitudes who found new life in the seductive sweetness of Sakyamuni's personality. The metaphysical basis of Christian Science is too crude, too contradictory to be accepted by the normal reason. What of that? It is not by metaphysical consistency that men live. With all its obscurity we find in the Sacred Book of Christian Science great truths — freedom from the fetters of sense and passion, the power of the soul over the body, victory of the mind over its tyrants fear and anger, the presence of God manifested with power; above all, the promise of an immense immediate good as the result of faith. These are the magnets to which the souls of men have sprung as waiting particles of steel. In spite of John Stuart Mill, the most powerful motive of religion will ever be the Practical Motive, and by the Practical Motive we mean believing because it is good and useful to believe, believing what is good and useful to believe.[1] We are never at a loss to find reasons for what we wish to believe. No one ever yet accepted a form of religious faith which promised to do him nothing but harm. The more good any particular form of religion accomplishes, the more men will believe in it, and the less good any particular church

---

[1] See Theodor Fechner's *Drei Motive und Gründe des Glaubens*, Leipzig, 1863.

or religious institution does, the less the faith it is able to inspire. Here lies the source of the power of Christian Science. It does unquestionably bestow certain great benefits on believers: it makes men happy, it improves tempers, it frequently weans men from evil habits, it can reduce or remove pain, it cures certain types of disease and it gives courage to endure these which it cannot heal. It concerns itself with the present and its effects are direct, practical, immediate. Therein lies its great superiority to preaching that is vague and impractical and which deals largely with a distant future. If we should promise every worshiper in Emmanuel Church next Sunday the gift of a ten-dollar gold piece, no matter what the character of the preaching there would be no vacant pews. Why? Because the congregation would be sure of obtaining a coin which passes current here and now — something which represents to them an immediate personal good. In precisely the same way, were we to say to certain persons, if you will believe and do thus and so you will receive a marked benefit in five days or five weeks, you will sleep well, you will be free from pain, you will escape from your vices, you will possess a peace which the world cannot take from you, and our prediction in every instance proved true, those persons would have a personal faith in us and in our ministry which were not easily shaken. We have heard many cultivated and intelligent persons discuss Christian Science. They begin by abusing it, but they end by admitting there is something in it, something it is evident which they do not understand.

As a matter of fact we have approached this subject from a totally different point of view. Our movement

INTRODUCTION

bears no relation to Christian Science, either by way of protest or of imitation, but it would be what it is had the latter never existed. We have taken our stand fairly and squarely on the religion of Christ as that religion is revealed in the New Testament and as it is interpreted by modern scholarship, and we have combined with this the power of genuine science. This we consider a good foundation — the best of all foundations.

CHAPTER II

THE SUBCONSCIOUS MIND

ALONGSIDE of the religious movement we have alluded to, and no doubt profoundly influencing it, there has occurred one of the most interesting developments of psychology which have taken place in the history of that ancient science. This has consisted in the recognition of powers in man beyond those usually employed in his normal consciousness. To this obscure domain of the soul a great variety of names unfortunately has been given — the unconscious mind, the subconscious, the subliminal, the subjective, etc. While it would be a mistake to affirm that the existence of powers so designated is universally admitted by psychologists, yet it is certain that there is a growing disposition in this direction. Even those writers who formally deny the principle are not able to dispense with it in their explanation of what goes on in the human mind. We believe with Professor James that the subconscious powers of the mind really exist and that the recognition of them forms the most important advance which psychology has made since the days of Fechner and Weber.[1] For this discovery suddenly transformed psy-

[1] While accepting the conception of subconscious elements in mind we fully recognize the fact that the existence of such powers is not directly demonstrable. In the following chapters this view is developed merely as a working hypothesis for which evidence is offered, but it has no direct

chology from a purely theoretical science, a preoccupation of the learned, into a powerful instrument for the improvement of human life. Henceforth this particular child of philosophy can no longer be termed a sterile virgin. I remember a lecture on psychology delivered by Professor James a good many years ago which Dr. James began with some such words as these: "Perhaps you will ask me what are the practical benefits conferred on the world by this interesting science. So far as I am able to discern, absolutely none." To-day, if he so willed, Professor James might easily rank with the greatest neurologists in the treatment of a large group of diseases, and this solely by virtue of his consummate ability as a physiological psychologist. Spinoza says that every advance toward perfection gives us happiness, and it is safe to say that the buoyancy which characterizes contemporary thought, the hopeful outlook amid all dangers that threaten us, the sense of the added cubit to man's stature, are due largely to the recognition of powers for good within his soul of which he was not formerly aware.

1. As to the nature of these powers, opinion ranges from Janet who, true to the traditions of his school, sees in subconscious activity only a pathological phenomenon, the concomitant of hysteria, to those who discern in it the proof of a higher nature, the spiritual man, made in the image of God. While the scope of this work precludes theoretical discussion of the subject, we will here enumerate

---

bearing upon our practice and it is accepted only in the modified form of "dissociation of consciousness" by Dr. Coriat. An element in our inner life which can produce mental effects without consciousness may well be named subconscious or unconscious.

some of the evidences of unconscious mental action, as to which most unprejudiced observers agree. In animals and insects there has long been recognized a mind unlike our own in that it is not individual nor progressive, but which is sufficient for the purposes of their wonderful lives. In spite of his exaggeration and his willingness to accept the marvelous, no one has discussed this subject with more ability than Edouard Von Hartmann.[1] Von Hartmann defined instinct as a purposive action of whose purpose the actor is unconscious. A trout elects to lie in a dark, shady pool and he quickly takes on somber hues in harmony with his environment. He passes out onto the sunny riffles and he becomes bright again. I have seen old fishermen who could tell the very pools and rapids from which a string of bass had been taken by the colors of the fish. The physiological means by which such changes are effected pass our comprehension and the greatest physiologist can give no account of them except that they are effected through the eye, as blind fishes are incapable of such transformations. How much less can the fish know the processes by which such pigments are deposited on his scales as will render him least visible to his enemies or his prey, or the necessity of his so painting himself. So in man a thousand purposive activities go on as to which we are in total ignorance, and to bring these within the sphere of our consciousness is only to derange them. The very regularity, invariableness, and certainty of these processes differentiate them sharply from the uncertain and intermittent character of our conscious acts. We go to sleep and all our bodily functions

[1] *The Philosophy of the Unconscious.*

go on as usual. Our heart continues to beat, our lungs are rhythmically expanded and contracted, all the digestive processes go on. Blood is supplied to every part of the system in exact proportion to each part's present need. Even in the deeper narcotic sleep of ether there is no failure, no cessation of each part to do its work. Grant that each organ mechanically responds to its stimulus, what power co-ordinates and controls them all through the long rhythms of sleeping and waking, and from the tropics to the poles maintains our inward temperature at the exact degree necessary to our health?

I desire to stretch out my arm and I have no difficulty in doing so. But do I know the complicated mechanism of nerves and muscles and tendons and bones which must be set in motion to perform this act? And even if as an anatomist I do know all this, have I any knowledge of where the lever of this machine lies or how to grasp it, or does such knowledge make my acts a whit better than those of a man who has never studied anatomy? On the contrary, is it not true that our more refined and difficult acts, such as balancing oneself on a bicycle, playing golf or the violin, are never perfect until they have passed the state of conscious effort and have become as we say automatic, *i.e.*, under the control of the subconscious mind?

2. Again let us consider the power of our organism to maintain its own equilibrium, and to recover its equilibrium when attacked by disease or injury. The animal organism may be called a machine, but a machine which can regulate its own action, can repair its own waste and injuries, and substitute one part for another which has become defective, is controlled by a different principle

from that which regulates the machines made by men's hands. However physiologists may ridicule the old so-called Vis medicatrix naturæ, and to-day one hears this spoken of with respect, it will ever remain the real means by which the sick recover health. "We amuse our patients," said one modest physician, "while nature cures them." Ambroise Paré wrote on the wall of his hospital: "I dressed the wound and God healed it."[1] It has been frequently stated by physicians that of all sick persons probably two-thirds would recover of their own accord without any medical assistance. Rural practitioners, especially in more sparsely settled regions, are in a position to observe this fact. A physician who formerly practised in a lonely hill country in New England once told me that in his early life he was constantly surprised to discover that his patients recovered from severe forms of disease such as diphtheria, pneumonia, and typhoid fever without any assistance from him. When a member of the family was taken ill a red flag was displayed. If he happened to see it while making his rounds, well. If not, the patient usually recovered anyway. I have observed the same in Newfoundland and Labrador. It is not merely that diseases have their term, are self-limited, but that the human body has means at its disposal to check and expel them, and since we have come to regard many forms of disease as due to the invasion of pathogenic microbes we no longer think of a malign principle in the body itself. The mere functioning of a diseased organ has a tendency to restore that organ to health.

This Vis medicatrix, to give a name to our ignorance,

[1] Quoted by Schofield. *Force of Mind*, p. 176.

must work through the instrumentality of the nervous system, since no other part of our organism possesses a mechanism sufficiently complex and universal, but these processes never emerge into consciousness, but must be regarded as due to the action of the subconscious mind. In fact as we descend in the scale of conscious life we find the recuperative, reparative energy intensifying, and acting apparently with greater purposive freedom. If a worm be cut in two the amputated part with all its organs will be replaced. In reptiles the loss of a leg or a tail is quickly made good by the growth of a new member. Even in man, in whom the scope of the subconscious mind is less, we see a thousand means employed to heal the injury or to check and eliminate the encroachments of the enemy. "Lymph is poured around the broken bone, abscesses are sealed up with an impenetrable wall; new vascular channels are dug in a diseased limb, gouty poisons are extracted in the convoluted kidney tubes."[1] Above all, in the marshaling and directing of the so-called phagocytes or white corpuscles of the blood, and in the self-production of antitoxic substances, we see a powerful effort on the part of nature to resist the invading armies of disease germs, and to secure immunity from the same in the future. Even pain and the painful symptoms of sickness are benevolent warnings which sharply remind us of our condition and compel the repose which we require, or which deter us from admitting into our system substances which would be injurious to us. These statements are made not in the interest of a theodicy, but simply as physiologic facts. They not only point toward

[1] Schofield, *Unconscious Therapeutics*, p. 57.

the existence of a subconscious mind, but they indicate how great a part that mind plays in the curing of every form of disease. Anything which weakens or depresses our subsconcious mind exposes us to disease by rendering us less able to resist its encroachments. And on the other hand we possess such allies and resources within ourselves that apart from surgical interference the physician's chief function is to awaken in his patient the will to live and to employ every element of resistance which the system itself affords. Sir William Gull goes so far as to say, "What shall doctors do? Rest and be still. The workman that made the machine can repair it."[1]

As an example of this let me relate the following. Not long ago a serious abdominal operation was performed on a lady by an eminent surgeon in the presence of other surgeons of national reputation. Naturally every means to avoid sepsis was employed which their art suggested. In spite of their precautions the wound became badly infected and a culture revealed the presence of no fewer than three species of pathogenic microbes. The patient's temperature rose to a dangerous degree and her condition became very serious. As a last resort the opsonic treatment was employed which reduced the sepsis and the temperature. The patient, however, did not rally and her life was despaired of, one unfavorable symptom being that from the beginning she had evinced no desire to live. At length, one day, she turned to the gentleman who had performed the operation and said to him: "Doctor, are you prepared to be the physician of the soul as well as of the body?" and being assured as to this, she relieved her

[1] Quoted by Schofield, *op. cit.*, p. 65.

mind of a burden which had oppressed her, with the result that from that very day she began to mend and in a short time she was completely restored to health.

3. *Memory.* If we limit our conception of the soul to its conscious activities after the manner of the older psychologists, it is difficult to see what part is played by those latent memories which form more than ninety-nine hundredths of our soul's treasures. What becomes of these possessions when for years at a time they no longer emerge into consciousness? Do they cease to exist? and are they created anew in the old guise and wearing the old garments when we happen to think of them? Writers who deny the subconscious mind imagine that they avoid this difficulty by saying that such memories exist potentially, that they are latent, etc., but this explains nothing.[1] The plain truth is that not the millionth part of the mental possessions of an educated man exists in his consciousness at any one time. If you were to take a pen and a block of paper and sit down with the determination of writing without external assistance all that you really know or

---

[1] Professor Pierce of Smith College, in his interesting paper entitled "*An Appeal from the Prevailing Doctrines of a Detached Subconsciousness*" (1906), seems to think that the recurrence of our latent memories in consciousness can be accounted for by the modification of brain and nerve substance effected by the original experience or by a series of experiences. No doubt all our memories have an organic basis, or rather it is certain that every psychical event is attended by a corresponding physical event. But to suppose that these traces in the brain or other modifications of brain substance are able under stimulation to transform themselves into thoughts is an error which after Tyndall and John Fiske ought not to be revived and which one is surprised to encounter in so refined a thinker. It is an example of the difficulty of maintaining a consistent denial of subconscious mental activity.

can remember you would be surprised to see how soon you would reach the end of your resources. The experience and laborious acquisitions of years can be expressed on a few sheets of paper, just as the achievements of a century are recorded in a few pages of an encyclopedia. As a matter of fact the little lamp of consciousness illumines only a tiny fraction of the soul's domain. Here and there a few points are illumined while all around the great dewy fields are wrapt in the darkness of night. This or that chamber of the soul's many mansions is lighted, then again it is wrapt in the darkness of night. So man lives in this world largely a stranger to himself. Not only do we possess and by means of the necessary associations can we recall to consciousness innumerable experiences which once claimed our attention, but apart from these there is an even vaster stream of experience consisting of fleeting impressions, trivial circumstances, vanished faces which made scarce an impression on us which are also preserved. The delirium of fever, a familiar perfume, the peculiar lucidity which comes to the drowning, a dream, returning to the scenes of childhood, etc., sometimes overwhelm us with a flood of memories of events so unimportant that they made scarce an impression on us when they occurred. Coleridge's account of the serving maid who in delirium fluently spoke the Rabbinical Hebrew which years before in the house of a learned pastor had fallen upon her unheeding ear, is the classical example of this. During all these years these memories have lurked in the obscure depths of our subconscious mind. It is probable that we forget nothing. Nor is the physical basis of our memories confined to the brain. Wherever there is nerve substance to be modified there is memory. On this rest all the marvelous aptitudes of our nervous system. I once took a terrible walk with an Indian through seven miles of pathless forest in Newfoundland on a night so dark that we had to hold our hands before our faces to avoid injury. The Indian walked steadily on, now skirting a deep ravine, now turning up the mountain to avoid an invisible swamp, now dodging a windfall, never baffled, never at a loss, and never stopping to consult the compass. At the end of several hours he brought me out of the woods within a hundred feet of the point at which we had entered them. I asked him how he did it and he replied, "Dunno, dunno, when I walk like dat my feet tink." In other words the impression on his moccasined feet conveyed by the texture and configuration of the ground over which he had passed but once awoke memories which enabled him to reconstruct in the dark an accurate image of the whole region. The mere facts of memory are sufficient to justify the conception of the subconscious mind.

We have all had the experience of attempting to recall a forgotten word or name. While we are consciously searching for it, it obstinately escapes us. We give up the search and think of something else and in a little while the desired name springs into consciousness. A few weeks ago I was spending Sunday in a town where a member of our class was sojourning in a large sanitarium. On going to bed on Saturday night it occurred to me that I had promised to pay this gentleman a visit. His name, however, which was a peculiar one, had wholly escaped me. I lay awake for an hour trying to recover it by placing the patient's face and physical appearance before me. In vain, it would not come. The next morning, however, while I was preaching and very much engrossed with my sermon, I suddenly heard almost as if a voice had uttered them the words "Mr. Blank." A medical friend was treating a nervous patient who in her disturbed mental condition constantly repeated snatches of poetry. Wishing to test the accuracy of her memory the physician committed her quotations to writing and later endeavored to verify them. After a good deal of trouble he succeeded with all but one quotation, as to whose source he could form no conjecture. Completely baffled he gave up the attempt until one morning, when in a fit of abstraction over another problem, he felt himself impelled to walk to his bookcase and take down a volume which at the time he did not recognize. He turned over the pages and his eye soon fell upon the desired lines, which were unimportant. It was a volume of Longfellow with which he was familiar, though the lines in question had made no impression upon him.

The most striking example of subconscious memory occurs in the so-called state of dissociation. A person is profoundly hypnotized and certain suggestions are made to him. Advice is given to him or he is told to perform certain acts when he awakens, and also that he will possess no recollection of the suggestion. He performs the acts, but does not know why he is moved to do so, nor if the hypnosis has been complete can he remember the advice given to him which nevertheless produces its effect. The next time he is hypnotized, however, he can repeat in the minutest detail the suggestions given to him in a former hypnosis. Thus it appears that conscious and subconscious memories are distinct and may exist independently of each other.

This is more plainly exhibited in dissociations which are more or less permanent. This will be discussed later. Dr. Morton Prince's "Dissociation of a Personality" has been so extensively read that it is only necessary to refer to it. Forel and Boris Sidis have recorded other similar examples. In the case of Miss Beauchamp the dissociation was so profound as to produce a decided change of personality, or rather a series of personalities some of which were totally ignorant of the others, while some shared the others' consciousness and memories.

4. I shall now allude to certain processes of the conscious mind in which the subconscious plays an interesting part. Few persons who think and who create are able to work constantly for the reason that they cannot depend upon their minds to furnish them with the necessary ideas. Even Balzac had his periods of production and of intense creative activity when he labored like a miner in the bowels of the earth, and his periods of exhaustion and stagnation. Goethe's "Faust" owes its supreme excellence doubtless to the fact that it was not written at one time: it represents the best thoughts, the noblest inspirations of Goethe's mature life. But most great poems are very unequal. They have their great passages, as has Marlowe's Faustus, in which the poet's soul reveals itself with all its power, and they have many dull lines which would never make their fortune. Even we who are no geniuses have similar experiences in our little efforts. If we sit down to write in cold blood without inspiration or reflection the

writing is forced and the result disappointing. But what we call reflection is seldom the conscious thinking out of a subject with all its details. It is rather the saturating of the mind with the matter in hand and then turning away from it and allowing it to work itself out as it will. If I may allude to so uninteresting a subject as the preparation of a sermon — my habit is to select a text and a subject as early in the week as possible. I try to keep this before my mind until I find my mind beginning to work, the thought fructifying, the parts forming. Then I dismiss the whole matter until I begin to write, when if I am lucky it is almost as if another person were dictating to me. All I have to do is to write with great rapidity and to criticise. The thought and even the language are supplied. Dr. Algernon S. Crapsey, who appears to think on his feet as well as any man I ever knew, once told me that in preaching he usually had the feeling of standing a foot or two from the speaker and of listening to another voice sometimes with surprise and even with disapproval. If this spell is broken and he is recalled to self-consciousness the sermon is spoiled.

In discussing this subject with a philosophical writer the other day this gentleman informed me that he has had many similar experiences. He was recently engaged on a series of philosophical monographs for a new encyclopedia, but he had great difficulty in composing them. The ideas apparently would not come or were incoherent and incongruous. As the articles had to be finished by a certain date this caused him much annoyance and he decided that he would dismiss the subject from his mind and wait until it suggested itself. Nor did he have to wait long, for in a few days he awoke with a strong impulse to write, and sitting down he was delighted to find his monograph writing itself, coming forth logically and symmetrically from his mind without any hesitation or effort on his part, the very language apparently given to him. He was afraid that on reviewing this work in cold blood he might find it like a dream composition, which seems very brilliant to the sleeper, but sheer gibberish a few moments later. His own judgment and that of the editor of the encyclopedia was that it was one of the solidest and best pieces of work he had done.

We all know the importance of sleeping on a difficult problem and the proverbial experience of many peoples declares that sleep brings wisdom. These experiences occur to every man who thinks and who creates, be he poet, philosopher, artist, composer, or writer of fiction. This sense of spontaneity and affluence, this uprush of powerful thought and feeling without any conscious effort of our own, is what we call inspiration, the breaking on us of another and a greater spirit. The ancient poets knew this. In their moments of rapt vision and utterance they felt themselves carried away by a higher power than their own which they called the Muse (the Inventress, the goddess of memory) and there is a certain touching illuminating quality in such compositions which distinguishes them from the studied efforts of conscious reason. Hence the time-honored comparison of inspiration with insanity.

In these phenomena psychologists have rightly recognized the action of the subconscious mind, and as in such creations of thought the subconscious is closely associated with the conscious intelligence they afford particularly good material for the study of the former. The works of genius bear the imprint of the Universal Spirit. Their most distinguishing note is their universality. They are not addressed to one generation nor are they limited to one place, but are at home everywhere and are contemporary with all times. But although this is true and although the subconscious mind from every point of view is more generic, and in closer touch with the universal processes of nature than our conscious intelligence, yet these two, the conscious and the subconscious minds, are most closely united, and normally form one personality, which, however, may be dissociated. The whole mind (conscious and subconscious) has been compared to a floating iceberg in which the portion which emerges above the waves is supported by the larger mass which is submerged. There is truth in this figure: its defect is that, the iceberg being homogeneous, it fails to distinguish the real differences which exist between these activities. To produce results of permanent value or even to function normally the conscious and the subconscious must operate harmoniously together. The subconscious mind, as Hudson affirms, does not originate thought, it can only elaborate and develop it along the lines imposed by reason. Left to itself it can only originate dreams by night and the delusions of the insane by day. Moreover, it must follow strictly the general tendencies of waking thought. The artist does not solve mathematical problems in his sleep. The last baffling difficulty in the way to invention is removed by the man who has pursued the train of thought up to this point. The novelist receives his inspirations in prose, the poet in verse, the painter in form and color, and the musician in harmony and melody. Moreover, with all their universality these compositions bear on every line the traits of individual genius. Along with his universal genius, his pure intuition of spiritual truth, Shakespeare possessed an astounding empirical knowledge of life, the result of close and shrewd observation. Balzac introduces a wealth of detail into his novels which would make them wearisome were it not offset by profound revelations of the moral life. This perfect balance of the inward and the outward, of intuition and observation, is to be found only in the greatest creators. In lesser men one element preponderates over the other. One thing however is certain, — the activity of the subconscious mind is no short cut to renown, no substitute for hard work. Before we can fly we must walk, yes run. It is only when the soul is lifted to a pitch of ardor by the most intense effort of thought and abstraction that the subconscious mind intervenes to complete our task and to do for us what we cannot do for ourselves. This is also true in great degree of its therapeutic activity.

Few poets or creative artists have described their own mental processes with psychological insight. These words of the poet, Ola Hansson, are therefore the more valuable:

"It is, I believe, a matter of extraordinary difficulty to determine how and when the poet conceives the ferment which impregnates his spirit, and which in the course of time results in a poetical work. I know from my own experience that it is usually impossible for me to determine the instant of the first germination of the idea in me which later runs as the scarlet thread through my work. Yet there is a certain determinate moment when the process begins. Now there is something growing in my mind. Something has affected me as the revelation affected Saul on the way to Damascus. Suddenly men and life assume new relations, new illumination, new perspectives. But on the other side of this stage, the emergence of poetic thought above the threshold of consciousness, ranges a whole chain of small hidden processes of which I had only a general and vague impression. In all stages of this process of growth, on both sides of the threshold which lies between consciousness and unconsciousness, something is present to which we may well give the name suggestion. Whether it be a brightening of the atmosphere or an expression in a human face, or a crisis in one's own life, or in the life of another, or a passage in a book, or a hypothesis in a scientific work — the general result in every case has been that something which hitherto lay bound in me, awakened from its magic sleep, living and fruitful as a germ after it is impregnated. Then all the faculties and energies of my personality concentrated themselves as by a magic spell on this one germinating point. All the blood of my mind flowed round this embryo, weaving its tissues and envelopes until at last the moment came when the new organic creation took the form and lineaments of a concrete conscious thing.

"At the same moment, the poetical idea became a suggestive Kobold, an almighty ruler, a parasite, if I may use the expression, in me. From that hour onward, it was nothing less than the center of the universe, the lighthouse on the sea of existence, the fountain of truth, the goddess of fortune (Glucksherd), the magic princess in the fairy castle, the promised land east of the sun and west of the moon, the gospel of the future. In its mode of operation, it can best be compared to the wand and the eye of the hypnotist.

"In early times men called this the sacred moment of conception or inspiration; on it follows the period of gestation and labor.

"From now on one goes the whole way hand in hand with the suggesting Kobold, hypnotized, will-less. This whole world, this whole life which one knew hitherto and still knows in hours which lie outside the magic circle, to be artificial, chaotic, full of contradictions and inexplicable, now stands before one, definite and luminous as a St. Elmo's fire, as a magic glow, as a far-beckoning light appears at night to one demented. The whole infinite complex of life's interpretations and theories of the universe, of human individualities, and personal fates and their determining factors, of historic knowledge and one's own experiences, all converge into this one point at which one stares till he is blind, which draws all things to itself, and which freed in us in the moment of deliverance I have described, becomes the focus of our inner life." [1]

5. *Perception of the lapse of time.* Ability to estimate the lapse of time during our waking hours is an accomplishment which few persons possess. Apart from external aids such as timepieces and the movement of the

---

[1] Taken from Hanssen's interesting discussion of the subconscious element in art which he contributed to Hans Schmidkunz' *Psychologie der Suggestion*, Stuttgart, *Von Ferd. Erke*, 1892, s. 260 ff.

heavenly bodies, our reckoning of time is probably effected by the addition of the units of our perceptions. As these constantly vary they afford no fixed criteria, and our time-sense is therefore very inaccurate. In sleep, however, it is different. Our subconscious mind possesses an appreciation of the passage of time which our conscious mind cannot approximate and of which at present we can give no explanation. Almost all persons whose duties call them to awake at a certain hour of the day or night, after a little practice have no difficulty in doing so. In my early life I acted as chaplain of a college and my duties required me to awake an hour and a half earlier than I was accustomed to do. For the first few weeks I employed an alarm clock, but finding that it disturbed my sleep I dispensed with it and in the course of six years I overslept only once, and usually I awoke within five or ten minutes of the time I proposed to myself.

This capacity is also shared to a marked degree by the animals. Both dogs and horses are frequently aware of the recurrence of Sunday and resent being compelled to work on that day. While living in the country I owned a game-cock who used to sleep in a tree directly under my window. Every night at about the hour of twelve he would awake, flap his wings and crow two or three times, when he would go to sleep again. I timed him frequently and he was seldom ten minutes out of the way. I gave one of his offspring to an iron worker who had to waken at three in the morning to go to the mill. Every evening the cock was placed on the foot of the bed where he would waken his master summer and winter with great regularity. A very intelligent Micmac Indian who for many years had observed the flight of waterfowl and the migrations of the caribou in Newfoundland informed me that their movements take place with astonishing regularity from year to year.

Even more striking is the appreciation of time through hypnotic and post-hypnotic suggestion, a very interesting account of which is given by Bramwell.[1] "The suggestions (Delbœuf's) were to be carried out after the lapse of 350, 700, 900, 1500, 1600, 1150, 1300, and 3300 minutes respectively, were made at varying hours of the day and night while some fell due at night after the lapse of several days. Three of the suggestions were fulfilled at the moment they fell due, four were carried out, but not at the exact time. In these an impulse to carry out the suggestion arose at the right moment." The two young women on whom the experiments were made were imperfectly educated and could with difficulty tell time by the clock. It would therefore have been impossible for them to reduce the minutes to hours and, by comparison with the moment when the suggestion was made, calculate the time when it would fall due. Bramwell's own experiments on the subconscious time sense are not less interesting. One of his patients was directed at the end of five hours and twenty minutes to make a cross on a piece of paper and to write down the time she believed it to be without looking at a clock or a watch. The suggestion was made in the so-called somnambulistic state and the subject retained no recollection of it after waking. It was carried out at the moment it fell due. Five minutes before the appointed time the patient became restless and

[1] *Hypnotism*, p. 114 ff.

said "I must do something, but I don't know what," and on making the cross at the right moment said to her mother: "It's all silliness." Out of fifty-five experiments performed by Dr. Bramwell on the same subject, forty-five were completely successful and in no case did the error exceed five minutes.

6. *The action of the subconscious mind in certain experiences of life.* In the course of our lives most of us are confronted with tasks or emergencies which require strength, courage, resourcefulness in excess of our ordinary powers, or we undergo experiences which without conscious effort on our part transform us, shatter the habits of a lifetime and lift us to a higher plane of being. A woman is engaged in the ordinary duties of her vocation with just sufficient strength for daily needs when an unusual demand is made of her. Perhaps several of her children are very ill at the same time. For weeks she seldom undresses herself, she snatches her food at irregular hours. She sleeps but little, but night and day is engaged in the hardest kind of work, which taxes her moral nature even more than her physical nature. Yet she does not break down and she knows that she will be sustained until the emergency is past, and she performs tasks which without the stimulus of love and responsibility would be impossible.

Or we are intensely interested and preoccupied in what we are doing and we lose all sense of weariness and effort. Sometimes in hunting in the Rocky Mountains I have mounted my horse at daybreak and have spent the whole day in the hardest kind of walking and climbing, returning to camp at nine or ten o'clock at night without serious sense of fatigue, apparently quite able to set out again at once had the light permitted. This was due to the intense excitement of the chase, for on other occasions, *e.g.* in breaking camp, half that amount of work would completely exhaust me. This is the reason why, except in the single point of mountain climbing, the tenderfoot can frequently wear out the seasoned guide to whom the pursuit of game is an old story and who is therefore more keenly alive to fatigue.

Or our life is threatened, or someone we love is exposed to sudden danger, and we exhibit a coolness, a resourcefulness, a capacity for swift and intelligent action which astonishes the onlookers. Heroic actions are performed, clever expedients are conceived and executed with the rapidity of thought. Our friends compliment us on our courage and composure, but the chances are that we were totally unaware of what we were doing. In company with a guide I was once caught in a long rapid through which it was considered impossible for a canoe to pass. I can remember the first sickening sense of fear which passed away almost instantly when I began to wield my paddle; then my mind became a blank until the moment when I found myself floating in a pool half a mile below, with only a few teacupfuls of water in the canoe. I have looked at that terrible water since and I cannot understand how we came through it alive.

Again, a new affection enters our life with all its cleansing energy. Old habits fall from us, our temptations and vices lose all power over us. Our moral nature has received such an increment of strength from the uprush of new and powerful feelings and motives that that which was almost impossible before we perform with scarce an effort. Maternal love also springs from the same subconscious sources and operates in a manner no less marvelous and awe-inspiring.

In this connection I should like to call attention to sexual love and attraction. No doubt the most brilliant and suggestive discussion of this subject is Schopenhauer's classical chapter. Schopenhauer recognizes the instinctive, subconscious basis of genuine love and passion that distinguishes it sharply from friendship which is based on rational considerations. He exalts and lauds love's mystical rapture, its sublime renunciations and sacrifices, even its crimes. Love is not the offspring of cultured reason, it is not bound by the conventions of society. It frequently enters our lives as a vast elemental force sweeping all before it and leaving ruin in its track. At last Schopenhauer comes to the interesting question why it is that two persons fall in love with each other. What is there in these two human beings that differentiates them from the rest of mankind to such a degree that the world itself depends upon their possession of each other, and all other men and women are absolutely indifferent to them? Schopenhauer answers this question by affirming that the Universal Unconscious Mind perceives that these two persons are best adapted to produce between them a perfect offspring, and that the Will which is fundamental to the universe impels them to this act. There is doubtless truth in this statement, which is only a more poetic rendering of the law of sexual selection. We agree with Schopenhauer as to the subconscious basis of all genuine love.[1] It is this which gives love its infinite quality, it is this which makes it blind to the ordinary considerations of reason and conscience. It opens to us a new and mysterious world of rapture and despair. We feel ourselves swayed by impulses of which we can give no account and over which we have little control. The world for us begins anew, and we wander for a while in that magical garden which opens once in our lives to receive us all. It may be doubted, however, if to-day the production of the perfect child who is yet to be born forms the sole ground for the irresistible attraction which so powerfully draws two human beings together. The majority of women and a good many men have passed beyond the stage where mere physical perfections enthrall them, and as for talent, brilliancy, and moral excellence, these, alas, offer no guarantee of their perpetuation in offspring, as the children of the most gifted parents constantly prove. And yet all permanently happy unions have their subconscious basis. There is something in every loved man or woman which cannot be grasped by reason or expressed in words. We intimate this by saying that the person in question is congenial to us, *i.e.*, that he or she partakes of our genius or spirit. Without this affinity in the subconscious realm, the deeper union of hearts never takes place. With it beauty and even intellectual brilliancy may be dispensed with. It is this which lifts true love out of the physical and the sensual, and which gives it its profound moral significance, for the

---

[1] In spite of Schopenhauer's scientific mistakes, it is interesting to note how many of his philosophical conceptions have been justified by subsequent science.

subconscious mind is purer than the conscious and if any part of our being is permanent, we may believe this to be such.

7. *The Subconscious Mind in Religion.* In every form of religion there is a preponderating non-rational element, and it is in this sphere that the most characteristic phenomena of religion — faith, awe, reverence, fear, love, ecstasy, rapture — take place. This sphere is constantly invaded by reason, but it obstinately defends its right to existence. No sooner is mystery banished from one domain of religion than it reappears in another. This constitutes the struggle of religion and science which at bottom is the necessary reconciliation of the needs of the conscious mind with those of the subconscious. Libraries have been written on this problem, for the most part by men who lacked the key to its solution. Again and again philosophers have attempted to analyze and explain religion, *i.e.*, to make it purely rational, but their attempts have failed, for in religion as in music and poetry there is an infinite element which defies analysis. Its motive power springs from the obscure depths of the subconscious mind, and to cut this nerve paralyzes its functioning. Here the instinct of the religious believer must be respected. He does not regard these rationalizing investigations as constituting religion, for he feels that the springs of his religious life lie elsewhere, in the obscure recognition of the Infinite Spirit by the finite spirit, in a sense of dependence, of guilt, of love and filial trust, in all those deep emotions which refuse to be translated into words, but which act as the most powerful motives of life. To banish these would be to take the

mystical and poetical element out of life, and to sap religion at its root. But this cannot be done. When the rationalizing process has been carried to a point at which the religious life is really threatened there is always a reaction, of which we see a striking example to-day. The longer and more persistent the rationalistic attack, the more vigorous is the mystical and spiritualistic revolt, and yet each such struggle brings the day of final reconciliations a little nearer by forcing upon men the legitimacy of the conflicting claims. On the other hand, were reason to ignore the claims of religion, or in other words were the conscious mind to become dissociated from the subconscious in this highest region of their activity, the result would be disastrous to both. Science would become petty and uninteresting and religion would surrender itself to vagaries and superstitions of every kind. But this reason cannot do for it recognizes in religion its supreme problem. Naturally those who look upon man's spiritual evolution as a transition from unconsciousness to consciousness will take a different view of this subject; but we do not share this conception. We believe that those elements of being which belong to the realm of the subconscious, will and emotion, are fundamental and permanent, and that to eradicate these would be to annihilate progress.

8. *The Physiological Action of the Subconscious Mind.* In this section we come to those operations of the subconscious mind with which from a therapeutic point of view we are most concerned. These facts have been elicited largely through the instrumentality of hypnotic suggestion, since it is by this means that the necessary dissociation of

the subconscious mind most readily takes place. While it would be a mistake to suppose that our conscious mind can effect no changes in our physical functions, since the heart's action can be altered by conscious attention and the cheek is suffused with blood in consequence of the spoken word, yet it is certain that the action of the subconscious mind is far more profound and universal. I shall not now rehearse the long list of physiological changes which can be effected by suggestion as these will be stated more fully in a subsequent chapter; here I will mention only a few which have occurred under my own observation. The temperature of the body can be elevated or lowered, and the pulse quickened or retarded. Perspiration can be produced, the action of the intestines can be stimulated, resulting in the removal of constipation. The occurrence of the menstrual period can be retarded or accelerated, its duration and volume regulated, and its painful symptoms alleviated. Many forms of pain depending on functional or trophic disturbance can be removed and parts of the body rendered insensible to pain. The sense of hearing in certain forms of deafness can be quickened. Some forms of eczema can be removed, and some forms of asthma can be checked at once. Stammering can be controlled, and nervous dyspepsia can frequently be cured. To this short list which is taken almost at random from our clinical notes, Bernheim, Forel, Bramwell, and Dubois add many other similar examples in support of the physiological action of suggestion. They prove beyond question that our subconscious mind acts through the instrumentality of our whole nervous system, both cerebro-spinal and sympathetic, and that through this complex mechanism it can effect important changes in our physical functions. Its action on the brain is seen more clearly in its modifications of consciousness, its control of the sympathetic system is indicated by trophic changes such as I have enumerated. Neither can it any longer be denied by men who are in possession of the facts now embodied in the orthodox literature of medicine and psychology.

Before bringing this long chapter to a close, let us look back over the path we have traversed and draw a few inferences as to the strange power of which we have been so long ignorant, though it resides within us and manifests itself in so many of the most important acts of our lives. It must be evident to anyone who surveys even the brief series of facts we have brought forward, that the subconscious mind is no pathological phenomenon, the psychical concomitant of hysteria. Janet came to this conclusion as did Charcot before him from a too limited induction of the facts in question. While the Nancy school, especially Liébault and Bernheim, and other practitioners like Forel, Bramwell, Moll, Lloyd, Tuckey and others were testing these principles of psychotherapeutics by applying them to thousands of patients, Charcot and his disciples contented themselves with hypnotizing a dozen or fifteen hysterical young women, and from these limited observations they have drawn their limited conclusions. According to their view only hysterical patients can be hyponotized. On the contrary, all experienced practitioners in this field state that between ninety and ninety-five per cent of all peoples on whom the experiment has been tried can be influenced hypnotically.' Janet must therefore regard all mankind as suffering from hysteria. The element of truth in Charcot's statement is that hysteria is a disease of the subconscious mind. This, however, is not his discovery. A general survey of the facts leads us to a very different conclusion. A power which quickens our intellectual processes, which heightens our will power, cannot be regarded as pathological. The subconscious mind is a normal part of our spiritual nature. There is reason to believe that it is purer, more sensitive to good and evil, than our conscious mind. While normally these two energies are closely united, they can be dissociated in their functioning and in their memories. Although the subconscious mind has more direct control of our physical processes than the conscious, it would be a mistake to limit its action to this sphere, or to regard it as the mere psychical concomitant of the sympathetic nervous system, though it may well be this. On the contrary, we have seen the important part it plays in religion, in memory, and in the higher creations of thought. Neither should we regard it as a mere generalized mind-stuff without personal characteristics. Though it is doubtless more generic and in closer contact with the Universal Spirit than reason, yet its creations bear the imprint of individual genius. While it acts in conjunction with reason, its mode of activity is very different. Apparently it cannot originate thought, but the materials given it can work to the desired end with the astonishing facility, ease, and swiftness which belong to the acts of instinct. Further speculation into its nature and its relation to consciousness would lead us too far from our purpose.

CHAPTER III

SUGGESTION

The most important fact which has yet been discovered in regard to the subconscious mind is that it is suggestible, *i.e.*, it is subject to moral influence and direction. In this it does not differ from our ordinary consciousness, except that under certain conditions it is more amenable to external control, and it is in closer contact with our physical functions. All human beings are influenced by their affections and by their relations with others, but some much more than others. There are positive dominating personalities whose mission in life seems to be to influence others, and there are receptive, passive natures which readily yield themselves to such influence. So, in the subconscious realm, some persons are far more suggestible than others. At the outset of this discussion I should like to remove from the mind of the reader, if it is necessary, the idea that there is anything morbid or uncanny in suggestion. On the contrary it is something which consciously or unconsciously we practise every day of our lives. A little girl falls down and hurts herself. Mother kisses the spot and "makes it well." We control our children, if we are wise, not by harshly rebuking their innocent naughtiness, but by diverting their minds, *i.e.*, suggesting something better. Politeness compels us to control our annoyance under a pleasant demeanor and in a little while it passes away. We are kept awake by unpleasant thoughts and we turn away from them by suggesting to ourselves thoughts that are more agreeable, and we go to sleep. A few words of commendation and praise brighten the whole day. If we can forget our pain for a little while the pain is apt to cease. In its therapeutic aspects suggestion is like all science, a particular application of common knowledge.

The psychological principle on which suggestion rests is known as dissociation, the concentration of the mind on some things to the exclusion of others. This can readily be extended to the isolation of the subconscious mind from the conscious, and as the former is the more potent factor in the removal of disease, it is to the subconscious mind that suggestions are usually addressed. Yet I would not by any means limit suggestion to the treatment of disease. Its power is coextensive with life itself. The most valuable lessons we learn are not given us in the form of didactic instructions, — they are those germinal thoughts which drop into our minds as the seed corn drops into the soil prepared for it, which the mind appropriates and transforms and which end by transforming us.

In therapeutic practice the action of suggestion rests largely upon faith. Whatever the method employed, its success depends upon the belief in the mind of the patient that it is likely to attain the desired result. A curative suggestion is an effect obtained through the conviction that it is about to take place. I tell a young girl that she is blushing and the chances are that she will blush immediately. I place a man in a comfortable reclining chair, cut off the stream of external sensations by darkening the room and insuring quiet, and I earnestly tell him that in a few moments he will be asleep. If he knows that hundreds of other persons have undergone this experience he will be more certain to accept my assurance and to obey the suggestion. I visit a woman who has been bed-ridden for months or years, convince myself that her inability to move does not proceed from true paralysis and I assure her that she can arise and I earnestly command her to do so, which she proceeds to do. A patient comes to me in violent agitation with palpitating heart and distress of mind. I soothe him by a few gentle and quiet words and tell him that his nervousness is passing away, that his heart is beating quietly and regularly and that in a few moments he will be calm and happy. He listens to me, believes me, and the prediction is fulfilled. Another patient is suffering from acute pain. I divert her mind, place my hand on the suffering part to heighten the impression that something is about to be done for her, or to direct her subconscious mind more strongly to it, and I confidently inform her that the pain is diminishing, that it is going down by degrees and that in a given time, five minutes, it will have disappeared. This also is completely successful. Still another is suffering from constipation. I inform this one that the action of the intestines can be controlled by the mind, that many persons have been cured by suggestion and that for the next few days he will have two evacuations daily. At the end of a week he returns and asks me to reduce the number to one. These are not fancy pictures, they are simply recitals of actual occurrences. They point to the fact that the mind has immense power over the functions of the body and that the active instrumentality which is faith can frequently be directed by suggestion. Great as is the efficacy of this instrument in a large group of disorders, its action is strictly limited. The physiological changes involved in the cases I have alluded to are doubtless due to the stimulation or inhibition of various organs through their controlling nerve centers by means which we do not as yet fully understand. If, however, these organs through disease or lesion are incapable of responding to such stimuli, no results will follow. It is useless to address suggestions to a brain withered by paresis, or to command a hand shaken by paralysis agitans to stand still. If the patient above mentioned had been suffering from valvular disease of the heart, my word would have no effect upon the heart's action. A toothache caused by the irritation of a nerve frequently can be cured by suggestion, but the pain caused by the pressure of an abscess cannot be so removed. For the same reason purely organic mental cases such as idiocy, paresis, etc., can never be improved by suggestion, because such diseases rest upon organic degeneration. Yet in many forms of organic disease, *e.g.*, in tuberculosis, the importance of suggestion as a subsidiary agent is not to be overlooked. Pain can be checked, coughing can frequently be controlled or diminished, sound sleep can be obtained. Above all the patient can be inspired with the firm conviction that the means employed will be successful and that he will be restored to health. Moreover, it is well known that the injury of one organ will frequently derange or inhibit the function of another, which latter may be restored by suggestion.

Further, the value of suggestion as an adjunct to surgery is now generally recognized. The most successful surgeons are beginning to appreciate the importance of the moral preparation of their patients for operations. By the calming and stilling of the patient's natural apprehensions and by direct suggestion, some of the worst effects of ether and the knife can be avoided or reduced to a minimum. Moral shock can be eliminated. Resistance to etherization and the ensuing nausea can frequently be overcome, with the result that the patient suffers less and recovers more rapidly. This is especially to be remembered in the case of nervous and timid persons and in diseases which tend to disturb the mental and moral faculties, *e. g.* in operations for exophthalmic goitre which Möbius defines as "crystallized fear." Quite recently three women were about to be operated on for this disease in a hospital in the middle West. The first patient reached the etherizing chamber in a state of terror which the operating surgeon cleverly diagnozed as "stage fright." Her temperature rose to about 104°, her pulse registered more than 200 beats, and it was very evident that an operation was impossible. The patient accordingly was taken back to her room where she died within an hour. The second patient underwent the same experience and also died. The surgeon, a very able and skilful operator, was in despair. He had still another patient to be treated: the omission of the operation meant death, and its performance in the light of his two previous experiences seemed likely to result in the same melancholy end. He at once determined to prepare this woman for her operation by reducing mental activity to its lowest terms and this resulted in complete success, the patient's pulse falling, while she was on the operating table, to 84 beats. In this instance sedatives were employed, but the same result could probably have been attained by moral influence and suggestion. The means, however, are of secondary importance; it is the result which counts.

It is, however, in the sphere of the functional neuroses that suggestion finds its legitimate field. Here its importance is the greater, because in these disorders the beneficent action of drugs and medicines is but slight, and what power they possess is due largely to their suggestional effect. These nervous sufferers with their insomnias, their shifting hysterical pains, their phobias, their hallucinations, their manias, depressions, and harmful exaltations, their intense irritability, their profound weakness, their moral perversion, their morbid feelings, their bad habits, are the despair of the ordinary practitioner and they will continue to be such until the physician enlarges the sphere of his culture and qualifies himself to treat the whole man. There is no class of patients so neglected and I may say no class of patients who can be more easily treated than many of these, provided the method be correct and be sufficiently elastic and individual. In almost all such cases the real cause of the disorder is moral or psychical. The cause of the disease being central, it is useless or next to useless to attack it at the circumference. One may remove local pain by local treatment only to experience the mortification of having the pain reappear at a new point. The ordinary sedatives may afford a necessary night's sleep, but they cannot remove insomnia, on the contrary they are antagonistic to natural sleep. Powerful tonics may act as a stimulant, but what the exhausted nerves need is rest, not stimulation. And when we approach the moral and psychical aspects of these disorders we see more clearly the futility of chemical and mechanical agencies. What drug or medicine, electric current, bath or system of exercise can remove the moral effect of shock, dispel melancholy and remorse, uproot destructive habits, eradicate fixed ideas, bring peace to troubled consciences, or supply a motive for living to one who has lost such motive and with it all desire to live? The plain truth is, moral maladies require moral treatment; physicians apprehend this, and usually abstain from administering medicines in cases where they are likely to do no good. The difficulty is that on account of their ignorance of psychological methods few physicians feel themselves competent to undertake such treatment. The time is coming, however, when a knowledge of physiological psychology will be considered as necessary to the art of healing as a knowledge of anatomy.

In saying this I by no means wish to ignore the value and importance of many subsidiary aids and adjuncts, of which from the beginning we have made the freest use. Psychical disorders give rise to innumerable physical disturbances, *e.g.*, in the digestive tract, and these may require physical and local treatment. Even if the effect of electricity or massage in these cases is largely due to their influence on the mind, that does not diminish their value, since a curative suggestion can often be best administered in this way. Dr. Weir Mitchell, who is the teacher of us all, has proved the great value of rest, isolation, and abundant nourishment, in a brilliant series of cures extending over a long term of years. But on the other hand Dr. Mitchell's patients owe even more to their contact with his remarkable personality, as is proved by the fact that his rest cure, valuable as it is in itself, in other hands fails to produce the astonishing results that are associated with his name.

I said a little while ago that the active agent in all so-called moral recoveries is faith. Physicians, whatever their school of practice, ought to recognize this principle and pay more attention to their moral relations with their patients, for these are frequently more valuable than their prescriptions. Dr. A. T. Schofield beautifully says, "When the eye of the patient meets the eye of the physician the cure begins if it is likely to take place." Physicians like other men owe their success in life to two sources, — to what they are and to what they know. Of these the latter at present engrosses almost their whole attention, to the neglect of the powers of their own personality. Many things are taught in the medical schools which at present have absolutely no bearing upon the curing of disease, while principles which are useful in the treatment of all diseases, and indispensable to the cure of some, are totally ignored. Yet any physician learned in the literature of his profession knows how constantly the fashions of medicines vary and how few are indicated in any form of disease with infallible certainty. Remedies which were constantly given a generation ago are seldom heard of now. When they were frequently mentioned and prescribed by celebrated men they worked many cures. Now no one expects much of them. The same fate will befall drugs that are popular to-day. Only a few old standbys such as iron, quinine, opium, and its derivatives, mercury in its various forms, the bromides and iodides, arsenic, strychnia, digitalis, etc., maintain themselves from generation to generation. Yet we ought not to ignore the psychical value of medicine. A prescription recommended by a trusted physician with the assurance that it will accomplish the desired result acts as a powerful suggestion. This is the cause unquestionably of many of the cures effected by homeopathy and especially by patent medicines which are compounds of inert or even deleterious substances. The glowing advertisement excites the patient's imagination. The marvelous testimonials bearing witness to striking cures inspire faith in the purchaser. A remedy that has relieved so many others will surely help him, and it not infrequently does so. When these remedies are analyzed their physiological potency is usually seen to be nil, and without their psychical appeal they would probably cure no one. The same result is often obtained in anticipation of the expected action of a well-known drug. A patient told me he could not go to sleep without sulphonal. I asked him how soon the dose affected him and he said in five to ten minutes. As sulphonal dissolves but slowly it was plain that it was not the physiological action of the drug that affected him but his expectation of its action. I therefore requested one of our physicians to dissolve a very few grains of sulphonal in a bottle of water, which I gave him telling him to take only one teaspoonful in case he could not sleep. Finding that this succeeded quite as well, I explained to the patient what

I had done and easily persuaded him to discontinue the use of sedatives altogether.

One reason why American physicians are so slow to avail themselves of psychical influence in combating disease is that they have been educated in a too narrowly materialistic school of science which assumes that only material objects possess reality and which thinks that the mind can safely be ignored. The trend of science to-day is in the opposite direction. The importance of the mind as a chief factor in health and disease is so apparent to all persons who allow themselves to be influenced by the facts that it cannot longer be ignored. The next great development of medicine will be along psychical lines. The way is already prepared in the disinclination of educated physicians to prescribe drugs and in the disinclination of educated patients to take them. At this crisis, when the physician realizes what a powerful and delicate instrument suggestion places in his hands, he will not be slow to avail himself of it, but to use this instrument successfully he must have faith in the soul and its powers and he must cultivate his own moral nature. The value of suggestion lies in its character and in the character of the man who makes it. Mere routine phrases and parrot-like repetitions have no effect on the sick. It is true, psychology is as yet a very imperfect science, and it may be that the question how the mind affects the body is forever insoluble to man. But on the other hand, what is more obscure or uncertain than the physiological action and the therapeutic value of the great mass of drugs which from time to time have constituted our materia medica?

This brings me to the discussion of faith as a therapeutic agent. Although in every form of disease faith in the physician and in the means he employs is of the utmost importance, yet mere blind and undirected faith seldom cures the sick. I have had abundant opportunities to test this, as many persons come to me full of faith confidently expecting that a single interview, one prayer, or the placing of my hand on the affected part, will remove a malady of years' standing. This, I need not say, seldom takes place, although occasionally it does occur. A woman, *e.g.*, came to me about six months ago and told me that she had suffered agonizing pain in her head for four or five days in the week for a period of fifty-five years. Her sufferings were so great that when her daughter sickened and died she was unable to care for her or even to attend the funeral. I believed her affliction to be a kind of reverberation of an old pain, the perpetuation in memory and imagination of a former condition. She was suffering acutely at the time, and having seated her in a comfortable position and having made her very quiet, I placed my hands on her head and assured her earnestly that the pain was diminishing, that it was in fact disappearing, and that in ten minutes it would be gone and that it would not return. The suggestion succeeded, the pain punctually ceased, and the patient has informed me from time to time that it has not returned. A man who was not able to visit the church wrote me from a distance that he and his wife were slaves of alcohol, and begged my assistance. I wrote him that he could break off this habit, that he would be helped in his struggle against drink, and that his first duty when restored was to help his wife to overcome her temptation. After six weeks I was gratified to receive a letter from my correspondent stating that since he had heard from me neither he nor his wife had tasted alcohol, and that greatly to their astonishment they found that they did not desire to do so. I could give other striking examples of immediate recovery, but I admit they are exceptional and unusual. In our practice we neither look for nor desire sudden and spectacular cures, partly because of the publicity which attaches to them, partly on account of the moral effect on other patients, which is apt to be bad, and lastly because such cures are seldom permanent. Although we try to awaken faith on the part of our patients, we do not desire blind or fanatical faith. We lay absolutely no claim to personal power, we explain as fully as possible the nature of the means we employ, and call attention to the limitations of such methods, and accept as patients only persons suffering from functional disorders. We encourage the patients to acquaint themselves with the principles involved, by maintaining a good library of standard works which we freely lend them. We avoid all fetiches and material adjuncts as means of suggestion and rely only upon moral, spiritual, and rational means. Faith may be strong, but it needs accurate and skilful direction in order to be useful as a therapeutic agent; hence the need of careful diagnosis, which is not merely physical, but also moral. This is not a task which every shepherd is qualified to perform. It requires careful observation of temperament, capacity, and idiosyncrasy which will tax the resources of the most gifted man. This study of conscience, this analysis of a life's experience in order to discover the cause of the present disturbance and to trace its history, requires time, sympathy, and some psychological acuteness. When the cause of the malady has been determined, it requires no less thought and skill to devise means of removing it. Here again the temperament, the culture and the moral nature of the patient must be taken into account. In this work there is no such thing as routine method or a system that applies to all cases. Each patient presents a new problem and requires individual care. Treatment which would be beneficial to one might have no effect or a bad effect upon another. In order to obtain the necessary co-operation of the patient, the thought presented must be such as the patient's mind is able to grasp, and it must gain his approval, otherwise it will be rejected. Motives which powerfully affect one man will have absolutely no effect upon another. Nor is it necessary merely to satisfy the reason: the will also must be aroused, possibly from the slumber of years. The task we are attempting is above all a moral undertaking. In the majority of cases, before the patient can be restored to health it is necessary to eradicate powerful habits, to supply new motives, to supplant the most intense egotism by new and real interest in others, to hew out new paths in the brain, sometimes to create or recreate a will. This requires an effort on the part of the physician greater than is involved in writing a prescription. It demands moral qualities of the highest order, intuition, sympathy, kindness of heart, and an absolutely inexhaustible patience. Character can be imparted only by those who possess it. But on the other hand, like every other moral victory it brings its own reward. No relations with men and women are so sacred as those which pertain to the moral life. No physician can do this work conscientiously and successfully without reaping a rich reward in his own character.

In order to obtain the best results in psychotherapeutics the physician and the patient must work together. There are many things which the patient can do for himself which will be discussed in the chapter on auto-suggestion, and there are many things which he cannot do by himself, but which an able and trusted adviser can help him do. Sometimes the patient can carry his recovery to a certain point, but he cannot advance beyond it. The cure tarries and he becomes discouraged. Then the co-operation of another personality is needed and with this help the recovery is completed. I believe this was what Christ had in mind when he said: "If two of you shall agree on earth as touching anything that they shall ask, it shall be done for them by my Father which is in Heaven."[1] At all events I have seen some startling illustrations of the truth of this word.

In regard to the nature of the faith proposed to the patient, honorable men will differ according to the ends they propose to themselves and according to their personal prepossessions. No right-minded person could desire the physician to demand of the patient a faith which he himself does not share. It has frequently been stated that it is the intensity of faith rather than its character or its object which is important in the treatment of disease, or, as Dubois puts it, "It matters little what banner we raise provided we hold it high." There is a

[1] Matt. xviii. 19.

sense in which these words are true. It is no doubt the intensity of faith which is valuable as a therapeutic agent. If we look no further than the control of pain, the removal of symptoms or even the cure of disease, any faith which will accomplish these results is sufficient for our purpose. But in the task we have set ourselves we do look further than this. Our work is essentially ethical and spiritual. Our chief interest in the men and women who seek our care is a moral and religious interest. In other words, we desire not merely to give them temporary relief, but to do them permanent good, to open to them the possibility of a new life, not merely to restore them to health but to give them motives for living. If we look at this reconstruction with reference to life as a whole I am of the opinion that it does make some difference by what form of faith these necessary changes are effected. I know a hospital in which a number of persons have been cured by two tuning forks. It is suggested to the patient that these are powerful magnets, contact with which will remove pain and cure many forms of disease. With a certain class of patients this works well, but I should expect no moral regeneration, no new and higher life to proceed from such a source, and on the educated who would recognize them, such objects would have no curative effect at all. When a man has become profoundly discouraged and his own life has lost its spring and motive and he realizes his inability to help himself, some ideal aid he must have. The great majority of normally constituted men and women find or may find such support in religion. Others find help in a noble philosophy, in art, in science, in music, in literature.

Since we have learned more of the nature of faith we are more sure than ever that it does make a difference what form of faith a man lives by. There are forms of faith professed and practised in this country which are almost worse than disease. On the whole I think I would rather be sick than crazy. On the supposition that the character of faith is a matter of indifference it is a little hard to see why physicians should object to Christian Science, which is certainly able to inspire faith strong as the strongest. It is always pleasant to see an old truth in a new light, and one of the greatest pleasures of my life has been to discover how exquisitely the religion of Christ is adapted to the sick, especially to moral and nervous sufferers. This is doubtless because Jesus lived much with such persons and had them constantly on his mind. It is not long ago that religion was regarded as a predisposing cause of melancholia, hysteria, and insanity (Maudsley), but to-day we know that the type of character created by Christ, calm, loving, patient, unselfish, fearless, trusting, is the type best able to resist every form of nervous disease and moral evil (Schofield). Therefore it is that we offer this religion to those who seek our aid, seldom without success. In fact the willingness of even worldly-minded and apparently irreligious men and women to accept the character and teachings of Christ and to live by them has been one of the happiest experiences we have been permitted to enjoy. Again and again have I heard a man who had not thought seriously of religion for years exclaim, '"I don't know whether I am going to recover my health, and the curious thing is I don't care now nearly as much as I did. But if I live I am going to be a better man than I have been in the past." As a matter of fact we possess in our religion the greatest of all therapeutic agents, if only we deal with it sincerely. The thought of a loving God within us, above us and about us, Who desires our peace, our happiness and salvation, and Who has greater and better means than ours to remove our anguish which He incessantly employs, is a consolation greater than our greatest need. I am tempted to quote a few words from a letter which was written by a lady who sought my aid in an intensely nervous condition caused by long-standing insomnia and the use of alcohol and morphia, and which reached me as I was writing these words. "I am astonished at the power which is doing this recreating for me, because I am perfectly conscious that it is in no wise my will. You most certainly set free some potent imprisoned spring of action. I feel no struggle, only a simple process of accomplishment."

Returning now to the more technical aspects of suggestion, I would repeat that its successful employment depends upon a certain degree of dissociation in which the command or assurance dominates our mind to the exclusion of other thoughts. I believe this is as true of waking suggestions as it is of suggestions given in sleep. I once read an old book of travels and voyages in which it was stated that John and Sebastian Cabot had discovered several fine pearls in America which they presented to the King of England. The statement made no impression on my mind when I read it, but in the night it suddenly occurred to me that if the Cabots had picked up pearls in the rivers they visited four hundred years ago, I might be able to do so now as it is highly probable that no one had disturbed them since. The following summer I sailed along the coast where I believed the Cabots had made their landfall and examined the beds of several rivers which, as I expected, contained large unio mussels, and from these in the course of a few days I extracted more than three hundred good pearls. Hundreds of persons had read that volume without perceiving the significance of this remark. What made the suggestion effective in my case was strong conviction that nothing stood in the way of its accomplishment. So when Dubois assures his patient that a symptom, *e.g.* a tendency to constipation, no longer exists or is about to be removed, Dubois' authority as a physician, the positive character of the assurance, and the well-known fact that he has cured hundreds of persons by the same means, tend to produce a state of dissociation by inhibiting the doubts and misgivings which would naturally arise were such a declaration to be made by an ordinary person, and the promised result probably follows. This, of course, is pure suggestion and is to be co-ordinated with a long series of similar phenomena. Dubois, probably from the wish to give an air of greater originality to his work, calls it persuasion, but the name is of no consequence. Dubois' brilliant recital of cures effected by waking suggestion is undoubtedly genuine, and we are in a position to substantiate many of his statements and to add to his list of disorders amenable to this treatment. Any adequate treatment of suggestion therefore must include both of its phases, sleeping and waking.

I would remind the reader at once that this problem, the causal connection between mind and body, is at bottom insoluble to man. If, as Tyndall said,[1] "the passage from the physics of the brain to the corresponding facts of consciousness is unthinkable, the reverse passage from the changes of consciousness to changes of our physical organism is just as incomprehensible." As to this whole question, Dubois Reymond, one of the greatest physiologists of the nineteenth century, has said, "Ignoramus et ignorabimus."[2] Yet after the manner of all science, we may leave the fundamental problem and describe the empirical processes as far as we are able to follow them. It is well known to-day that every mental change is preceded and followed by physical changes. A sensation finds its way to the brain, it emerges as a thought and that thought results in an action of some sort. The more powerful its centripetal action, the more powerful the centrifugal reaction. A man receives an affront or an insult which evokes an outburst of passion. His mind is shaken with angry thought, but the effect does not end there. He trembles, his brow darkens, his hand clinches, his features become pallid, showing the convulsed action of the heart. Only by inhibition of the higher centers of the brain is his fury prevented from manifesting itself in violent deeds, and even then the storm does not die away without profoundly depressing his muscular and nervous system. What was the cause of this great discharge of nervous energy? Undoubtedly the moral emotion awakened by the affront to his personality which might have been offered without the least physical violence. The older physiologists who wished to eliminate the per-

[1] Lecture delivered in 1868, pub. in *Fragments of Science*, 419.
[2] *Über die Grenzen der Naturerkentniss.* 7th ed., 1891, pp. 40 ff.

plexing mental factor attempted to account for such phenomena by describing them as pure nervous reflexes of which the state of mind was the effect not the cause. A Danish philosopher expresses this by saying:[1] "What the mother feels who mourns for her dead child is in reality the fatigue and languor of her muscles, the coldness of her anæmic skin, the inability of her brain to think clearly and quickly. All this becomes evident from the consideration of the cause of such phenomena. Take away from the frightened person the bodily symptoms, let his pulse beat slowly, his gaze be firm, his color healthy, his movements quick and certain, his thoughts clear, and what becomes of his fright?" Statements to this effect are so obviously perversions of facts that they need no refutation, especially as to-day by simple suggestion we can produce the same physical symptoms of which the mind is the sole cause. The well-known fact is that the mind is able to control to a marked degree the functional activity of our physical organs.

In our normal life the phenomena most closely resembling the changes effected by suggestion are the results of powerful emotions such as I have described. The ordinary operations of our minds have rarely any appreciable influence upon our physical condition; but emotions such as fear, anger, despair, hatred, act directly upon our nervous and muscular mechanism, profoundly affect our secretions and excretions and stamp themselves upon the very tissues of our organism, producing in fact very much the same conditions that are produced by suggestion.

[1] C. Lange, *Über Gemütsbewegungen*, German by Kurella, 1887, quoted by Paulsen, *Introd. to Philos.*, p. 82.

SUGGESTION

The moral and physiological effect of these phenomena is yet to be considered. Here I would call attention to the fact that powerful emotion also is attended by marked dissociation. It occupies the mind to the exclusion of all else and the subject is frequently insensible to pain and to the dictates of self-preservation and reason. Soldiers carried away by the excitement of battle often fail to feel their wounds and injuries; in the edifying autobiography of John L. Sullivan, that hero states that he never felt a blow received in the ring. Two bull moose, elk, or caribou while fighting will allow themselves to be approached without alarm, and during the mating season they lose much of their habitual caution. Standing in an open marsh I have called up a wild bull moose to a distance of a hundred feet from me, and I only ceased calling for fear that he would attack me. Persons suffering from intense grief forget to eat and are frequently insensible of weakness, weariness, and pain. Intense fear both in animals and man can paralyze limbs, inhibit flight, and even produce the rigidity known as catalepsy. In all these phenomena, dissociation, anæsthesia, analgesia, paralysis, catalepsy, and other marked somatic changes, we have the true counterpart of the phenomena produced by suggestion. In both cases we may well refer such changes to the action of the subconscious mind.

These changes certainly take place through the instrumentality of the nervous system, both sympathetic and central. They are effected either by the direct stimulation or inhibition of the action of the glands and organs or through the contraction or dilation of the blood-vessels and lymphatics which regulate the supply of nourishment afforded each part. How these results are obtained passes our comprehension, but that they really take place there can no longer be any doubt. When I say to a patient, your pain is diminishing, it will soon cease, I am no more giving scientific directions for the accomplishing of this result, than in the act of stretching out my arm I am giving the power that effects it anatomical and physiological instructions as to the means by which the act is to be performed. All that is necessary is to put the suggestion before the mind in such a form that the mind will accept it and act on it. But to do this the mind must believe that the act proposed to it is possible and right. Otherwise it will reject the suggestion and the act will not be performed. For this cause it is necessary as far as possible to guard against counter-suggestions of reason, paralyzing doubts, the persistence of old habits, and all those moral and intellectual inhibitions which would thwart our purpose and render our attempt futile. Waking suggestions therefore must be brief, and it is frequently better to give them indirectly as hints which will be seized by the mind, than to issue them as commands. The more one can gain the faith and co-operation of the patient, the better the suggestion will succeed. For this reason suggestions conveyed by electrical machines, placebos or ideas contained in books are often of great curative value. The reader appropriates the thought that is congenial to him and acts upon it, or rather it acts upon him. In order to avoid the danger of opposition and counter-suggestion some practitioners prefer to treat the patient silently. If the nature of the treatment and the character of the suggestions thus silently offered are fully explained to the patient in advance, I can see no reason why such suggestions should not be effective, but to imagine that there is a telepathic bond between the operator and every subject he attempts to treat, and that thoughts arising in the consciousness of the former are reflected in the mind of the latter, is, in the light of our present knowledge, a baseless assumption. In cases in which the practitioner is ignorant of the disease he hopes to cure, and the patient knows not the means by which he is treated, cures when they take place must be credited to the general account of faith.

Again, in order to deepen the dissociation and to guard against adverse influences many of the ablest neurologists prefer to give their suggestions through the medium of hypnosis. In this condition the action of the higher cerebral centers which may cause disturbance is more or less inhibited, and it is believed by many that suggestions so given are addressed directly to the subconscious mind and that they will be more vigorously fulfilled. While I have absolutely no prejudice against hypnotism in safe hands, and while I know its employment to be almost necessary in certain disorders, I doubt very much whether it is necessary or peculiarly beneficial in the treatment of the ordinary neuroses. The method of suggestion which I have found to be most effective in dealing with the large number of nervous persons who come to us is first to make the patient calm and quiet. This in itself is a decided advantage, especially if one explains to the patient how to attain to this condition at home. If a very nervous person who is suffering from acute moral or physical agitation can become profoundly still for an hour, the benefit is frequently noticeable. The bad habit is broken at least for a time, and I have more than once had the pleasure of seeing recovery begin after one or two such treatments. I place the patient in a comfortable reclining chair, instruct him how to relax his arms, his legs, his neck, head and body, so that there shall be no nervous tension or muscular effort. Then standing behind him I gently stroke his forehead and temples, which has a soothing and a distracting effect. Without attempting to induce sleep I inform him that his body is resting and that his mind too will rest, that he will not let his thought run on unchecked, but that it will lazily follow my words, and that when I make a useful suggestion to him he will repeat it to himself. I then tell him that all nervousness is passing from him, that everything is still within him, that his heart is beating quietly and regularly and that he is breathing gently and slowly. I suggest to him that he is entering into peace, that his mind is abstracted and his thoughts are becoming vague and indistinct. As soon as I see that these suggestions are effective I pass to the curative suggestions. If the patient is suffering pain I assure him that the pain is diminishing and that in a little while it will be gone. If I am treating a patient for insomnia, I tell him that he will sleep soundly to-night, that he will feel drowsy and fall asleep soon after he goes to bed and that if he awakens at all in the night he will make a few suggestions to himself and immediately fall asleep again. In short I make the suggestions as positively and simply as possible and under these conditions I usually find it advisable to repeat them more than once. During this treatment, which usually lasts from fifteen minutes to an hour according to the difficulties I encounter, a small proportion of patients will fall asleep and take a short nap, as some persons are so constituted that they will sleep anywhere if they are allowed to rest quietly. I have never observed, however, that such sleep had any particular significance.

I ought perhaps to add that I personally attach a religious importance to this state of mind. When our minds are in a state of peace and our hearts open and receptive to all good influence, I believe that the Spirit of God enters into us and a power not our own takes posssession of us. Thus I am tempted to explain the marked moral and physical improvement which I have frequently seen follow such brief periods of complete repose, and especially moral changes which occur with very little effort on the part of the patient. When a man who has struggled unsuccessfully for years against sexual vice or alcoholism suddenly finds himself free, it is evident that one of two things has happened to him. Either the old temptation has died within him, or a new spiritual energy has entered into him which lifts him above its power. Again and again I have heard men and women who had undergone this experience express surprise that it had taken place with so little effort of their own and, like the woman whose letter I have cited, they say this change has not taken place through their own effort or volition but through the instrumentality of a higher power. We may call this suggestion, but I can hardly believe that the mere assurance of a human being can effect moral changes so stupendous and to the unaided victim so impossible. A woman who had been bedridden for years through a form of hysterical paralysis, and who had been apparently restored to health and strength, told me that when she became profoundly still and concentrated her mind on the thought of God's presence within her, she frequently felt such a sudden increment of strength that it frightened her. In this connection it is to be remembered how earnestly Jesus warned men against injurious agitation and passion, against anger, fear, and anxious care, and the importance which He attached to calm and peace. We have just begun to fathom His motives, but there can be no doubt that in His colossal task of the moral regeneration of the world He counted on a higher power than man's unaided will. To-day we recognize the universe to be a great storehouse of invisible energy, contact with which has enormously increased the potentiality of human life. Is it probable that all those energies are mechanical? Does not the whole moral and religious life of man testify to the existence of unseen spiritual powers which are friendly to us? Such unquestionably was the belief of Christ. It is natural that the scientific discovery of the mechanical aspects of this Power should come first. ("Howbeit that was not first which is spiritual, but that which is natural and afterward that which is spiritual.") But the discovery of the other will follow. Many perfectly sane persons believe that we are on the brink of that discovery to-day, and that just as our own physical life has already been transformed by the employment of energies which have always existed though we had not recognized them, so our moral and spiritual life is destined to be evermore profoundly transformed. We shall learn the secret of Christ's personal life. Whatever

SUGGESTION

the surprises of the future, faith which opens our heart to the universe, love through which we escape from the narrow limitations of self into the life of humanity, and the possession of an inward peace which the world cannot take from us, will never lose their ancient power.

There is a very easy and rational way by which many childish faults and nervous weaknesses can be removed, that is by making good suggestions to our children while they are in a state of natural sleep. This may strike some persons with surprise and it raises interesting questions as to the relations of natural and induced sleep, but I have employed this method so many times with success that I feel justified in mentioning it. By this means I have removed childish fears, corrected habits of masturbation, bed-wetting, biting the nails and sleep-walking. I have checked nocturnal emissions and nervous twitchings, anger, violence, a disposition to lie, and I have improved speech in two stammering children. My method is to address the sleeping child in a low and gentle tone, telling it that I am about to speak to it and that it will hear me, but that my words will not disturb it nor will it awake. Then I give the necessary suggestions in simple words, repeating them in different language several times. The child rarely awakens and if it does it usually drops to sleep again immediately. I have had the best results with children I know well and for this reason I think it best for the mother or some other loved and trusted person to make the suggestion when this is possible. The difficulty in employing this method with grown persons is that they usually awake when spoken to. With some children, however, one can carry on a conversation. When questioned they will answer very much as persons do in hypnosis. This is a perfectly harmless and, in competent hands, an effective means of improving certain undesirable habits and tendencies in children.

I wish now to attempt to remove two objections to the employment of suggestion which rest on misapprehension or ignorance. Many persons who have no practical knowledge of these matters imagine that through suggestion one person can acquire an undue power over the will and conscience of another. This they think will lead to dependence, a weakening of the will and even to the undermining of character. Other persons ask, if suggestion is so powerful an instrument for good, why may it not also be equally powerful for evil? At the present time these are matters of exact knowledge and observation, and no one lacking such knowledge ought to expose himself to merited rebuke by passing *a priori* judgments on them. It is true these misapprehensions have been encouraged, if not created, by the misleading language employed by some earlier writers on hypnotism, especially those of the so-called Salpêtrière School of Paris. The theories of this school, as Bramwell says, are now generally disregarded by those practically engaged in hypnotic work. At no time did Charcot and his colleagues employ hypnosis extensively for therapeutic purposes, and most of their views and statements have been superseded or corrected by later investigators. They made little use of suggestion, but believed in a kind of necromantic power inhering in material objects. Like certain quacks in

America, they believed that medicines are able to exercise an influence within sealed tubes. They asserted that symptoms can be transferred at will from one patient to another or even to a glass of water,[1] that a sealed tube of laurel water when presented to a Jewish prostitute compelled her to adore the Virgin Mary, etc., aberrations which on the part of scientific men, especially after the sober and rational views of Braid, seem incredible. In speaking of the dozen or fifteen hysterical young women on whom their experiments were conducted, they allowed themselves to use very misleading language, calling them "pure automata," "things," "absolute machines," etc. But it is the conviction of recognized authorities on this subject (Bernheim, Forel, Moll, Bramwell, Lloyd Tuckey, etc.) that no such state exists and that Charcot and his disciples were deceived in this and other beliefs. Bramwell observes, "Where the act demanded is contrary to the moral sense, it is usually refused by the normal subject, and invariably by the hypnotized one." Moll, Forel, and Bramwell have so ably argued the case of hypnotism and have so abundantly proved how unreal are its supposed "dangers" in experienced and conscientious hands that it is only necessary to refer to their works.[2] In my own experience I have never seen any instance of weakening of the will or of enfeeblement of personality through suggestion, though I have seen innumerable examples of the strengthening of character

---

[1] See *e.g.* Ernest Hart's *Hypnotism and Humbug.*

[2] Moll, *Hypnotism:* Scribner, N. Y., 3d ed., 1906. Forel, *Hypnotism and Psychotherapy:* Rebman, N. Y., 5th ed., 1906. Bramwell, *Hypnotism:* Alex. Moring, 1906.

and liberation of the will from bondage and evil habit. It ought to be remembered that the operator has no power in himself. He cannot impose his will upon the subject, whether the latter be sleeping or waking. He can only evoke powers which are dormant in the patient's soul or invoke divine powers as one chooses to look at it. If he were to suggest anything contrary to the subject's moral sense, his suggestion would be absolutely rejected. Neither is there any danger in my judgment that the patient will become dependent upon the physician so that his presence and services cannot be dispensed with. In this respect the effect of suggestion is the reverse of that of the drug habit. On the contrary, as the moral nature awakens and assumes control, it becomes independent and needs no longer external support and assistance. The danger lies in this direction rather than in the other, as the patient sometimes believes himself stronger than he is and wishes to discontinue the treatment too soon.

The second objection to suggestion both waking and sleeping is that if good and helpful suggestions will be accepted and acted on, evil and harmful suggestions may also be imposed on passive and unresisting minds. It is one of the encouraging facts in regard to human nature that this natural apprehension has proved to be unfounded. I do not mean to say that criminal suggestions might not be accepted by criminal minds, though it is difficult to see why this should be attempted, as criminals do not need the aid of hypnotism to be incited to crime. Neither do I deny that crimes may be perpetrated on the deeply hypnotized, just as they may be perpetrated on the sleeping, though as Forel observes such acts would be full of danger as one can never judge absolutely of the mental condition of the hypnotized nor predict what memories they may bring with them into consciousness. Nor lastly do I deny that a perversion of character might take place in hypnosis through the repeated efforts of a cunning and wicked person, though the corruptor would meet with far greater difficulty than if he attacked his victim in his or her normal consciousness. But I do assert with distinctness and confidence that no virtuous man or woman will accept a suggestion which is repugnant to his or her moral nature. On the contrary, what we observe in hypnosis is an elevation of the moral faculties, greater refinement of feeling, a higher sense of truth and honor, often a delicacy of mind which the waking subject does not possess. In my opinion the reason for this is that the subconscious mind, which I believe is the most active in suggestion, is purer and freer from evil than our waking consciousness. Every once in a while the story of crime committed through hypnotism is recorded in the papers. I have investigated several of these and have found either that they were pure fabrications or that hypnotism was not employed. The mere fact that the few established instances of the criminal use of hypnotism, the Cynzski case, the murder committed by the half insane Gabriele Bompard, the beggar Castellar who induced a poor girl to follow him, etc., have been cited for years by the text-books shows how insignificant is the number of crimes committed through hypnotism in comparison with those committed every day by other means. Von Lilienthal, who has published perhaps the best statement of the forensic aspects of hypnotism,[1] concludes that the laws at present contain sufficient provisions for the protection of society against its abuse. Into this aspect of the subject I shall not go except to say that two important legal uses of hypnotism, its application in the detection of crime and in the reformation of the criminal, have been but little employed in this country. The latter consideration is a very important one. We have succeeded so well with many persons of criminal tendencies at large in society that it would be well worth the effort to apply the same methods to those confined in prison. The abuse of hypnotism is certainly attended with less danger than the abuse of medicines. Many useful drugs, if taken in too large doses, or when they are not indicated, are dangerous poisons, but this is no reason why they should not be prescribed in proper quantities by competent physicians. In fact hardly a therapeutic agent can be cited, not even the rest cure, which in unskilful hands may not produce harmful results.[2] In this country, what has tended to bring hypnotism into disrepute more than anything else is the curious indifference of public opinion which has permitted irresponsible vagabonds to employ it in exhibitions which are degrading to human nature.

A great deal of importance has been attached to the fact that suggestions of imaginary crimes are frequently

[1] Von Lilienthal, *Hypnotism in its Relation to Jurisprudence* in the *Journal of Collective Legal Science*.

[2] Dr. Mitchell says: "In dealing with this as with every other medical means, it is well to recall that in our attempts to help we may sometimes do harm, and we must make sure that in causing the largest share of good we do the least possible evil. The one goes with the other as shadow with light and to no therapeutic measure does this apply more surely than to the use of rest." — *Fat and Blood*, 8th ed., Phila., 1907, p. 73.

accepted by hypnotized persons. A girl is commanded to put a certain piece of sugar which she is told contains arsenic into her mother's tea, and she obeys. From this it is argued that a virtuous young woman in a state of hypnosis does not scruple to commit a detestable crime. The weak point of these experiments is that the experimenters forgot to ask the patients of their opinion as to the nature of the act they are performing. Bramwell, however, whose discussion of the subject is the best I have seen,[1] took this precaution. He suggested to his patient, Miss D., that she should steal a watch placed conveniently for the purpose on the table. This she refused to do. He asked her later why she had not obeyed his suggestion, and she said, "Because I knew it would be wrong." The same patient in hypnosis told Dr. Bramwell that his suggestion of stealing the watch was only an experiment, but that she would not obey it because she would not do what was wrong even in jest. She admitted, however, that she would put a lump of sugar into her mother's teacup even if Dr. Bramwell said it was arsenic, because she knew it was sugar and such an act would not be even doing wrong in jest. Bramwell cites a number of instances[2] in which his suggestions, though perfectly innocent, were rejected because in some way they offended the moral sense of the subject, e.g., the case of a young woman who refused to see a décolleté photograph of herself, who said: "I never should have my photograph taken in such a low-necked dress, and did not wish to see it, or describe

[1] *Hypnotic Theories* in *op. cit.*
[2] *Hypnotism*, p. 330 ff.

it to you, as the idea offended me." Of course the kind of suggestion which will be accepted or rejected depends largely upon the normal individuality of the subject, but even in the most striking examples of imaginary crime, *e.g.*, that cited by Forel, in which "an old and very suggestible man discharged two blank cartridges at Mr. Hoefelt," we may be sure, as Forel himself admits, that the patient was well aware that the operator would not ask him to commit a real crime. On this subject Moll says: "There is no doubt that subjects can be made to commit all sorts of imaginary crimes in one's study, but these laboratory experiments prove nothing, because some trace of consciousness always remains to tell the subject he is playing a comedy."[1] Bramwell sums up the result of twelve years' experiment and observation in these words: "I have never seen a suggestion accepted in hypnosis which would have been refused in the normal state. I have observed that suggestion could be resisted as easily in the lethargic as in the alert stage. I have frequently noticed increased refinement in hypnosis; subjects have refused suggestions which they would have accepted in the normal state.

"Examination of the mental condition in hypnosis revealed the fact that it was unimpaired."

"Although I am willing to admit that it is possible that harm may be done through the mismanagement of hypnotic cases, I have personally seen no evidence of this either in my own practice or in that of others. Further, I have never seen the slightest bad effect follow carefully conducted hypnotic experiments."[2] In general it may be

[1] *Hypnotism*, p. 371.   [2] *Op. cit.*, p. 330; *op. cit.*, p. 436.

said that while virtuous and normal persons are well protected against evil suggestion, the defective and morally weak may be injured by the unscrupulous. This is a subject of which the laws will have to take cognizance. Far more important to us, however, is the suggestion of mob violence conveyed without the instrumentality of hypnotism, by which the nature of honorable and humane men is temporarily transformed, causing them to commit barbarous and inhuman deeds.

I pass now to a more speculative consideration of the moral and physical changes effected by suggestion. The scope of this work precludes a discussion of the innumerable views advanced to account for hypnotic phenomena, and this is less necessary as a full and admirable discussion of the leading theories is contained in Bramwell.[1] The facts to be accounted for are of the most varied character and it is safe to say that no sufficiently comprehensive and exact explanation of them has as yet been given. Indeed the very nature of so-called hypnotic sleep has not yet been determined, but this is not to be wondered at when we remember our ignorance of natural sleep. The belief of the older mesmerists in an external invisible agent, an odylic force, etc., need not detain us. The purely physical theories, such as Charcot's, Heidenhain's, and Ernest Hart's, may also be rejected, since we know that hypnosis can be induced without mechanical stimulation, that the hypnotized are not automata capable only of reflex action, and lastly that the observed physical changes take place through suggestion and not as the result of mere nerve stimulus. Neither, on the other hand, is suggestion in

[1] *Op. cit.*, 273–424.

itself, as Bernheim seems to think, the sole factor to be considered, for, as Bramwell says, there are certain conditions within the subject, willingness to obey and the ability to do so, which are necessary to the successful employment of suggestion. Moreover, the state of hypnosis itself, whether it be induced by suggestion or by mechanical stimulation, presents certain problems which must be reckoned with.

The relation of hypnosis to natural sleep is a most interesting question. Bernheim regards the two states as practically identical. This view is open to objection on the ground that hypnotized persons usually preserve a degree of intelligence and invariably a moral sense which are not present in normal sleep and dreaming. Yet it must be admitted that the conditions to which one is subjected are very different. The sleeping person lies in a quiet, dark room cut off as far as possible from all sense stimulation, while the mind of the hypnotized subject is invaded by the suggestions of the operator. I have been hypnotized several times for intense fatigue when I was unable to obtain natural sleep, and after the suggestions had been given I was allowed to sleep for several hours. As far as I was able to recall my sensations they differed decidedly from those experienced in a sound nap in the daytime, in that, although profoundly relaxed and unable to move, I did not really lose consciousness. On one occasion I failed to awake at the command of the operator. I heard the order to awake plainly enough and knew what it meant, but I calculated correctly that it was not necessary for me to awake so soon, and I enjoyed my rest so much that I did not wish to be disturbed. Only when

I perceived that the operator was about to dash water in my face could I make the necessary effort. My experiments with sleeping children lead me to believe that there is less difference between induced and natural sleep than is usually supposed. Of course it may be said that my assurance that the child will hear me, but will not awake, causes it to pass from natural sleep to hypnosis. In view of the difficulties others have met in effecting this transition this seems to me unlikely. A little boy of my acquaintance, now about nine years old, talks a good deal in his sleep as the result of vivid dreaming. By entering into the situation presented in his dream it is often possible to engage him in conversation without awakening him. New situations can be suggested to him which he will accept and develop sometimes in a very lively and natural manner. At the present time I am treating a woman of sixty-three for nervous debility and melancholia attended with acute insomnia. I began by visiting her in the afternoon, but finding that my suggestion as to sleep did not produce the desired effect I changed the hour to nine in the evening and treated the patient after she had gone to bed, suggesting that she would fall asleep at once and sleep all night. This has succeeded much better as the patient usually falls into a quiet sleep while I am with her or a few minutes afterward, and does not awake until morning when she finds herself much refreshed. What I wonder is, where hypnosis if it exists ceases and natural sleep begins.

It is probable that the majority of persons who are not good sleepers put themselves to sleep by suggestion, either by concentrating their minds upon the thought and expectation of sleep or at least by excluding all disturbing and exciting thoughts. Bramwell, in arguing against the identity of natural sleep and hypnosis, cites Hirsch's objection that young children do not put themselves to sleep in this way. That is true, their mothers and nurses do it for them. They divert the mind and render the infant slightly dizzy by rocking it. They croon into its ears monotonously repeated lullabies whose sole burden is the oncoming of sleep. If the wakeful child is old enough to understand they give it verbal suggestion. In short, they exhaust the methods of the hypnotists old and new.

The question has been raised whether hypnosis is to be regarded as sleep at all, as in this condition consciousness persists. In reply it may be asked whether consciousness is ever totally extinguished in natural sleep. It is true we are frequently unaware of a single dream during the night, but that may be due to a more vigorous amnesia than that which usually obliterates our dreams a few moments after we awake, an amnesia which can also be readily effected through suggestion in the deeper phases of hypnosis. My friend, Dr. Mumford of Boston, has informed me of extensive experiments on this subject which were once made in the Massachusetts General Hospital in that city. When patients had to be awakened in the usual routine at night they were immediately asked about their dreams, and in every case they were found to be dreaming. I think it very doubtful if hypnotized subjects ever really lose consciousness even in the deeper stages of hypnosis. In my own experience I have invariably retained a pretty clear perception of what was going on around me. In spite of the operator's command that I should hear nothing but his voice, I have heard whispered conversations, the ticking of a clock, etc., and have been able to study my own organic sensations. In fact about the only indication which convinced me that I was really influenced was the fact that I did not feel a pinprick, could not lift my eyelids or resist commands in regard to the movement of my limbs, though I tried to do so. In this my experiences tallied closely with those of Professor Bleuler's,[1] although I think some of my hypnoses were deeper than those he describes. I have asked many persons immediately after hypnosis as to their sensations and they have almost invariably told me the same thing. In fact in the lighter forms of hypnosis it is difficult to make patients believe that they have been influenced at all, as the state of consciousness is so different from the profound sleep they had anticipated. Sometimes, however, they are surprised to discover how much time has elapsed. The only exception that has come under my personal observation is in cases of deep lethargy into which a few persons pass as soon as they are directed to go to sleep. While in this condition such persons show little if any mental activity. It is usually impossible to elicit any rational response from them, and they frequently fail to hear or at least to obey the simplest suggestions. I believe this condition to be pathological and not due to suggestion, as in several instances I have seen the same persons pass into it when merely seated in a comfortable position, without any suggestion of sleep being given to them.

Comparing the most striking phenomena of natural and induced sleep one observes in both the same inertia and relaxation, fixation or closing of the eyes, reduced

[1] Forel, *Hypnotism and Psychotherapy*, chap. xv.

action of the heart, measured and regular breathing, which, however, can be disturbed by both dreams and suggestions. Whether in hypnosis one finds the cerebral anemia supposed to be present in natural sleep is questioned by Heidenhain [1] on the grounds that hypnosis has followed inhalation of nitrate of amyl which causes hyperemia of the brain, and because no change appeared in vessels at the back of the eye during hypnosis. In dream consciousness we have a condition analogous to the thoughts, images, and hallucinations which can be evoked in hypnosis by suggestion. Sully [2] objects to this that the greater part of our dream material in nightly sleep comes from within the organism, not from without as in hypnosis, that the natural dream is more complex and varied than the hypnotic, and that the hypnotical subject tries to translate his hallucinations into actions in a manner that finds no parallel in natural sleep. All these statements may be questioned. Dreams, for example, are believed to arise from two sources, from stimulation of the external senses, and from organic feeling or central action causing or continuing an association of ideas. Of these the former class of dreams occur far more frequently than the latter. Maury, Preyer, and others have shown by classical experiments how readily the dream consciousness follows sense stimulation. A bottle of eau de cologne held to Maury's nostrils caused him to dream that he was in Farina's shop in Cairo. Sprinkling of his face caused Leibner to dream of a shower, etc. Maury, moreover, relates a number of things which returned to his memory

---

[1] Cited by Bramwell, *op. cit.*, p. 306.
[2] Cited by Bramwell, p. 310.

SUGGESTION

in dreams, though when awake he knew nothing of them. Exactly the same phenomena occur in hypnosis without the intervention of spoken suggestion. Moll's experiments in this field are interesting.[1] He hypnotized a person and blew with a pair of bellows without speaking. The subject translated this sound as the exhaust of a steam engine, and by an association of ideas dreamt that he saw a train and the railroad station at Schönberg. Moll drummed with his fingers on the table and the subject dreamt of military music, a parade, etc.[1] Thus two of Sully's statements fall to the ground. Most dreams proceed from external stimulation, and, as Miss Calkins of Wellesley has shown, through the ear rather than through the eye as in hypnosis. Dreams in hypnosis may be as complex as ordinary dreams of normal sleep. Neither is it strictly true to say that the normal dreamer shows no disposition to translate his hallucinations into actions. Somnambulists it is well known execute difficult and dangerous feats which they would not dare to undertake or could not execute in their waking moments. Nervous persons who never walk in their sleep frequently act out their dreams by laughing, weeping, and gesticulating. If the covering is removed they will draw it on again. If a fly or mosquito alights on them they will brush it off again. I have seen my little boy strike out vigorously with his fists when dreaming of fighting. Though not a good rider I have slept soundly on horseback and for more than two hours at a time while the pack train was moving over rough country in the Rocky Mountains, only awaking when my horse suddenly dropped his forefeet down a

[1] *Op. cit.* 211 ff.

declivity. Forel[1] describes in a very interesting manner his experiments with a dormouse sunk so deep in lethargic sleep that it could not be awakened. Forel placed the little animal on the top branch of a small fir tree, and although asleep the contact of the sole of its foot with the branch caused it to cling to the branch with its claws. As it sank into a deeper sleep the muscles of the clinging foot gradually relaxed until the dormouse seemed about to fall. Then, however, its nervous system was pervaded by a sort of instinctive flash and its other foot seized the next lower branch when the same scene was repeated, the dormouse going profoundly to sleep again and saving itself only when just about to fall. It slowly lowered itself from branch to branch until it reached the floor of the cage, when it continued to slumber. This experiment was repeated several times on two dormice with the same result; neither fell and neither awoke.

Thus it appears that hypnosis and natural sleep resemble each other in their physical phenomena and in their dream consciousness more closely than most writers are disposed to admit. Their most fundamental difference consists in the preservation and even the heightening of moral consciousness in hypnosis, and in a capacity for logical thought which dreams do not possess. Both these peculiarities are of great interest. There are few more curious aspects of human nature than the moral character of our dreams. No one apparently is protected against these strange metamorphoses of character which cause us in our sleep to perform acts cheerfully and without remorse which we shudder to think of when we are

[1] Forel, *op. cit.*, chap. xiv.

awake. Our dream consciousness is not controlled by moral judgments, in our dreams we lose for the most part our sense of right and wrong. A trifling circumstance affects us prodigiously while the commission of a crime seems to us quite natural. In hypnosis, however, we see the very reverse of this. The hypnotized person not only preserves his mental rectitude, but his sense of right is heightened, his moral faculties are more sensitive, his delicacy and refinement of feeling are increased and he will frequently refuse suggestions which waking he would accept without scruple. Yet we see an interesting analogy to the moral character of our dream consciousness in the willingness of many hypnotized subjects to commit imaginary crimes. This moral apathy, I believe, proceeds in both cases from the same source. We are warned by an inward sense of the utter unreality of the whole performance. This would not apply to immoral acts actually performed by somnambulists, but these are pathological in their nature, and must either be referred to the perverted waking consciousness or regarded as a moral degeneration resulting from the causes which produce this condition.

The intellectual activity of our dream consciousness is also marked by certain striking characteristics, most noticeable of which is the absence of logical consistency. In our dreams we accept without suspicion the most improbable situations. We pass from one scene to another without sense of incongruity or inconsequence. This is probably due to the fortuitous stimuli which find their way to the passive and sleeping brain, awakening now one and now another association center, which are uncoordinated by attention. We have seen that the same conditions can be produced in hypnosis through the stimulation of the external sense. In spoken suggestion, however, the suggestion claims the attention of the subject, steadies his thought and gives it a purposive and logical character which dreams seldom possess. I would call attention, however, to the fact that apart from our dreams a logical and purposeful mental activity of a very high order frequently occurs during sleep, resulting in the solution of problems, the composition of poems (Voltaire and Coleridge) and the working out of many valuable ideas. These trains of thought seldom if ever emerge as dreams. They are of a more permanent fabric than the stuff which dreams are made of, and they are doubtless to be referred to the action of the subconscious mind.

As the field of hypnotic experimentation has broadened, its phenomena have become richer and more complex, but their very richness and complexity point more inevitably to the one cause which is sufficient to account for them. We have to consider not merely the somatic changes and the dissociations of personality which can be produced by hysteria, but the elevation of moral character, the improvement of certain intellectual processes, abnormal appreciation of the lapse of time, recollection of forgotten events, the overthrow of old and powerful habits and the formation of new ones, the cessation of pain, and the positive removal of innumerable functional disorders. It is obvious that effects of this character point to a psychical cause, in fact to a mind that possesses qualities moral and intellectual. It is equally evident that this mind functions otherwise than our ordinary waking consciousness, for not only are its activities unattended by a sense of effort and conscious attention which characterizes the latter, but it operates in a field whither consciousness cannot follow it, attaining its results through the instrumentality of the sympathetic nervous system, the unstriped muscles, vaso-motors, glands, etc., which lie outside the sphere of consciousness and over which conscious volition has no control. Moreover, it is to be remembered that these phenomena take place not as the result of mechanical nerve stimulation, but by suggestion. All this points in the same direction as the facts already recorded, to a subconscious activity which is essentially moral, but which controls our physical functions to a far greater extent than our consciousness. This is the only hypothesis which is sufficient to account for the facts, but in accepting it we by no means reject all physiological theories as to the manner in which the subconscious mind functions. Bramwell,[1] for example, ridicules Boris Sidis' ingenious theory of dissociation through the contraction of the minute fibers of the nerve cells, on the ground that the facts to be explained are increased volition, memory, intelligence, etc. Yet, granting this, it is certain that dissociation takes place in hypnosis, and Sidis' explanation of the physical concomitant of this condition, the isolation of association centers, may well be correct. Frederic Myers[2] and

---

[1] *Op. cit.* 305.
[2] *Human Personality in the Light of Hypnotic Suggestion. Proceedings of the Society for Psychical Research*, vol. iv. *The Subliminal Consciousness*, ibid. vii, p. 298. vol. ix, pp. 3, 26. *The Subliminal Self*, vol. xi, p. 33 f.

Delbœuf [1] have written with their usual brilliancy and perspicacity upon the possible origin of our subjective consciousness. Delbœuf suggests that in lower forms of life the animal was just as conscious of what was taking place in its interior as of what was happening at its periphery. With the progress of development, however, its attention would be directed more or less exclusively, on the one hand to the organ which placed it in direct relationship with the external world, and on the other to the means of attack or defense which it learned to use from day to day with greater certainty and vigor. At the same time the cares of the interior would be got rid of more and more completely, and would be confided to a servant who had been trained to look after them, and whose zeal could be depended upon. In a highly developed animal such as man, the importance of conscious life distracted the attention from the phenomena of vegetative life; the continual obligation to provide for the necessities of existence absorbed the will, while the mechanical regularity with which internal organs acted rendered conscious attention regarding them unnecessary. The care of the vegetative life had been handed over by the will and nervous mechanism which had learned to regulate themselves, and which in general fulfilled their task to perfection. Sometimes the machine went wrong, and intervention became desirable. The power which formerly regulated it had, however, dropped out of the normal consciousness, and if we desire to find a substitute for it we must turn to hypnotism. In the hypnotic state the mind was in part drawn

[1] *De l'origine des effets curatifs l'hypnotisme. Étude de physiologie experimentale.* Paris, 1887.

aside from the life of relation while at the same time it preserved its activity and power. Voluntary attention could be abstracted from the outer world and directed with full force upon a single point, and thus the hypnotic subconsciousness was able to put in motion machinery which the normal consciousness had lost sight of and had ceased to regulate. If a contrary opinion had till now prevailed, this is because observation has been exclusively directed to the normal exercise of the will. The will, however, in the hypnotic state can regulate movements which have become irregular, and assist in the repair of organic injury. In a word, hypnotism does not depress but exalts the will by permitting it to concentrate itself upon the point where the disorder is threatened.[1]

Myers suggests that the stream of consciousness in which we live may not be our only one. Possibly our habitual consciousness may be a mere selection from a multitude of thoughts and sensations. The self below the *threshold* of ordinary consciousness Myers terms the subliminal consciousness, and the empirical self of common experience the supraliminal. He holds that subliminal consciousness and memory possess a far wider range of physiological and psychical activity than the supraliminal. The latter is limited by the need of concentrating itself on recollections useful in the struggle for existence, while the former includes much that is too rudimentary to be retained in the supraliminal memory of an organism so advanced as man's. The recollection of processes now performed automatically, and needing no

---

[1] Slightly abridged from Bramwell's statement of Delbœuf's views, *op. cit.*, pp. 568–9.

supervision, passed out of the supraliminal memory but might be retained by the subliminal. The subliminal or hypnotic self can exercise over the nervous, vaso-motor and circulatory systems a degree of control unparalleled in waking life.

Further, Myers suggests that the *spectrum* of *consciousness* as he calls it is indefinitely extended at both ends in the subliminal self. Beyond its supraliminal physiological limit lies a vast number of complex processes belonging to the body's nutrition and well-being. These our remote ancestors may have been able to modify at will, but with us they seem to be withdrawn from the field of volition. If we wish to modify them we employ drugs and medicines. At the superior or psychical end lies an unknown mass of impressions which the supraliminal consciousness is unable to receive directly and which it must apprehend through messages from the subliminal consciousness. Myers arranged hypnotic phenomena in three grand divisions. 1. The great dissociative triumph of hypnotism in the inhibition of pain under conditions of nerve and tissue with which it is otherwise inevitably connected. 2. The associative or synthetic triumphs of hypnotism in the production and control of organic processes which no effort of normal consciousness can effect. 3. The intellectual and moral achievements of hypnotism in the removal of physical cravings for alcohol, morphia, etc., and the eradication of destructive habits and tendencies. This is believed to be effected through the paralysis of the lower appetitive centers by hypnotism and the exaltation of the will.[1] These views are im-

[1] Abridged from Bramwell's statement, *op. cit.*, pp. 358 ff.

portant because they have contributed largely to the development of the doctrine of the subconscious mind.

The chief criticism I should make of Myers' and Delbœuf's illuminating theories is that they identify the subconscious mind too closely with the phenomena of hypnosis. It is true that in the hypnotic state the dissociation of the subconscious mind from consciousness is most complete and its activity most striking, but we should not forget how large a part is played by the subconscious mind in our normal lives and without the intervention of hypnosis. It is certain, *e.g.*, that far more diseases have been cured by the emotional effect of strong faith and expectation than have been cured by hypnotism. Intense preoccupation or excitement can render one as insensible to fatigue and pain as hypnotic suggestion. Innumerable events of our past lives are flashed on us by subconscious memory without external aid. Permanent pathological dissociation certainly occurs, and with the greatest achievements of the subconscious mind, the inspirational creations of genius, hypnotism has nothing to do. I mention these facts because it would be an error belittling to our subject to identify the subconscious mind with its hypnotic activity, as Charcot identifies hypnosis with hysteria.

Myers' and Delbœuf's suggestion that the physical functions now regulated by the subconscious mind were perhaps originally within the field of consciousness and under the control of the will may be true. At all events conscious emotional states still possess somewhat the same power. It can hardly be doubted that dissociation which inhibits counter-suggestion and concentrates the whole power of the will upon the act to be performed is an important factor in all curative suggestions. Bramwell questions this on account of the undiminished intelligence of hypnotized subjects, but it is only necessary to remember the gross hallucinations to which they are subject to perceive how limited the sphere of their mentality is and how incapable such subjects are of comparing and analyzing their sensations. The rapid changes in the coloration of fishes to harmonize with their environment might be cited in support of Myers' theory. This may be regarded as a conscious act in so far as it is effected through vision. I would also call attention to a fact which so far as I have noticed has been overlooked in the discussions of this question, *i.e.*, the tendency of injured animals to sleep. The sick or wounded bird or animal as a rule falls into a profound sleep, thus escaping from pain, and in this sleep recovery takes place. Animals also appear to possess a capacity for the inhibition of pain which we do not know. It is unusual to see in them indications of suffering after the injury has occurred. Fowls will pick up food only a few minutes before death. Horses after receiving ghastly wounds in battle have been found contentedly cropping grass. In general it is interesting to observe how the trend of modern thought tends to substantiate Schopenhauer's position that the unconscious volitional element in man is fundamental, while the conscious, rational element is acquired, and that the former which normally regulates our functions is also most active in the elimination of disease.[1]

[1] See *e.g.* W. Hanan Thomson's work, *Brain and Personality*, Dodd, Mead and Co., New York, 1902, in which Dr. Thomson shows how true this is in the development of the higher brain centers controlling speech, visual and auditory memories, etc.

CHAPTER IV

AUTO-SUGGESTION

WE have seen how powerfully suggestion operates when administered in the waking state or in a hypnotic sleep. Let us now consider a third form of suggestion in which the idea presented to the mind takes its origin, not, as in the other two forms, from without, but from within, is produced by the activity of one's own brain. To this process has been given the name Auto-Suggestion, a barbaric but convenient term, of Greek and Latin origin, meaning a hint offered by the self to the self. It differs from suggestion only in this, that the point of departure of the hint is *within* the individual, whereas in the case of suggestion it is *without*. At bottom, suggestion and auto-suggestion are the same. The mechanism of the brain which carries into effect the suggestion offered in a hypnotic or in a waking state carries into effect also auto-suggestion; in the one as in the other there is the same mental state of heightened suggestibility; and common to both are the same morbid and healing effects. Auto-suggestion may be defined, then, as a self-imposed narrowing of the field of consciousness to one idea, by holding a given thought in the mental focus, to the exclusion of all other thoughts. This statement, of course, does not solve the problem of auto-suggestion: it is intended simply to express what is meant by the word. The thing itself, the psychical process covered by the word, remains and is likely to remain for a long time the standing riddle of psychology. What it is in its ultimate nature, how it operates, and what are its physiological or nervous concomitants, no man knows. That it is a reality, however, and a reality of the highest psychical and ethical significance, no man may doubt.

To be convinced of its reality one has but to take a glance at the history of ideas and especially of religious ideas. The amulets and charms of savage men owed what efficacy they possessed to the fact that they were the symbols of an inner mental state, the objects to which the desire or yearning could attach itself — in a word, they were auto-suggestions done into wood or stone. With the rise of polytheism, auto-suggestion takes the form of dreams or even of self-induced hallucinations in which the god appears and says the redeeming and saving word to the suppliant. And when we rise still higher, what is the goal of the ancient Vedantist philosophy of India, the union of the individual ego or soul with Brahman, the cosmic Divine essence, what is the Neo-platonic ecstasy in which the soul flees from earth and time and becomes a citizen of the eternal world, what are the transcendental visions of Swedenborg, his angels and demons, heavens and hells — what are these but elaborate and profound auto-suggestions? Nor has the Christian religion left this element in the psychical organism unaffected. Some of the phenomena of the Apostolic age, such as "the speaking with tongues," are to be thus psychologically explained.

So too in a measure may we account for the intrepidity the more than human endurance with which old men and children, young men and maidens, faced death in the Roman amphitheatre in a form so terrible that its mere description turns cold our blood to-day. Auto-hypnotism may well have been the means by which the Divine mercy spared them the worst agonies of their fate. And when we come later to the mystics and monks of the Middle Ages, much in their experience which has been rejected by the scientific mind as incredible, and accepted by the religious mind as miraculous, is now seen to be neither one nor other, but a reality to be explained in terms of psychical processes. Perhaps the most striking of these phenomena is that of stigmatization which has, however, been paralleled in our own time in the case of some hysterical patients. From St. Francis of Assisi and Catherine of Siena to the famous case of Louise Lateau there has been a succession of susceptible souls who by intense mental concentration on the sufferings of the Saviour, on the wounds in his hands and feet and side, have in some way, inexplicable to physiology, so affected the bodily organism as to reproduce in it the sorrows of the Crucified. And thus in a very real sense they may be said to have borne "branded on their bodies the marks of the Lord Jesus."[1]

[1] For a philosophy of auto-suggestion the reader is referred to F. W. H. Myers' *Human Personality and Its Survival of Bodily Death*, vol. ii, pp. 311-314.
"There will be effective therapeutical or ethical self-suggestion whenever by any artifice subliminal attention to a bodily function or to a moral purpose is carried to some unknown pitch of intensity which draws energy from the metetherial world." *Ibid.*, vol. i, p. 218.

Actual observation and experiment in our own time have confirmed the testimony of history as to the reality of auto-suggestion. We know, for example, that the hypnotist with a few words whispered to his subject can induce in him a headache or colic or an attack of indigestion, nay, that the same pathological states can be induced by waking suggestion in the case of specially suggestible people. Why then should not an idea arising internally — an auto-suggestion — bring about the same effects? And as a matter of fact we find this to be the case. The psychical disorder called hypochondria is really the fruit of vicious auto-suggestion. "Feelings of uneasiness or even pain originate in the mind a suspicion of disease existing in particular parts of the body, it may be the lungs, stomach, heart, brain, liver, or kidneys. Slight irregularities and functional disturbances in the action of these organs being noticed, are at once suggestive, to those hypochondriacally disposed, of serious and fatal disease progressing in the part to which the attention is conveyed. This deviation from a natural state of certain functions frequently lapses into actual structural disease, as the effect of the attention being for a lengthened period morbidly concentrated on their action."[1]

Take two typical illustrations. A youth is struck by the fact that the majority of the members of his family die of heart disease at a given period of life, and he is forced to believe that a like fate awaits him. But the day is as yet distant: he is young, and the idea does not unduly worry him. Still it exists in the subconscious

[1] Forbes Winslow, M.D., *On the Obscure Diseases of the Brain and Disorders of the Mind*, pp. 221 sig.

region of his mind: and occasionally it reappears as the years pass by. But the time approaches when his family weakness is accustomed to disclose itself: the auto-suggestion gathers strength unless the healthy elements in consciousness can suppress it. Often the imagination creates nervous cardiac pain, and the sufferer feels palpitations and flutterings and these will give a basis, a point of support for the auto-suggestion, and at once a conviction that the disease is real, and the fatal hour has struck, seizes the mind with overpowering force. And this conviction reacts on the physical organ, giving rise to all kinds of nervous complications. The man sinks into chronic invalidism — the victim of an auto-suggestion.[1] The other illustration is afforded by a sufferer known to us whose trouble is to be traced to the reading of a medical work — a practice which the non-medical person would do well to avoid. Nowhere is the adage so much to the point as here: "A little knowledge is a dangerous thing." Our lady friend, while feeling, from some accidental and temporary cause, depressed and melancholy, happened to read that slow and difficult speech is a sign of approaching paresis or paralysis. She at once felt that such a fate would be hers, and sure enough, soon afterwards she developed a slow, drawling utterance which of course tended to confirm the original self-suggestion. The experts were agreed that there was no organic disease present and convinced the patient of that fact: nevertheless, the self-suggestion had done its work and the speech defect persisted. The remedy was found in reversing

[1] See Lefevre: *Les Phenomenes de Suggestion et D'Auto Suggestion*, pp. 112 seq.

the psychical process that brought about the mischief, in substituting a true for a false auto-suggestion. Illustrations of this order may be found among all sufferers from nervous disorders. Indeed hysteria has been defined as "a form of unconscious auto-hypnotism." And the miseries of neurasthenia are immensely increased by the same morbid cause. Dubois has given abundant illustrations of this fact in his interesting work, "Psychic Treatment of Nervous Disorders." And his great success in dealing with these disorders has been due to his singular skill in leading his patient to substitute good auto-suggestions for bad ones.

But the power of auto-suggestion is seen in normal as in abnormal humanity. Many of the little mannerisms and habits from which we seem unable to shake ourselves free are to be explained in this way. One person can not sleep except when lying on his right side, another can eat mutton but regards veal with aversion, and a third, if he is to be comfortable while traveling, must sit with his back to the engine. Such are some of the tricks we play upon ourselves. Unhappily the force of auto-suggestion is operative in more important concerns. The fanatic whether in politics or in theology is the bond-slave of his self-suggestion: the whole universe is for him concentrated into a single red-hot spot — his consciousness is narrowed to this point and for him everything else is not. The heresy hunter, the dietetic "crank" who would reconstruct the order of human life on the basis of "predigested" cereals, the temperance or teetotal "faddist" who believes that the utter abolition of alcohol would mean the dawn of millennial glory —

these familiar figures in English and American life are all intelligible in the light of the psychological principle which we are now discussing. What these men are suffering from is a dissociation of consciousness, more or less, and they become normal men once consciousness is unified and they see life steadily and as a whole.

So far we have noted the mischievous effects that auto-suggestion can work. But it is also a power for good. As a therapeutic agency and uplifting ethical force, its value can hardly be exaggerated. The various troubles, physical and mental, which are amenable to its influence make a long list. A few may be named: the milder neurasthenic and hypochondriacal states, functional disturbances of the digestive apparatus, constipation not dependent on organic disease, mild insomnia, certain forms of neuralgic headaches, the milder types of melancholia, irritability of temper, lack of self-confidence, constitutional nervousness, swearing, perverse self-will, vicious habits, stage-fright, and various types of lesser obsessions. In these and other troubles the patient can, as Shakespeare says, "minister to himself." What a gospel of hope is here for the depressed and unhappy! What a chance of redemption for those who are the slaves of circumstance or of their own folly! In saying this we are not giving rein to an airy optimism: we are keeping well within the limits of sober reasoning and scientific fact. All functions of the bodily organism are controlled by the nerves, which end in the brain mechanism which in turn is dependent on ideas. If, then, mischievous ideas set in action the automatism of the brain and thus create a morbid state, does it not follow that good ideas, opposing auto-suggestions, will neutralize these first and thereby dissipate the nervous or mental trouble? In other words, if one state of mind can produce a disease another state of mind can effect a cure.

In a remarkable essay,[1] Dr. Coste de Lagrave, a French physician, describes a number of experiments which he made upon himself during several years — experiments by which he was able to cure himself of certain physical weaknesses and to evoke latent qualities of soul and intellect. For example, following on an attack of dysentery he developed neurasthenia. Prominent among the symptoms was an extraordinary sense of fatigue: he could with difficulty walk a mile a day; the fatigue obstacle was insurmountable. One evening he suggested to himself that he would be able to walk without fatigue. On the following day he walked about seven miles with ease — a journey broken only by one hour's rest. On another occasion when riding with the regiment to which he was attached he suffered greatly from cold feet. Disposing himself as comfortably as possible on his horse's back, he closed his eyes, induced a somnolent state and then suggested to himself that his feet should be warm. In about half an hour he felt a distinct sensation of warmth in them. This lasted for ten minutes: unhappily, his mind called away to other things, his poor feet at the end of that brief respite returned to their original state of frigidity. He did not resume the effort at auto-suggestion owning to the accompanying mental fatigue. "I preferred," he says, "to have cold feet." In the intellectual

[1] Read before the first Paris International Congress of Experimental and Therapeutic Hypnotists. See the proceedings, pp. 290–311.

sphere he found auto-suggestion of the highest value. It was his duty to entertain a certain great lady, but his efforts at doing so proved a miserable failure: he was tongue-tied in her presence, and his first visit was very short. Thanks to auto-suggestion, however, on the second occasion he burst forth into conversational eloquence that lasted an hour and a quarter! But perhaps his most striking experiment was his self-suggestion that he should have abundance of ideas, and that he should have ease in putting them on paper. He found that the amount of literary work he was able to accomplish was in proportion to the duration of the auto-suggestion. On the other hand, he noticed that when he failed to make his auto-suggestions he could not write ten lines and was compelled to turn to something else. So powerful did his act of auto-suggestion become that he was able to produce dreams and even hallucinations. "I no longer lived," he says, "among the living but in another world — a world that thought and reasoned quite differently from this one." This last experience so frightened him that he ceased his experiments in the region of dreams and fancies. Our observation, so far as it has gone, confirms the testimony of this scientific witness.

Many have come to us suffering from disagreeable habits of various kinds, from fears and inhibitions such as stage-fright, from nervous weakness and lack of vital energy, and they have been put in the path of self-cure by being taught how to practice auto-suggestion.[1] It is hardly necessary to remark at this point that auto-suggestion no more than any other form of suggestion is an

[1] See Appendix A.

omnipotent power. It has its limitations. In the first place, the organs by which the auto-suggestion is realized must be themselves in a healthy state organically. The hypnotist may call upon his subject to move his arm or leg, but if the motor zone of the patient's brain is destroyed, the command will remain unfulfilled. The same thing holds good in the case of the auto-hypnotist. Hence the importance of examination by a competent medical authority, before undertaking the work of self-cure. Otherwise, failure and despair may attend the effort. In the second place, we must note the limitations in the mental realm. The auto-suggestionist must have the intellectual acquisitions in connection with the idea which he seeks to realize. Otherwise he is addressing a vacuum — the most hopeless of all tasks.

If an illiterate man is put into a hypnotic sleep and is ordered to preach a sermon before a large congregation, he will probably misquote a few half-forgotten scraps from the Bible, his exegesis will be loose, his arguments will be painful platitudes, and his illustrations, to say the least, will be racy of the soil from which the preacher sprang. So too with the auto-suggestionist: he must have the prior intellectual accomplishments which fit him to play the wished for role. We cannot say with Dr. Johnson that a man can become anything he chooses, a great musician, a great mathematician or a great poet. Nevertheless it is equally true that a man can *if he will* approximate to greatness along lines in harmony with his nature. "*If he will*" — "Ay, there's the rub," the reader may say. "My misery is that I cannot will. I am blown this way and that. I seem incapable of gathering up my forces and directing them to some tolerable end. From my birth I have been a weakling, a moral and physical failure. To bid me will is merely to mock me." What answer can be made to this cry of wretchedness? What but this: "You are a moral being, endowed with reason and conscience, and these insist that you ought to have self-control, that you ought to organize your nature on a moral basis. But if you ought, you *can*, otherwise the Creator has put us to permanent confusion. Appeal, then, to yourself: rouse the capacity to will that lies dormant within you: rise up and obey the behests of your better self." The power to will comes by willing just as the power to think comes by thinking.

"The education of the will," says Emerson, "is the object of our existence." And there is no better aid in this education than the practice of auto-suggestion. For what, after all, is the will? It is simply the effort to concentrate our attention on and thus select one idea rather than another. Now in auto-suggestion the predominant element is the concentration of thought on, or the narrowing of consciousness to, a single idea. So that in a sense we might say that auto-suggestion is simply the will in action. It is a roundabout way of getting the will to work. And the blessed path which auto-suggestion takes is that of the removal of inhibitions or checks on the activity of the will. Here is to be found the secret of that new sense of power which has come into so many lives to-day through the medium of Christian Science, Faith-healing, Metaphysical Healing, the Raja Yoga of Indian theosophy and other forms of mental gymnastics. These systems are so many aids to the training of the will by auto-suggestion so that the reserves of mental and moral energy within us may be made available for physical and spiritual health. Within all of us are these reservoirs of power, but ordinarily we cannot release their current, they are inhibited by various psychical influences. "Most of us feel," says Professor James, "as if we lived habitually with a sort of cloud weighing upon us, below our highest notch of clearness in discernment, sureness in reasoning or firmness in deciding . . . We are making use of only a small part of our possible mental and physical resources. In some persons this sense of being cut off from their rightful resources is extreme and we then get the formidable neurasthenic and psychasthenic conditions, with life grown into one tissue of impossibilities." This distinguished writer goes on to show how "levels of new energy" which have remained unutilized may be tapped by the will set to work by various suggestive methods.[1] Thus modern psychology puts its imprimatur on a very ancient doctrine, though in doing so it strips it of its occult and mysterious atmosphere. From this point of view, auto-suggestion may be described as a means by which the pent-up energies within us may be released to innervate afresh the whole man, or, to use psychological language, as the method by which the inhibitions may be lessened and the threshold may be lowered so that the stored-up energy may be made available for the restoration of mental and physical equilibrium.

The reader may ask: What of the dangers attending

[1] See a notable essay, "The Energies of Men," in *The Philosophical Review* for January, 1907.

auto-suggestion? Do not the newspapers print stories from time to time of persons who by self-hypnotism have done themselves irreparable injury, have even died in the act? Doubtless: but have not newspaper stories come to be synonymous with "fairy tales"? Take the following as a safe rule especially as regards psychological matters: *Read newspapers with the utmost scepticism, suspending your judgment until after the closest investigation.* An excellent illustration of the need for this rule has been made public recently. A story was widely published to the effect that a certain gentleman had hypnotized himself and could not awaken from his sleep, and finally that he died from the effects of self-hypnosis. Such a statement was calculated to impress the popular mind and to create all sorts of absurd fears much to the detriment of the general weal. An investigation was made. It turned out, on the authority of the attending physician, that the gentleman died of tumor of the brain and the story referred to was pronounced to be a concoction, "pure and simple, the finished product of Yellow Journalism, published again after repeated denials of its truthfulness."[1] The average man regards all psychical phenomena with suspicion as uncanny and other-worldly, and the average editor supplies the sensational pabulum that a superstitious credulity demands.

A few practical hints may be added: —

1. Some forms of acute pain are amenable to auto-suggestion. Liébeault tells how he cured himself by auto-hypnotism of such a painful disorder as facial neu-

[1] See *Journal of the American Society for Psychical Research*, p. 430, September, 1907.

ralgia. As a rule, where there is pain the curative suggestion must be made by another.

2. Assuming the absence of acute pain and of any organic disease, auto-suggestion may be entered on with confidence. The best condition for its induction is that of somnolence, whether preceding sleep or accompanying awaking. At night, then, and in the morning, immediately before sleeping and immediately after beginning to awake, the half-sleeping and half-waking or "hypnagogic" state is most favorable to success. By practice one can induce this state at other times.

3. Lying in bed or in a comfortable arm-chair, with the eyes closed and the limbs relaxed, formulate and repeat mentally the thought that contradicts the unhealthy state of consciousness or that expresses the virtue or quality you desire to possess. The auto-suggestion must be made over and over again, not with a sense of stress or strain, but calmly and with quiet assurance. Suppose you are a victim to mental sluggishness; you desire to read and study, to realize worthy ambitions, but when the time comes for work your brain refuses to act and thoughts will not come. What are you to do?

Choose a time when the brain is most suggestible and that is generally when you feel an inclination to sleep, then calmly formulate in your mind some such proposition as this: "I am organically sound: the nervous system is intact; the bodily organs are discharging their proper functions, therefore I ought to have a mind clear and alert, able to grasp ideas and to relate them logically: therefore, such a mind can be mine. Henceforth I will think easily and correctly: study will be a delight and work a joy." Your trouble will yield to repeated suggestions of this order, which create, as it were, a psychic line of least resistance. That is, it will become easier for you to think well and quickly, than to think with difficulty or not at all.

4. *Auto-suggestion must be persistent and systematic.* This is an indispensable prerequisite to the best results.

5. Some degree of belief in the reality and efficacy of the suggestive principle is necessary. The subject must admit into his mind the thought that he can be helped so as to prevent the inhibition of the auto-suggestion by the higher faculties: the thought admitted puts in motion the cerebral mechanism.

6. Finally, the success attending auto-suggestion varies with the mental constitution and the degree of suggestibility of the subject and the nature of the trouble to cure which the suggestion is made.

CHAPTER V

THE FUNCTIONAL NEUROSES

As we hope that this book will be of some service to nervous sufferers, we are loath to introduce into it any descriptions of disease. But on the other hand the chief object we have proposed to ourselves is an account of the work undertaken for the benefit of the sick in Emmanuel Church, and to give this without any discussion of the disorders we attempt to treat is impossible. The sick are therefore advised to skip this chapter and they would probably do so without advice.

Every one knows how difficult it is to describe nervousness, partly because its forms are so protean, its phenomena are so rich; partly because they are so elusive. Nor is this to be wondered at when we remember the infinite delicacy and complexity of the nervous system, and its intimate connection with our moral life. On these accounts, nervous affections are apt to be more diffused than others, their symptoms more variable, their forms more fluid and indistinct. The nervous system is general and possesses a great variety of elements, and its diseases also are general and less susceptible than others of definite classification. They may affect one organ or the whole system, sensibility, locomotion, intellect, and character. The difficulty of classifying nervous disorders is shown by the fact that their nomenclature is constantly changing.

A little while ago everyone spoke of nervous prostration. Now almost every form of nervousness is referred to as neurasthenia. The disorder known as psychasthenia is not mentioned in the older books, while hypochondria of which we used to hear so much has become unfashionable. This fact should be carefully borne in mind. Though the several recognized types of nervous disorders present some more or less constant forms and symptoms, yet these forms tend constantly to merge and to blur the picture. They have been compared [1] to the old so-called temperaments, the sanguine, the phlegmatic, the choleric, and the melancholic.[2] No doubt these represent real aspects of human nature. The difficulty is that few human beings possess them in their pure forms. The same is true of nervous disorders. We speak of the neurasthenic temperament, the melancholic, the hysterical, etc., but it is to be remembered that the diagnosis is determined by the dominant note, while the minor symptoms may be identical. Möbius has prepared a kind of schematic representation of the several neuroses, both functional and organic, in which their types are classified and their general relations indicated by intersecting circles, or by straight lines, e.g., those leading from St. Vitus' dance to epilepsy. The great

[1] — e.g., by the celebrated Paul Julius Möbius whose admirable work, both literary and scientific, deserves to be better known in this country. I have drawn on the latter freely in the preparation of this chapter and the two following chapters — especially on *Die Nervösität, Dritte Aufl.* Leipsic, 1906.

[2] "The ancient distinction of the four temperaments which psychology borrowed from the medical theories of Galen sprang from a fine observation of individual differences of men." W. Wundt, *Phys. Psychol.* II, 422.

central circle, Nervousness, it will be observed, intersects all the others, and within this circle lies a smaller one called nervous weakness or neurasthenia, as this lies at the center of all the neuroses without presenting in itself their peculiar phenomena. This scheme is interesting

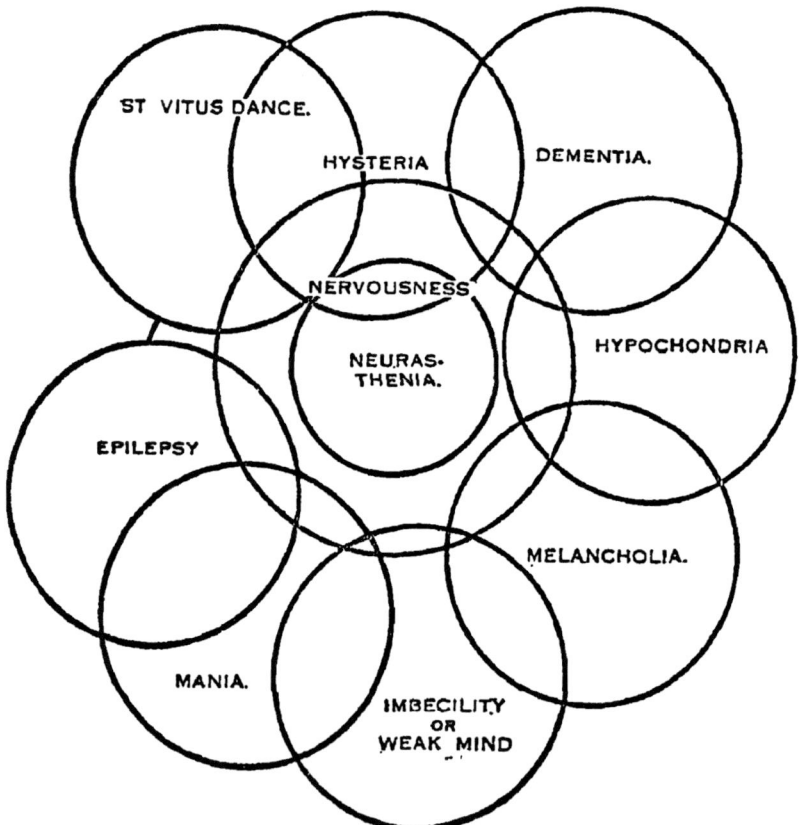

and instructive provided it be remembered that it is only a mechanical device which does not pretend to express everything.

A neurosis is an affection of the nervous system whether it is functional or organic, local or general, in its character.

Functional neuroses or functional nervous disorders are those which involve no change in the form and structure of the elements and organs of the nervous system, or rather, since every effect must have its cause, they are those which involve no change which can be perceived. What we ordinarily call nervousness is less a disease than a condition, the result of overstrain or over stimulation of our nervous system, and here the difficulty of defining nervous disorders appears. The most healthy person may feel the subjective depression, the sense of irritable weakness and exhaustion which we call nervousness. But when this condition is not removed by normal rest, when it becomes acute and gives rise to a general physical debility, it is called neurasthenia.

Neurasthenia, as the name implies, indicates a condition of nervous weakness and irritability. It is the most common and least specialized of the functional neuroses. Möbius expresses this by placing neurasthenia which he calls nerve weakness at the center of his chart, on the ground that all other nervous disorders are attended by irritability and exhaustion. Persons suffering from neurasthenia are easily excited and they tire easily. They are apt to suffer from depression and from pains in the back and limbs, from headache and insomnia. Their enfeebled condition exposes them to other maladies such as digestional disturbances, vertigo and palpitation of the heart, weakness of vision, and in severe cases it may amount to absolute prostration. Neurasthenia is frequently attended by loss of flesh, which, as Dr. Mitchell points out,[1] is an important symptom in itself and because

[1] *Fat and Blood*, p. 15.

it is apt to be attended by anæmia. What is the cause of this weakness and exhaustion which cannot be removed by normal rest? Apart from hereditary predisposition, it is almost invariably psychical in its origin. The patient has been subjected to a nervous strain too great for his powers. He has experienced some moral shock, or has undergone an experience which has given rise to anxiety, worry, or fear, any of which may result in profound depression, the weakening of the normal powers of resistance. In fact all the functional neuroses are to be regarded as diseases of the subconscious mind. By recognizing this we simplify diagnosis, and we are in a position to understand why it is that one form of nervous disorder passes so readily into another. When the psychical poise is established the physical symptoms usually disappear. In many cases this is most readily attained by the admirable system of treatment devised by Dr. Mitchell; but as Dr. Mitchell affirms,[1] no treatment of neurasthenia succeeds which ignores its moral aspects.

2. Hysteria, although pre-eminently an affection of women, has no necessary connection with the reproductive organs (hystera = womb). The interesting characteristic of hysteria is that the thoughts of persons suffering from it create morbid physical and mental conditions, *e.g.*, violent pains and partial paralysis, in short the very conditions which can be produced by suggestion. This fact led Frederic Myers to propose his interesting theory that hysteria is at bottom a disease of the sub-

[1] "The physician who neglects to consider the moral and mental needs and aspects of each case will find that many will relapse." — *Fat and Blood*, p. 79.

conscious mind, a theory which is now generally accepted. "It is a striking characteristic of the hypnotic self that it can exercise over the nervous, vasomotor, and circulatory systems a degree of control unparalleled in waking life. Are we aware in practice of any malady or group of maladies in which these functions, these capacities, are the subject of special disturbances? Are there anæsthesiæ appearing, shifting, and disappearing as rapidly as the suggested anæsthesiæ of hypnotism? Are there anomalous vasomotor disturbances which seem to follow the patient's mere caprice? The reader will answer with the word hysteria, and meaningless or misleading though that term be, it is in fact our first and obvious reply. Not, indeed, all, but almost all the phenomena which can be induced by suggestion in the hypnotic state occur spontaneously in hysterical patients."[1] Charcot and his disciples also recognized the intimate relation of hysteria to hypnotic phenomena, but instead of regarding hysteria as a disease of the subconscious mind, they attempted to force all hypnotic phenomena and other evidences of subconsciousness into the category of hysteria. The unanswerable objection to this is that more than ninety per cent of normal men and women can be hypnotized, while real hysteria is comparatively a rare disease. Myers' theory, therefore, that hysteria is a disease of the subconscious mind may be regarded as highly probable. Its phenomena are produced by morbid auto-suggestion over which normal consciousness has little control. The most constant symptom is disturbance of sensibility. The patient may be insensitive on one side of the body, she

[1] Quoted by Bramwell, *op. cit.*, pp. 364-5.

may become blind in one eye or be affected by mysterious pains and abnormal feelings in various parts of the body. One leg or even both legs may be paralyzed, although this is a mere nervous inhibition as is shown by the fact that the paralyzed limb is able to execute all other movements than those involved in standing and walking. The patient may suddenly lose her voice and as suddenly recover it. On the other hand, sensibility may be heightened, certain portions of the body become exquisitely sensitive and the patient keenly perceives her own organic processes. Palpitation of the heart, marked difficulty of breathing, pain in the stomach, strange sensations in the intestines may ensue. In severer cases partial or general convulsions may occur which are frequently mistaken for epilepsy but which produce little if any effect on the personality. The nervous instability of the hysterical is well known. They frequently laugh uncontrollably and their laughter turns to tears with no apparent reason. Persistent vomiting, hiccoughing, etc., frequently occur. In short there is scarcely a functional disturbance which may not be produced by hysteria or an organic disease whose symptoms cannot be counterfeited. A friend of the author was about to operate for the removal of a moderately large abdominal tumor. When the patient was etherized the tumor disappeared — a case of hysterical phantom tumor. The very general character of hysterical symptoms leads us to suspect a general cause like the subconscious mind which is able to control all the machinery of the body. The pains, anæsthesiæ and other phenomena of hysteria are constantly shifting. As they are produced by suggestion, they can be removed by the same means. The underlying cause, however, cannot be so easily analyzed or disposed of, yet suggestion unquestionably is the best method of treatment. I have observed a marked difference, however, in hysterical patients. Some are controlled almost wholly by their own suggestions and are difficult to influence, while others yield much more readily.

The psychical symptoms of hysteria are hardly less pronounced. We observe an increased emotional excitability and rapid changes of mood. Hysterical persons are naturally keenly interested in their own sensations and feelings. They are frequently at the mercy of perverse impulses and deaf to reason. They are capricious, sensitive, and irritable and seldom wish to suffer alone. Although memory sometimes suffers in hysteria, the intelligence is seldom affected. Hysterical traits are found in all nervous disorders, especially in nervous exhaustion, but they usually disappear with the latter.

3. Of late years a third type of nervous disorder has been recognized which is known as psychasthenia.[1] This term is used to designate a form of nervous weakness in which the psychical element is dominant. Its distinctive characteristics are weakness of will and overscrupulousness, frequently accompanied by episodes of a strange sense of the unreality of all things. Psychasthenic patients find it difficult to come to a decision whether the matter be big or little, and this inability troubles them. They are apt to doubt and to question everything, even their own acts. I once treated a schoolteacher who was frequently tormented at night with the

[1] This word is not found in the Century Dictionary, 2d ed., 1895; it was coined by Janet.

apprehension that she had locked up one of her pupils in the school building, and in order to obtain sleep she was obliged more than once to visit the school in the middle of the night and assure herself that no child was confined there. Such persons are frequently compelled to perform an act a second time to assure themselves that they have actually done it. They are troubled and anxious about many things and frequently ascribe this to a "New England Conscience." In severer cases they become the victims of morbid fears and so-called fixed ideas, an unspeakably bitter bondage of which the well can form no conception. These phobias may attach themselves to almost any act or situation of life, though as a rule they are pretty well defined. Their victim may recognize their absurdity. He may keenly appreciate the fact that they are limiting his usefulness and cutting him off from every pleasure in life, but such knowledge gives him no power to resist them. I will give a few typical cases from our practice. A woman read of leprosy in the Bible and that one or two Chinese lepers had been discovered in this country. Immediately she conceived a violent dread of leprosy and also the idea that she and her children were exposed to it. She became afraid to touch almost every object and spent much of her time in washing her hands until she reflected that the soap might be infected, a thought which drove her to despair, as it seemed to destroy her last refuge. This case was cured by repeated suggestion.

A highly educated gentleman dropped a tin bucket down a well many years ago. In peering down the well he became dizzy and confused. This gave him an aversion to wells and also to tunnels. Dreading the latter he began to avoid traveling and his repugnance toward tunnels extended itself until he became unwilling to allow anything belonging to him to pass through them. Accordingly, if he wished to send a letter to the western part of Massachusetts he would forward his letter to another point and have it remailed in order that it might avoid the Hoosac Tunnel. The next development of his phobia was in regard to his own movements. If he set out to go from one part of the city to another, he must return by the same route however circuitous it might be. By the way he went, by the same way he must return, and this applied particularly to entering a room and departing from it. I have seen this gentleman tremble before a door because he could not be sure that it was the way by which he had come in, and because he could not accept my assurance as to the fact. Of course such fears are not developed without much curious reasoning.

A third patient who has come under my care has gradually shut himself off from almost every necessity of life, some morbid fear or thought interdicting one natural and innocent act after another. For years he has drunk no water, nor eaten meat or bread, nor slept in bed, nor taken a proper bath. Sometimes for weeks he cannot remove his clothing as every button gives rise to questions which require hours of anxious thought. The last time he undressed himself he was eight hours in the process, and all this as a result of fears which he feels to be baseless and in consequence of a train of reasoning which he knows to be utterly fallacious.

In such cases the question of sanity becomes very pressing. Fortunately most phobias and fixed ideas are limited in their domain and they require restraint only when they become dangerous to their victim or to others. Unquestionably mental twists of this kind are, like hysteria, to be regarded as diseases of the subconscious personality. Such suggestions do not proceed from reason, which may be unimpaired, since reason resists them and abhors them. They are suggestions issued by the subconscious mind, only in the case of phobia in the form of inhibition. As they are rooted in the subconscious they must be removed from it, and the best means to effect this is by hypnotic suggestion which gradually removes the suggested fear and strengthens the will to resist it. Mere argument is useless, and force and violence are worse than useless.

4. *Melancholia.*[1] The characteristic trait of melancholia is a morbid depression of self-consciousness, a sadness which is not the result of objective conditions. A sable pall seems to settle upon the world through which the sun cannot shine. Every event is the cause of new sorrow and to avoid pain the melancholic patient turns away from all external happenings and broods upon himself, sometimes refusing to speak for years. Weakness of the will, profound indifference to the ordinary interests of life, and callous insensibility to those he loved are further symptoms of this sad disease which cause fresh sorrow. Sunk in a sea of dark and gloomy thought, the melancholic sufferer often dreams of suicide but is deterred by his enfeebled will. Too much confidence, however, is not to be placed in this protection even in mild melancholia, as many have learned to their sorrow. Sometimes the disease reaches a crisis and ex-

[1] Or manic depression.

plodes in some violent or desperate deed. Melancholia not infrequently alternates with mania.[1] Two periods of life are especially exposed to it, the stormy period of early manhood and the oncoming of old age. In its severer forms melancholia is regarded as a true mental disease, and as such it is not amenable to psychical treatment. I have recently treated a patient who has undergone periods of more or less acute melancholia for more than forty years, the periods lasting for several months and recurring on an average once a year. In this case suggestion appeared to be very successful, but I am apprehensive that the disease will return as it does in all these periodic cases. The severer cases which have come to my knowledge have been either hereditary or they have consisted in a permanent modification of a temperament and character naturally inclined toward melancholy, and usually this has been attended by delusions and hallucinations of a depressing or dangerous character. These delusions are often of persecution, or they may attach themselves to religion. In the latter case sound and normal religion can hardly be held responsible for them, for it is not the normal conceptions of religion which trouble the minds, but a morbid perversion of thought which religion repudiates and seeks to remove. We all know apparently sane persons of so bitter and morose a disposition that a comparatively slight exaggeration of it would create a condition of true mental disease. These unfortunate beings are often the victims of melancholia, although the fact may not be known. A development of the disease, however, renders them dangerous to themselves and to society.

[1] *i.e.*, marked exaltation.

Apart from true constitutional melancholia the condition we have described may coexist with epilepsy or hysteria or it may be as a passing psychosis, the result of nervous exhaustion, excess, or painful moral experience. The latter forms are frequently curable by suggestion and moral influence. Indeed Voisin claims to have succeeded with several cases of acute and severe melancholia attended with dangerous delusions, which had been diagnosed as insanity.[1] Melancholia also is to be regarded as an affection of the subconscious mind. In constitutional cases this is apparent. But even in functional cases there is a dissociation which concentrates attention on a gloom and misery which exists largely in the mind, and which inhibit all joy-giving emotions.

5. Hypochondria is a curious word which has been used time out of mind to describe a form of melancholic disposition in which the attention of the patient is fixed on the conditions of his own organism. If the hypochondriac falls ill, he is confident that his sickness is severe or mortal. He carefully observes his symptoms, and loves to read medical works, referring to himself all the horrors he encounters therein. This introspection makes its subject and object apprehensive and egoistic. Sometimes he conceals this under a gloomy air, but more often he delights to tell his own woes and to describe his symptoms to the amusement or annoyance of his friends. Nothing vexes him more than the hint that his sufferings are imaginary, and in one sense he is right, for although often purely subjective in origin they may be very real. For

---

[1] See reports of Voisin's cases in Bramwell, *op. cit.*, p. 212, etc., and a list of Dr. Auguste Voisin's publications on p. 449.

not only can our physical functions be deranged by constant attention, but true morbid conditions can be created by fear and strong expectation, *e.g.*, the phenomena of hydrophobia, cholera, yellow fever, etc., which have been frequently observed in persons not actually infected. Hypochondriacal or somatic delusions, if allowed to rise on unchecked, may also result in monomania. Sufferers believe that their heads are made of glass, that they have insects under their skins, or frogs and lizards in their stomachs. Or they believe that the source of their painful feelings lies outside themselves, that they are victims of fiends and demons, that their enemies are trying to poison them, etc.[1] These severe symptoms are fortunately rare. The minor phenomena of hypochondria, however, are very common and they are sufficiently definite to deserve recognition. If they shade insensibly into melancholia on one side, they are frequently produced by the same conditions which cause simple neurasthenia on the other, and in such cases when the nervous exhaustion is overcome the morbid apprehensions disappear. The line of demarcation between hypochondria and hysteria is also frequently vague. This has led some neurologists to drop the unmeaning term altogether, and to substitute for it the more definite and significant psychasthenia which, however, is not of the same content.

6. Chorea or St. Vitus' Dance is characterized by involuntary irregular movements which cease in sleep. Several forms of this disease are recognized, especially the hereditary chorea which affects whole families, and is incurable, and the infectious form which usually appears

[1] Möbius, *Nervösität*, p. 16.

in children and is curable. In lighter cases of the latter the children are often regarded as mischievous or naughty. They make faces, scratch with their pens, and let things fall to the floor. In severe cases the muscles contract wildly and violently, causing strange movements which were formerly regarded as proofs of possession. Speech is affected or is entirely absent. The disposition is irritable, moody, melancholy, and subject to outbursts of passion. This disease usually attacks weak and delicate children and causes them to appear weak-minded.[1] The minor chorea is frequently contagious in the sense that one child acquires the habit from another, through conscious or unconscious imitation, or it may follow intense fright or an attack of rheumatism. This form of chorea is distinctly amenable to suggestion. Bramwell reports nine cases treated with success,[2] and we are able to add others. The appearance of chorea in later life is unusual, and when it occurs it is apt to be in the incurable form and on a hereditary basis.

7. *Mania.* Under this ill-omened name are included all those mental disturbances whose fundamental trait is the domination of a morbidly exalted self-consciousness (Möbius). For our purpose it is not necessary to penetrate far into this melancholy field. What leads me to enter it at all is the fact that a condition of stormy excitement known as manic exaltation occurs in the functional neuroses. These states though frequently recurrent are usually short-lived. While they persist the patient is completely dominated by a violence of speech,

[1] Based on Möbius' description.
[2] *Op. cit.*, pp. 260–1.

of thought and emotion. He will pour out a flood of excited, sometimes meaningless words. He will utter threats against himself and others, and frequently he is unable to control his movements, but walks violently back and forth like a caged animal. These states can sometimes be checked by moral means at their inception, but when they pass a certain stage they are uncontrollable and must be allowed to wear themselves out. This purely functional disturbance which resembles strong excitement and anger forms one of the intermediate states which lie between the functional neuroses and true mental disease.

The most constant moral symptoms presented by the various functional neuroses are weakness of will, *i.e.*, inability to make a decision, lack of concentration, *i.e.*, inability to fix the mind on one subject, weakness of memory, lack of self-control, irritability, rapid exhaustion, apathy, despondency, and fear. It is these moral sufferings and this sense of abject weakness which make the conditions we have described so terrible. Other sufferers hope on to the grave, these are frequently "sunk in despair unfathomably deep." These diseases have found expression in every literature, but no one has described the horrors of melancholia and insomnia with the tragic eloquence of James Thomson with whose writings [1] every neurologist should be familiar. A woman said to me a while ago: "Who could guess that the mind has so many doors leading directly into hell?" Nervous sufferers frequently receive but scant sympathy. Because their maladies

---

[1] *The City of Dreadful Night, Vane's Story, A Voice from the Nile, Essays and Phantasies,* etc.

rest on no palpable organic basis they are thought to be imaginary. If by imaginary we mean unreal, this is a great mistake. These disturbances are indeed subjective in that they are affections of personality, but in admitting this we do not regard them as unreal. On the contrary, our subjective feelings are the most real things we know. For my part, I would rather break my thigh and be infected with tuberculosis than endure for thirty days even sub-acute melancholia and insomnia, for I know that in the former case I should suffer less and recover my health sooner. By making light of nervous sufferings we simply repel and disgust the sufferers and render ourselves unable to help them. A certain amount of firmness and even of sternness is frequently necessary in dealing with neurotics, but as to our comprehension and sympathy there should be no doubt.

CHAPTER VI

THE CAUSES OF NERVOUSNESS (HEREDITY)

As the phenomena of nervousness are so general in character we may well suspect its causes to be likewise general. In fact in so far as nervousness is an affection of personality we may look for its causes in all the influences which affect our personality. Modern science has reduced these to two general categories, heredity and environment, and no less comprehensive complex of causality will account for the well-nigh universal nervousness which pervades our modern world. So far as I am aware the history of nervousness has not been written, but it would be a mistake to suppose that nervousness was unknown to the ancient world. Where insanity and suicide have prevailed we may be sure that the milder functional disorders were not absent. To cite a single example, no secondary personalities have impressed themselves more deeply upon the pages of the New Testament than the sad figures of the demoniacs, the paralytics, the epileptics, and the maniacs whom Jesus so frequently encountered. The Jews, with their wonderful excess of vital power, suffer much from nervous irritability at the present time and with them this is no new disease. The New Testament reveals the wide-spread neurotic conditions which prevailed at the time of Christ, and from all we know of the moral life of the pagan world at the beginning of the Christian Era it is plain that Graeco-Roman society was even more deeply affected. Antiquity, however, knew not syphilis.

While reading the description of the various neuroses just given, it must have occurred to more than one person to ask, whence come these strange affections of personality? Functional nervousness is not a disease of invasion like diphtheria or tuberculosis due to the presence in the system of pathogenic microbes. It is not a malady caused by the lesion or degeneration of vital organs. Whence then come these sad moods, these morbid states of mind, this melancholy, this irritable weakness, these unseasonable fears and sad transformations of character? These are questions which the physician who deals with such disorders has to face every day, and in fulfilling his calling his first inquiry is usually as to the family history of the patient. In other words, in all serious nervous disorders heredity plays a very important part. We have been so greatly cheered during the past few years with the good news that tuberculosis is not an inherited disease that a good many persons have encouraged themselves with the thought that this may also be true of all other maladies, but it is not true of nervous diseases whether they are functional or organic. As nervousness in all its forms is a very general condition, rooted in constitution and temperament, the conditions which lead to it are the more likely to be transmitted. Moreau of Tours tells a sad story of the times of the French Revolution. In 1789, a man, terrified by the first revolutionary excesses, shut himself up in his room which thenceforth he refused to leave for a period of ten years. When his daughter reached the age at which her father had incarcerated himself, she followed his example although the Revolution was then over, and remained a prisoner for the remainder of her life. This recital strikingly shows us how nervous conditions in parents repeat themselves in children, frequently in a severer form. Dr. George Carroll Smith, of Boston, in a recent paper[1] analyzes the history of one hundred neurasthenic cases taken at random from his own practice, and of these he finds forty-three "clearly hereditary" and fifty-seven "acquired." This proportion is probably not unusual, although it is to be remembered that nervous affections are transmitted far more frequently than is true mental disease. This is true of epilepsy, hysteria, neurasthenia, and neuralgia, alcoholism, a morbid impulse to suicide, certain criminal tendencies, migraine, chorea, developing in late adult life, muscular wasting and peculiar forms of spinal cord disease. It does not always happen, however, that these tendencies reappear in children in the exact form in which they appeared in the parents. On the contrary, these affections, like insanity, are frequently transformed in transmission. But when in one and the same family we find a constant tendency toward nervous disorders appearing now in the form of insanity, now as epilepsy, now as hysteria, or again as alcoholism, neurasthenia, or imbecility, it is necessary to suppose some constant and general cause.[2] Nor need the variety of these affections cause us any surprise when we remember how readily one

---

[1] The Annual Address before the Rhode Island Medical Society, June 13, 1905, and published in the *Boston Medical and Surgical Journal*, August 15, 1907.   [2] Möbius, *Nervösität*, S. 28.

nervous condition passes into another and how constantly their symptoms run together. Frequently the recurrence is delayed. The child may be healthy and he may grow to a fine and vigorous man, but at last the fatal hour may strike that summons him to follow the way of his fathers. I have in mind a family in which the father after leading an exemplary life for forty years suddenly developed a craving for alcohol which lasted for nearly twenty years when he entirely ceased drinking. Four fine sons, the two elder born before their father's downfall, have followed in his footsteps. In them all the morbid craving developed comparatively late, after thirty. But whereas the father reformed and is still alive, two of his sons drank themselves to death, one is paralyzed, while the fourth has completely disappeared. This illustrates one of the most pathetic aspects of the transmission of nervous ills. Disorders which were only temporary in parents are frequently permanent in children. As Möbius puts it, a passing delirium in a parent may establish inextinguishable marks of degeneration in offspring.[1] As we ascend the course of a degenerate family we usually come to a point beyond which health prevails. In other words, we can trace the inherited disease directly to some ancestor near or remote with whom it began. Morel gives such an example in the history of a family in which the great-grandfather was a drunkard and died in consequence of excessive indulgence. His son who was also an inebriate died insane, the grandson though temperate was a hypochondriac with murderous instincts. The great-grandchild was weak-minded and idiotic and with him the

[1] *Op. cit.*, p. 32.

succession fortunately ceased. Terribly significant is the appended chart of Dr. Doutrebente in which it is shown how the sickness of the father reappeared in the most manifold forms through two generations, with the result that a numerous family was extinguished in the third generation.

On the other hand it ought to be remembered that by no means all the children of nervously diseased parents inherit a diseased nervous system. Some are perfectly healthy, some even in degenerate families are men of genius. Frequently the defects of one parent are offset and almost nullified by the excellence of the other. Hence the results are apt to be far more serious when both parents are nervously affected. Again, when undesirable and even dangerous tendencies are plainly present in children their development can often be checked by a wise training and by a wholesome mode of life. Man is not merely the victim of fate, the product of hereditary influences over which he has no control, he is also a moral being endowed with a will which in innumerable splendid instances has resisted destructive tendencies and vanquished them. Environment also counts for much. In general the probability of transmission, and the severity of the transmitted disease, depends upon the severity of the disease or degeneration in the parents. (Möbius.) Yet it frequently happens especially in mental diseases that the malady is not propagated directly from father to son. Very often the affection appears in one generation in the aunt or uncle, and the next in the nephew or niece, or the disease may skip one or more generations and reappear in a subsequent one. This shows once more how exceedingly

FAMILY HISTORY

First Generation.	Second Generation.	Third Generation.	Fourth Generation.
Father very intelligent, a victim of hypochondria and delusion of persecution, died in an attack of mania. Mother nervous and excitable, especially in consequence of the fears she felt of her husband.	1. Child died suddenly in 16th year. 2. Child died suddenly in 18th year. 3. Child died suddenly in 15th year.	Extinct.	Extinct.
	4. Oldest daughter hypochondriacal, excitable, religious scruples.	1. Child died early. 2. " " " 3. " " " 4. " " " 5. " " " 6. ⎫ Married, all very intelligent, 7. ⎬ misshapen ears. Had 8. ⎭ children who died early. 9. Boy, eccentric and dissipated. 10. Boy who underwent three attacks of temporary delirium.	" " " " " " " " " "
	5. Mentally weak daughter, in an asylum from 20th year.	Extinct.	"
	6. Imbecile daughter.	Imbecile child, hermaphrodite.	"
	7. Mrs. L. delusions of persecution — suicide.	Intelligent boy, died of apoplexy at 24. Imbecile boy, passionate, kleptomaniac. Boy, artist, dissipated, lively, peculiar. Boy, nervously weak, died in an attack of mania.	" " " "
	8. Weak-minded boy.	Girl, degenerate.	
	9. Boy, distrustful, hypochondriacal, refused to live with his wife.	Extinct.	"
	10. Hypochondriacal boy.	Half imbecile.	"

Dr. Doutrebente, quoted by Möbius, p. 41.

general and diffuse nervous disorders are apt to be. In the former case (aunt or uncle) it is necessary to ascend higher to find the origin of the disease.

One of the causes of inherited nervous diseases is intermarriage. When a morbid taint appears in a family it can be checked and eventually extinguished by the constant infusion of fresh and healthy blood. But when near relatives marry, both of whom carry within them the same morbid germs, the obvious result is accentuation of the family weakness. Royal and noble families among which intermarriages are frequent are constantly threatened with degeneration, insanity and extinction through the operation of this law. (Niebuhr, Esquirol, Spurzheim, Quatrefrages, Möbius.) The Jews alone seem to be unaffected by consanguineous marriage. Incompatibility between parents, lack of sympathy and affection, are also unfavorable to the production of sound and vigorous offspring. On this subject Schopenhauer's observations[1] are very interesting. Children sprung from such unions, he affirms, are apt to be sad and inharmonious beings.

These, however, are secondary causes. They teach us the solemn lesson that diseased nervous conditions are transmitted, but they cannot tell us how such conditions are acquired, or how nervousness came into the world. To learn this lesson we must turn to the life history of the individual and trace the effect of environment upon the nervous system, but before we do this it is well to remind ourselves once more of the effect of our acts and states upon our children. In the moral world the law of causa-

[1] *Works*, Vol. III, S. 591 ff.

tion prevails with the same inexorable certainty that characterizes its action in the physical world. Nervous and moral conditions are transmitted and they frequently become graver in the process of time. The severest and most incurable forms of nervous disease are usually those which are attended by a bad family history. Many families bear in the persons of the majority of their members the stigmata of moral and physical degeneracy. From this point of view, the ancient doctrine that the sins of the fathers are visited on the children unto the third and fourth generation is true to the letter, for in the third or fourth generation such heavily burdened families almost invariably are extinguished. Nature, which apparently hates abnormality, sees to it that the abnormal and the degenerate do not propagate their degeneracy indefinitely upon this earth. We shall see, however, that by no means all nervous disorders are the result of moral delinquency. Many of them are imposed upon us by conditions of life over which we have practically no control.

CHAPTER VII

THE CAUSES OF NERVOUSNESS (ENVIRONMENT)

NERVOUSNESS in its manifold forms is often called a disease of civilization. "Without civilization there can be no nervousness; there is no race, no climate, no environment that can make nervousness and nervous disease possible and common, save when reinforced by man's work and worry and indoor life."[1] While there is a large element of truth in this saying, it is certain that the severer forms of nervous disease, epilepsy, melancholia, mania, and idiocy, are and have been well known to barbaric and savage life. Civilization has unquestionably enhanced longevity, yet the vaster and the more complex the environment to which we must adjust ourselves, the greater are the demands made upon our nervous system. In this sense nervousness is the child of civilization, and the more life demands of us the more nervousness is destined to spread both by the creation of new types and by the transmission of old ones. Unless we find some better means than we possess at present to calm and simplify our lives, the end of our civilization is in sight, for we cannot continue to use up our forces faster than those forces are generated. Humanity, however, has a wonderful capacity for renewing itself. When the disease becomes pressing the cure comes. In this case the relief

---
[1] Beard, *American Nervousness*, Putnam's, 1881, p. 193.

is already in sight. It will come in the discovery and use of those inexhaustible subconscious powers which have their roots in the Infinite. As a runner exhausts his "first wind" and then taps a new source of energy which carries him indefinitely on, so humanity will not falter in its race. Soon it will learn the great lesson of "hitching its wagon to a star," and then it will no longer faint and stagger on its way as it does now while it childishly insists on carrying its burden on the weak shoulders of flesh. Moreover it is to be remembered that work seldom injures, it is worry which undermines the health. Much has been written on this subject of the highest value by the so-called Metaphysical School, to which I am glad at last to pay my respects.[1] Here I shall only attempt to review some of the prevailing conditions of our social and moral life which act unfavorably upon our nervous system.

Among all the predisposing causes of nervousness, the first place must be assigned to drunkenness. No other source of mental and nervous disease can be pointed to with anything like the same certainty. Alcoholic poisoning is believed by many eminent physiologists to infect the reproductive germs, in opposition to Weissmann's theory which certainly finds no support in the history of nervous disease. Von Bunge, arguing this question, calls attention to the fact that the daughters of drunkards are seldom able to nurse their babies, their milk being deficient in quantity and in nourishing elements. Be this

[1] I allude to such writers as, Mr. Henry Wood, Mr. Charles Brodie Patterson, Mr. Horatio Dunn, Mr. Ralph Waldo Trine, Mr. Crane, and also to Mr. Horace Fletcher, Miss Anna Payson Call, Mr. Jordan and many others.

as it may, it is certain that the posterity of drunkards suffers to an almost incredible extent from the milder and the severer forms of mental and nervous disease. For this reason the great neurologists, *e.g.*, Forel, Möbius, and Weir Mitchell, have been great advocates of temperance. Möbius goes so far as to say, "In my opinion the widespread conditions of weakness which we call nervousness, neurasthenia, etc., in the majority of cases are due to the intemperate habits of parents. People are apt to think that the strenuousness of life, the demands of business and other influences, create nervous weakness. But it is very probable that the telephone, railroads, and the demands of business have no injurious effect upon well people. They may rack their nerves for awhile, but they certainly do not create the conditions which we encounter daily in our office hours. Examination reveals the fact that the majority of these patients have never been really well, that their maladies began in childhood."[1] Of course the more seriously the father has injured his brain and nervous system through alcoholic indulgence, the more serious the disorders he is likely to bequeath to his children. But it would be a great mistake to imagine that the habits of so-called moderate drinkers have no effect on posterity. To this cause as much as to any other is due the short life of so many prosperous American families, which frequently become extinct in the third or fourth generation. The founder of the family's affluence makes his way by intelligence, sobriety, and hard work, but he desires a different life for his son whom he brings up in luxury and pleasure. The son spends his time in enjoy-

[1] *Op. cit.*, pp. 44-5.

ing and perhaps dissipating what his father earned and he frequently bequeaths a diminished fortune and an exhausted nervous system to his children. During the past ten years, thanks to the influence of our fine boys' schools and to the example of our great President, there has been a marked improvement in the ideals of our young men who are doomed to wealth. But this melancholy drama has been enacted so often as to be typical of a certain phase of American life. Luxury tears down the house which self-denial has built. Nor is this spectacle peculiar to America. P. Buchner in his interesting examination of the conditions of life in Hamburg comes to the same conclusion. He says: "Generally the third generation (of affluent families) sinks back into the great impoverished mass out of which the founder of a commercial house arose. Hence there are few Hamburg families which have been able to maintain themselves for more than a hundred years. Of the old patrician families which established the Hanseatic League, not one remains to-day. Only new names figure on the Hamburg exchange." [1]

One of the most ominous signs of the times is the large amount of alcohol consumed by business men, not for pleasure, but as a stimulus to flagging powers or to stimulate digestion. In this way a man who regards himself as quite temperate will consume from four to six cocktails or other alcoholic beverages daily without suspecting that he is undermining his nervous system or that of his children. Yet we are constantly confronted

[1] *Der Hamburgen Handel*, Grenzboten LXIII, 15, 5, 80. Quoted by Möbius.

with defective and hysterical boys and girls who owe their enfeebled constitutions in no slight degree to their father's habit of moderate but constant tippling. Nervousness is regarded as peculiarly a disease of girls and women, but a nervous system which requires frequent alcoholic stimulation in order to function is certainly diseased. No nervousness is worse than alcoholic nervousness, and a man who can maintain himself only with the assistance of alcohol will not maintain himself long. Unfortunately, if he has children he will not suffer alone. Our civilization, as Möbius remarks, is built on alcohol, and as the flood of alcohol rises the prevalence of neurotic weakness rises with it.[1] To this rule as to all other generalizations on mankind, the Jews form an exception, as they are both sober and nervous. On the other hand, Americans on account of their peculiarly nervous temperament are less able to resist alcoholic poisoning than other peoples.

After alcoholism perhaps the most general cause of nervous affection is venereal disease and the moral and physical consequences of illicit sexual relations. The memorial presented to the diocesan convention of the Episcopal Church in Massachusetts in 1907 on the state of morals reveals the alarming extent to which virtuous married women are inoculated with venereal disease by their husbands, and our hospital reports tell the same story. From these infected unions when they are not

[1] It is useless to talk of more temperate habits while the drink bill of the nation steadily rises, dwarfing the expenditure for the necessities of life. Someone must consume all the liquor brewed and distilled in this country.

sterile springs a race of infirm, debilitated children who frequently bear on the body and soul the imprint of their father's sins. Apart from its corroding action on the mucous membranes, the epidermis, and the bones, the poison of syphilis not infrequently attacks the brain, the spinal cord and the nerves. Even those from whose systems the actual virus of syphilis has been eliminated continue to suffer from general debility and from a nervous dread of a fresh outbreak of the disease.

As the conditions of life grow more complex and the craving for luxurious living becomes more universal, marriage becomes more difficult and tends constantly to be postponed to a later period of life. The result of this is a constant increase of sexual vice. Prostitution is the cancer of our civilization, and apparently it is inseparable from it. It is the penalty we pay for our ideal of monogamy, which in the present state of humanity can never be perfectly realized. The result is the existence of a large class of sad and degenerate beings which polygamous countries hardly know, a class branded by every infamy, preyed upon by every brutal passion and by the foulest disease. That women of this class suffer from every form of nervous, mental, and moral disease, that their lives are short and that they are frequently shortened by suicide, goes without saying. No human being suffers so disproportionately for human frailty as the fallen woman.

Apart from recognized prostitution, many tendencies of contemporary society encourage temporary and irresponsible unions to an extent hitherto unknown in our American life. Among these tendencies I should include the increasing difficulty of marriage and the frequency of divorce, the loss of religious faith with its attending relaxation of ethical standards, the increasing love of pleasure, and above all the industrial conditions as they affect woman. Girls and young women who were formerly brought up in the privacy of the home and under parental control are now found in large stores and factories, and in offices where, freed from all moral restraint, they work side by side with men, often for wages which barely suffice for subsistence. The result is an immense increase in irregular or temporary sexual connections. Nor do I imagine for a moment that such relations are peculiar to the working classes. One of the revelations of our work has been the large number of men and women, frequently of the highest station, who are suffering from disturbances originating in the sexual life.

The effects of a "double life" upon the nervous system are unmistakable. "He who lives more lives than one, More deaths than one must die," says Oscar Wilde. Probably women, who have more at stake and whose moral sensibility is greater, suffer more from this cause than men. The intense excitement which attends such experiences, the remorse they frequently inspire, the burden of a guilty conscience, the element of falsehood and secrecy which they introduce into life, fear of discovery, dread of consequences, and the horror which attends the discovery of pregnancy all react powerfully upon the nervous system and they may lead to insanity. Goethe has depicted the depth of woe and guilt into which an innocent girl may be plunged through her affections, and in Margaret's madness and death he has given the tragic ending of these crooked paths. Balzac in the wonderful trilogy which describes the utter ruin of Lucien de Rubempré, and in his terrible Cousine Bette, has laid an even more unsparing finger upon this open sore of our civilization. Frequently more dangerous than the moral emotions I have mentioned is the deep-rooted dissociation of personality which results from the attempt to lead two lives. On the other hand it ought to be remembered that sexual perversions and outbreaks are often the effect and not the cause of nervous conditions. The first duty of one so affected is to seek the advice and assistance of an experienced neurologist, and to avoid as he would the devil those dangerous so-called "specialists" who batten upon sexual vice and upon the morbid fears of their victims. Of sexual perversions I shall not speak except to say that they are recognized forms of mental and nervous disease which can frequently be removed by suggestion.

One of the most certain causes of nervousness is the overtaxing of the mental powers in childhood. It is well known that the human brain at birth is quite embryonic. Many of the nerve fibers have not received their medullary sheaths, the higher centers of speech, of word and visual memory, are not yet formed. The brain is not yet organized by habit.[1] In short the most important work of life is performed during the first six years. Man is born with a brain and nervous system differing but slightly from that of the anthropoid apes, but the modifications which take place in the former during these years separate

---

[1] See *e.g.* Thomson's exceedingly instructive chapters, "The Faculty of Speech," "Nervous System Evolution," and "The Brain and Personality." *Op. cit.*, p. 75 ff.

him from the animal kingdom as a star is separate from the earth (Thomson). Every day is a voyage of discovery into an unknown world. The child's powers of observation, of attention and of memory are taxed to a degree which it is difficult for us to comprehend, and these difficult feats of memory, of imitation, of co-ordination and self-direction are performed through the instrumentality of organs which are yet imperfect, which are easily exhausted, and which require long and frequent periods of complete repose. In the face of these facts it is hardly necessary to say that during these tender years no additional burdens ought to be imposed, unless it be the acquisition of a second language which can then be acquired with the least difficulty. Above all things, the child's nervous system ought to be protected from all shocks and unnecessary stimulation. Those who care for it should be mild and free from nervousness. During this period an excess of mental application not only injures the brain, but checks growth and induces morbid precocities, *e.g.*, premature sexual development (Möbius).

The beginning of school life, therefore, before the age of seven or eight is neither desirable, nor in the long run profitable. At an earlier period, if any instruction beyond normal development and the moral training of the home be thought necessary, the Kindergarten which trains the senses and which teaches useful lessons without fatiguing the attention is the best school for the young child. In fact it is the concentration of attention which is most difficult to a child. The child's powers of observation and of imitation are keen, but the attention is very volatile, and the attempt to fix the mind for any length of time on one thing produces a sense of fatigue which is the chief cause of the child's aversion to school and study.

The American school system has often been compared with the German to the distinct detriment of the former in respect to thoroughness and comprehensiveness and as regards sound scientific method. No doubt the principles of pedagogics have been studied and applied in Germany more successfully than elsewhere, and it is certain that German school-teachers as a class are far more learned than ours, but on the other hand our American schools are not responsible for the wrecking of nervous systems, the almost universal defects of vision, and the not infrequent suicides of children which are produced by the severity of the German school system, against which German physicians and men of science continually protest. The educational problems presented in the two countries are very different. The German school undertakes the training of a homogeneous people in a country where specialized knowledge is the chief avenue to success. Upon the American school is laid the duty and responsibility of transforming the offspring of the most diverse races into American citizens, and of preparing its pupils for a life in which talent, moral character, and initiative play a larger part than learning. The first of these tasks it performs in a manner above all praise. No aspect of our civilization is more remarkable than our power of assimilating the various peoples of the earth and of transforming them into good and enthusiastic Americans full of love for our institutions. This miracle is performed for the most part by our public schools, which of late years have taken a far more liberal

CAUSES OF NERVOUSNESS (ENVIRONMENT)

view of their moral and social duties and opportunities. Studies of public school life like those of Myra Kelly are full of interest from this point of view.

One injurious element in the early life of our rich children is its extreme complexity. The young children of well-to-do people have as many engagements as their fathers and mothers. As soon as one task is ended they are hurried to another. Then come children's parties, dances, rich food, late hours, etc. All this excitement and confusion and distraction of attention unquestionably react injuriously upon the nervous system and upon character. For this reason it is often best for boys to leave homes where there is really no place for them and to enter schools where life is simple and wholesome and where they will be thrown under the influence of manly men. As humanity rises higher the labors imposed upon youth become more severe, but it is a poor preparation for life to overtax and cripple these faculties and powers on which our happiness and our usefulness depend.

A frequent source of nervous debility in boys, less frequently in girls, is the habit of self-abuse, a vice that is shared with mankind by dogs and monkeys. Pernicious as are the effects of this wide-spread evil on body and mind, they are by no means so terrible as interested and mercenary persons pretend. Victims of this sad habit should know the truth in regard to it, for the morbid apprehension and fears created by the wilful misrepresentations of charlatans often produce in them nervous conditions which are more harmful than the effects of the vice itself. The "Incurable spinal disease" of which one hears never proceeds from this cause (Möbius), weak-mindedness and imbecility very rarely. On the other hand no one can deny that serious moral and nervous affections follow the habitual practice of masturbation, and these are more serious in early life, and when, as is often the case, the victim is temporarily nervous and delicate. The physical symptoms are weakness, pallor and backache, and general debility. The effects on the brain and nervous system are more serious. They may dull the intellect, weaken the memory and the affections, produce listlessness, apathy, moroseness and morbid irritability, in short a general perversion of character. This habit may arise through a variety of causes, some of which are in themselves morbid. Parents owe it to their children, especially to their boys, to be sincere with them on these subjects. They may take it for granted that their reticence only exposes their children to revelations from impure sources. There is something morbid and base in our attitude toward the great mysteries of life which in themselves are pure and wonderful. Truth can never harm us. It is the lie long meditated in secret that corrupts us. I have heard many a young man who had fallen low exclaim, "If my father had only told me when I was a boy." In conclusion I would say that the widespread notion that sexual activity is necessary to the health of man at any age is a fallacy. Balzac, who knew human nature as well as another, speaks frequently of the great surplus of moral and physical power possessed by virgins. Neither are occasional losses to be regarded as dangerous or as indications of disease provided they are not too frequent. These, however, and the habit of masturbation and in general a tendency to impure and evil thoughts can in the majority of cases be removed by suggestion, and parents whose children are so afflicted ought not to hesitate to employ it.

We come now to the more general causes of nervousness in our environment and these may almost be said to be coextensive with our civilization. The well-nigh universal conditions of nervous weakness which confront us on every hand proclaim the fact that life as it is organized at present is too difficult for us. The brain and nervous system of man are capable of responding to an incalculable yet limited variety of stimulation, and it begins to look as if for us the limit had been reached and in many cases exceeded. This is the situation which confronts us to-day, and theoretically two courses are possible; either the reduction of the nervous tension under which we are living, or an increase of moral and nervous energy to meet life's demands. Accordingly Pastor Wagner and others have issued a powerful appeal for the Simple Life, but just as these lessons seemed likely to be heeded, our President drowned their gentle voices with his loud roar for the Strenuous Life, and it is easy to see in which direction the tide is turning. Here, however, we are not concerned with remedies but with symptoms.

The health and well-being of any animal organism depends upon its adjustment to its environment. After this adjustment is made, it perpetuates itself by the transmission of acquired faculties. A kind of equilibrium is established between the nervous system and the normal demands made upon it, which permits the formation of habits and innumerable unconscious acts. But every change of environment disturbs this equilibrium and demands new adjustments in the course of which innumerable individuals and sometimes whole species perish. During the past century the general conditions of human life have changed more profoundly than during any corresponding period since the dawn of civilization, and one general cause of the prevailing nervous irritability which we observe at present is the heavy task imposed upon the nervous system in adjusting itself to a new environment and in meeting new demands.

But our environment has not merely changed, it has become more complex. It is true the world presents far fewer natural obstacles to us than it presented to our forefathers. The difficulty of maintaining this country in peace and affluence is slight in comparison with the difficulty of wresting it from stubborn Nature and from implacable savages. Our present embarrassments would not seem serious to a generation which had beheld our soil drenched with the blood of citizens. And yet the critical hour for every nation occurs after its struggle with Nature and for its own existence ceases to be pressing. Man carries his conquest of the world to a certain point: he overcomes its hard obstacles, but its soft seductions usually in the end overcome him. Our fathers wrestled against flesh and blood and to virile men this struggle is the easiest. We must wrestle against effeminating luxury, against corrupting materialism, against our own debilitated nervous systems, against the vastest doubts which have ever dismayed the minds of men, against the very richness and complexity of the life we have inherited. Perhaps never, except in the years following the birth of Christ, has the world aged so perceptibly as during the century just ended. As we look back to the lives of our fathers and grandfathers, what charms us most is their simplicity, and as we look forward to our own lives, what terrifies us most is their complexity, and this complexity no Pastor Wagner can reduce. Knowledge has become so vast that the human brain can no longer contain a fraction of what a man may legitimately desire to know, and with this infinite expansion of knowledge, the old faith, which did not rest on knowledge but largely on ignorance, becomes more difficult. Every path of knowledge ends in doubt. We build our theories and our explanations of things up to the skies, yet over every explanation towers a gigantic question-mark. Who is able to follow all these paths through doubt to final reconciliation and peace? What eye but the eye of omniscience can trace all the infinite radii of truth to the point where they converge in God?

If the world of thought has become too great for our minds to grasp, the life we lead threatens to become too manifold in its interests, too exacting in its demands, for our weak organisms. In the early deaths and suicides of many of our ablest men, in the alarming increase of insanity and nervousness, in the diminishing and vanishing offspring of the cultured classes, in the general use of alcoholic stimulants and dangerous drugs, we already see a limit set to the dissipation of man's energies. These are the conditions under which life presents itself to the more favored classes. The less favored suffer from grievances which cry louder to Heaven. Without an uncharitable thought we may admit that the same system which has made one portion of society rich has made a large portion poor. One of the problems, therefore, with which the twentieth century is confronted is the problem of human happiness. It has taken us a long time to admit that there is such a problem, or if there be such a one that there is a possibility of its solution. But we are slowly learning that it is impossible for anyone to be happy in this world so long as he is obliged to lower his eyes in the presence of the misery of his fellow men. The noble already perceive that the highest and most satisfactory use which can be made of wealth is to expend it during life in the improvement of man. After a while we shall learn that it is better to leave our children pure examples and high ideals than abnormal fortunes. Fathers who have seen the melancholy experiment tried sufficiently often will not be anxious to corrupt and ruin their sons by leaving them too rich.

The whole tendency of the age in which we live may be summed up in two words, mechanical and material. We have not succeeded in making life more beautiful, indeed much of beauty is gone out of life. It may be doubted whether on the whole we have made life better or happier, but it cannot be doubted that we have made life more effective. Our planet supports a far greater number of inhabitants than ever before, and those inhabitants are better nourished, better clad, and better educated than in the past. All this has come about through the discovery and control of the immeasurable and inexhaustible mechanical energies of nature, first of steam and then of electricity. But these gigantic forces have not only enhanced incalculably the effectiveness of human life, they have shortened all its processes. The supreme end to which all practical inventions look is economy, economy of time, economy of effort, economy in the cost of production. Of the two great functions of steam, manufacture and transportation, the latter is of more importance than the former. And when steam proved too slow, the light wings of electricity were employed to bring distant human beings into instantaneous communication and to flash man's messages from one end of the world to another.

All this is wonderful, but to him who sees in man more than an acquiring animal, it cannot appear as an unmixed blessing. These mighty servants have ended by enslaving their masters. They have introduced an element of haste and of feverish unrest into human life which amounts to a disease. All our labor-saving devices have not procured for us either rest or peace, they act only as an incentive to new effort. The very processes of acquisition are so vast, so complex and so pitiless that a man once launched in them becomes part of a machine. He is hurried on in spite of himself and as soon as he becomes ineffective he is cast aside as so much scrap iron. Moreover the purely material complexion of our civilization has reacted unfavorably upon us, for man, strange as the phrase sounds to-day, is essentially a moral and spiritual being and he can never find his permanent rest in material things. Were the tendencies which have prevailed for the past century to prevail and to accelerate for another hundred years, they would then cease through sheer exhaustion. Nervous disorders propagate themselves with such fatal facility, they increase in severity so rapidly, that when a civilization becomes thoroughly neurotic, unless the causes of nervousness are removed its end is in sight.[1] The great problem of our age as of all ages is the problem of the spiritual life, but never since the downfall of Rome was that problem more pressing than it is to-day. Christianity arrived too late on the scene to save the Roman Empire, but it showed what a spiritual religion can do by creating a new world out of its ruins. Only Christ is strong enough to save the world to-day, but to do this He must be allowed to free Himself from the iron fetters with which human tradition has bound Him. He must be permitted to confront humanity with all His divine reasonableness, His pity, His sense of God's nearness. Salvation will come not in a return to a world that has passed away forever, in an ineffective milk and water existence, but in an enlargement of spiritual power through the recognition and appropriation of spiritual energies which surround us, as we have already recognized and employed the mechanical energies of the universe. We have learned that in the little world every spiritual event is attended by a mechanical event and *vice versa*. We may be sure that the same holds true of the great world. The unfailing characteristic of nervous debility is weakness, the secret of health is peace.

[1] As to the fact of the rapid increase of insanity and of the milder and severer neuroses, there can no longer be any question. Earlier writers like Maudsley encouraged themselves that this increase was only apparent, that it was due to new and improved methods of procuring vital statistics, to the multiplication of insane asyiums, etc. But people do not become insane because asylums are built for them, asylums are erected for the accommodation of madmen, and all recent literature recognizes the deplorable fact that mental and nervous disease including insanity and suicide is increasing much more rapidly than the population.

There can be no doubt that the decline of practical religion has had an injurious effect on the moral life and sanity of every people which has undergone this experience, nor is the reason far to seek. The morality and standards of living of every civilized nation are built on the foundations of religion, and when this is withdrawn or weakened the superstructure collapses. Religion, therefore, cannot be regarded as an illusion, as a temporary phase of human culture through which men and nations pass, and then are done with it forever. If this were true the downfall of religion would be the harbinger of new and higher life. As a matter of fact in the history of the nations it has been the precursor of spiritual night and death. The cause of the downfall of religion has been the same through all ages. Religion has identified itself so exclusively with the Traditional Motive as to be inaccessible to the other great motives of faith, the Practical and the Rational. As a result it has largely ceased to be useful, and it no longer represents truth. The Traditional Motive, believing because one has been taught to believe (Fechner), is very powerful, but it is not strong enough to hold the faith of the better portion of mankind forever. A religion exclusively of the past cannot dominate the present or represent reality to minds which have outgrown it. Hence it is repudiated.

On the practical effects of the weakening of religious faith as a cause of nervous and mental disease I would prefer to quote the words of some recognized neurologist and man of science. Möbius says: "We reckon the downfall of religion as one of the causes of mental and nervous disease. Religion is essentially a comforter. It builds for the man who stands amid the misery and evil of the world another and fairer world. Besides his daily care-full life it lets him lead a second, purer life. The consciousness of being within the hand of Providence, confident hope of future righteousness and redemption is a·support to the believer in his work, his care and need for which unbelief has no compensation. In comparison with the Last Things the incidents of this life seem small, and his outlook on eternity sustains him in passion and in sorrow. Meditation calms and refreshes him like a healing bath. In the congregation one member sustains another. Worship breaks in upon the daily drudgery with days of rest and of meeting, and orders the life of the individual and of the community by the establishment of fixed customs. *The more religion descends into life, the more it remains at man's side early and late, the more it affects our daily life, the more powerful is its consoling influence.* In proportion as it disappears out of the human life, and as the individual and the nation become irreligious, the more comfortless and irritating life becomes. If one disregards the few who make of speculation or of art a kind of religion, the people, with its religion, loses the ideal altogether, and there remains nothing but unsatisfying reality. The best comfort in sorrow and inward peace disappear. Then the highest good consists in worldly possessions, and the struggle for these becomes man's first and last. For the people, however, as Kant says, religion is the public standard of virtue, and when this standard falls, even if the morality which rests on natural goodness of the heart does not directly suffer, formal morality (legalität) receives the severest injury.

The morality of a nation suffers most seriously through the downfall of its religion, as experience has everywhere and always proved. To speak of the present, materialism, or, as it shamefacedly calls itself, the mechanical theory of the world expresses itself in the masses as brutality. The pure ethical impulses are too weak to control the massive egoistical instincts of men. Let us eat and drink for to-morrow we die is the logical watchword. Struggle of all against all, and the conscienceless subjection of the weak, must prevail in exact proportion as the mechanical theory of the world prevails.

"If we consider the effect of irreligion as increasing our helplessness to resist the storms of life, and as favoring dissipation and crime, its relation to nervousness cannot be doubted. For if chronic moral disturbances contribute to nervousness, these conditions must be regarded as causes."[1]

Another unquestionable cause is the strenuousness of our American life with its ups and downs, its incessant changes, its large element of uncertainty and the restless energy which it demands as the price of success. Many of our higher positions of trust are deliberately planned with the knowledge that no man will hold them long. Responsibility and anxiety remove their occupants in the course of a few years. Of late the vast combinations and aggregations of capital have introduced an element of uncertainty into business life which increases its moral strain. A man may labor successfully for years only to see the results of his labor swept away by causes over which he has no control. The swift transitions from

[1] *Op. cit.* 85 ff.

wealth to poverty and from poverty to wealth with the intense emotional crises which attend them are also very harmful in their effects on the nervous system. Men who live habitually on these emotions, *e.g.*, stock-brokers and gamblers who make and lose fortunes every day, naturally suffer most and exhibit many of the phenomena of insanity. The floor of a stock exchange, *e.g.*, on a day when values are fluctuating rapidly, might readily be mistaken for Bedlam. But even in the most legitimate and conservative business there is an element of uncertainty, a swiftness of change, a degree of fluctuation which does not exist in other countries.

The effect of the conditions of American life is plainly perceptible in the Jew, who is far more subject to nervous diseases in this country than elsewhere. I have discussed this question with Hebrew practitioners and the views they have expressed coincide with my own. The Jew, however humble may be the beginning of his business career, is too intelligent not to perceive the great opportunities for the acquisition of wealth which this country affords him. Accordingly he works unsparingly, he denies himself almost the necessities of life. He is frequently ill-nourished and in a state of constant fatigue. But he bends his whole energy to lifting himself out of his humble circumstances into affluence. He works all day and he schemes and plans at night, with the result that in spite of his magnificent vitality, his sobriety and freedom from venereal disease, he suffers greatly from insanity and other forms of mental and nervous weakness.

I would like here to call the attention of business men to the great importance of a secondary aim or interest in life. In fact I scarcely know of anything so conducive to longevity, the preservation of one's powers and capacity for enjoyment, as a variety of interest and occupation. The most incurable and impossible patients we have encountered have been business men who had confined themselves exclusively to business and who had never learned to play. When such men find themselves incapacitated for business they are the most helpless and unhappy of human beings, for the reason that they do not know what to do with themselves. Hence they easily fall victims to hypochondria, melancholia, and other nervous disorders. A man frequently looks forward for years to retiring from business, and he does so only to find himself restless and unhappy and perhaps to fall into an early grave. A radical change of habits and occupation is apt to be a dangerous experiment after fifty, and before a man attempts it he should be sure of something to occupy his thought and his time and to take him outside himself. Some men find such an interest when their own work is done in living for others. On the other hand a man can do a prodigious amount of work if he varies that work with play which really amuses him, or if he substitutes for mental toil occupations which involve muscle exercise. By such judicious habits men like President Roosevelt and Dr. Mitchell have performed an incredible amount of labor without injury to their health. But even more important than a change of occupation is a real secondary interest in life which keeps the heart young. Some men find such an interest in sport, in hunting and fishing, in sailing the seas and in exploring wild nature. Others find it in the cultivation of the soil, in breeding fine cattle, horses, dogs, sheep and fowls, others in art, music, literature, science, or travel. But some such avocation is almost indispensable to men whose main interest in life is absorbing and whose duties are exhausting. Over against the increasing strenuousness of life and concentration in cities, we may point to the return to nature and the soil, the revival of sport, the passion for games and out-of-door exercises which have added perceptibly to the stature of both men and women and are among the most encouraging signs of the times.

Although those whom we are accustomed to call "business men," *i.e.*, merchants, financiers, manufacturers, officers of corporations, etc., are the most heavily burdened, the duties of professional men, physicians, jurists, clergymen, actors, etc., are not slight and each of these callings makes its own demands on the nervous system. Few greater mental efforts can be imagined than are involved in preparing and pleading an important and difficult case in court. The exercise of memory, of rapid judgment, in short of all our higher faculties employed by great lawyers on such occasions, together with the power of sustained and convincing argument, tax the resources of the most gifted man and are frequently followed by utter exhaustion. The physician feels the burden of the gravest responsibilities. He cannot minister to his patients without to a certain degree taking their sicknesses upon him. Nor can he forget that human lives are constantly staked on his judgment and skill. If he is able and brilliant he is apt to be overworked. He suffers from mental and physical over-exertion and from almost constant anxiety. The actor and the singer stake their reputations every time they appear on the stage. Beside the incredible feats of memory they are constantly called on to perform, they must preserve an inward calm and repose in order to do their best work. Every art requires a long and wearisome technical preparation and an amount of labor of which the uninitiated can form no conception. Clergymen, if they are rectors or ministers of great and highly organized parishes, must be leaders of thought, organizers, financiers, scholars, able preachers. In other words, they must labor in constantly recurring tasks and duties, which are always the same and yet must always be done differently. Addressing the same audience week by week, they must not repeat themselves. Speaking on the oldest theme known to man, they must be able to make it ever fresh and new. Their working week consists of seven days, and their working day, if they are really interested in their work, ends at midnight or when they are too weary to write, to speak, to think or to act any longer, and then they go to bed with the sad consciousness of having left many tasks undone. In short, if we are really alive and awake to our opportunities, life demands of us all that we are able to give and to do. But such activity, unless we have the constitution of a rhinoceros or an incentive and enthusiasm which never flag, exhausts us and gives rise to insomnia, depression, brain fag, and every other form of nervous weakness.

Neurasthenia and nervousness in all its forms are frequently thought to be affections of the rich and of the great brain workers. This, however, is a mistake. There are other circumstances which act quite as unfavorably upon our nervous systems as those which I have enumerated. I now refer to the restrictions of a narrow lot, to loneliness and isolation, to the frequent repetition of uninteresting tasks, to the burdens of maternity and domestic cares and worries. These, like the constant dripping of water which wears away stone, are frequently the causes of mental and nervous diseases and disorders. Persons who live much alone are apt to become "peculiar." The wives of farmers, especially in sparsely settled regions where life is hard and barren, are peculiarly subject to insanity. Bookkeepers and accountants whose days are passed in performing simple operations on meaningless numbers are also apt to suffer from mental disease. Telegraph operators and mail sorters whose duties demand protracted close attention also suffer frequently from nervous disorders. In our practice the two classes of persons which most frequently seek our aid are unmarried women teachers and married women, mostly mothers, of moderate or restricted means. Among the former neurasthenia, nervous exhaustion, insomnia, mild melancholia, and psychasthenia are of common occurrence. The complaints I hear most frequently from such teachers are of the monotonous repetition of tasks, loneliness and sadness, of the difficulty of the moral control of their charges, of fears of growing old and helpless, of failure, of insanity, etc. The causes of nervousness among the married women above mentioned are more complex and they cannot so readily be distinguished. Sometimes this nervous condition is due to marital incompatibility, to the intemperance or bad conduct of their husbands, to shock, or to some painful moral experience. Frequently it is present simply because these women are unequal to the tasks and responsibilities imposed upon them and their nervous systems have succumbed to the strain. Perhaps they were always more or less delicate, and marriage, child-bearing, and family cares have resulted in further enfeebling them. The latter patients are among those most benefited by rest and change, although reorganization of the home life is frequently necessary. Many husbands are selfish towards their wives without intending to be. They are so accustomed to see the latter weak and hear their complaints that it does not occur to them that there may be a cause for such weakness and complaining. Domestic servants over forty years of age are quite frequently slightly demented. This is probably due to somewhat the same causes as those which affect teachers and to the performance of hard manual labor during menstruation. The nervousness frequently discoverable among students in women's colleges is also due largely to the latter cause, in this case to the overtaxing of the brain and nervous system during the menstrual period. Dr. Mitchell has written judiciously on this subject.[1]

Among the general psychical causes of nervousness intellectual over-exertion is probably the most fruitful. No element of our system needs rest more than the brain and certainly none suffers equally from excessive fatigue. When brain fatigue is attended by intense excitement, as is frequently the case in the lives of business and professional men, the injury to the brain and nervous system is severe and more permanent. All the depressing emotions, anger, fear, moral shock, anxiety, worry, sorrow, have a

[1] *Doctor and Patient,* 151 ff.

very unfavorable effect upon our nervous system and upon all our physical functions, and when as sometimes happens these sad feelings persist for years, their effect upon temperament and character may be permanent. We know to-day that every psychical event is attended by a corresponding nervous event. Joy, happiness, a sense of well-being, are invariably healthful and health-bringing. Grief, pain, anger, and anxiety have also their concomitants in the brain and nervous system and these are injurious or destructive in character. It is to be remembered, however, that such emotions are frequently not voluntary in the sense that they are wilful. They are often symptoms of a more general disease in which body and soul suffer together (Möbius). The psychical causes of nervousness, as we have seen, may also be of a different character. The effect of our environment instead of overtaxing our moral and intellectual powers may depress and starve us by its barrenness and monotony. This is frequently the effect of life on the prairie, especially on those who come from mountainous or hill countries. In the west there is a form of mental disease known as "prairie insanity."

The physical causes of nervousness are very numerous and can only here be alluded to. Whether mere physical labor, however hard in itself, produces nervousness may be doubted, although protracted labor which robs us of our sleep or rest is undoubtedly injurious. I have seen the experiment tried of causing men to work seven days in the week with very bad results. After a couple of weeks the men have become demoralized, weak, and inefficient, and the work (loading freight cases) was badly done. If, as von Jhering believes,[1] the Sabbath rest originated to meet the necessities of the laboring men in Babylon, we have an ancient precedent for its scrupulous observance which modern physiology fully endorses. In general, any employment which robs us of the needful modicum of sleep must be regarded as injurious. Dr. Weir Mitchell has proved abundantly the great value of rest and isolation in many of the functional and organic neuroses. There can be no doubt that the over-stimulation of our senses has an exhausting effect upon the nervous system. The tumult and uproar of our cities unquestionably has an irritating influence upon those who are inclined to nervousness. Schopenhauer has written an eloquent tract on the Din of Cities which ought to be reprinted and widely circulated. Elevated railways running through the principal thoroughfares of cities are the cause of untold sufferings. Beside torturing the sick and weak with their infernal uproar, they injure the eyes of thousands by the tiny filaments of steel which the brakes constantly shave from the wheels. Many of our street noises could be abolished or mitigated with great benefit to the public health.

Intense heat also has an irritating and depressing effect upon the nervous system. The extraordinary series of atrocious crimes against young children which occurred in New York last summer (1907) has given rise to many curious theories on the subject. In this outbreak suggestion was a far more potent factor than the heat of the sun. It is known, however, that summer is favorable to crimes of violence and also to suicide. The most marked

[1] *Evolution of the Aryan.*

effect of intense heat on the nervous system is in heat prostration and so-called sunstrokes which are attended by marked elevation of temperature, insensibility, intense headache, and convulsions, and which is frequently followed by a long period of nervous weakness.

Physical shock is also a common cause of nervous debility, and in these days of frequent railway and automobile accidents the so-called traumatic neuroses are of constant occurrence. In damage suits against railway companies injuries of this nature frequently receive slight consideration, yet they may be far more serious in their subsequent effect than broken bones. I know a young man of splendid physique who underwent a railway accident with apparently no effect beyond that which is generally termed "a good shaking-up." Within a year he became a nervous wreck unable to attend to his business and a burden to himself and to his family. This condition lasted for four or five years when it gradually improved, yet he obtained but trifling compensation because he had no wounds to show.

Other physical diseases such as heart disease, phthisis, and affections of the reproductive organs, especially in women, produce nervous conditions. In tuberculosis nervous disturbances are frequently present at the inception of the disease, but as the latter progresses irritability and depression give place to the unconquerable optimism which is characteristic of consumption. The association between affections of the female organs and nervousness is preserved in the word hysteria, but this relation is very general as many hysterical women have no organic disease, and many sufferers from uterine affections are

CAUSES OF NERVOUSNESS (ENVIRONMENT)

not hysterical. Fevers through the modifications they effect in cerebral circulation and through the inflammation of the brain and its membranes give rise to mental disturbances and to delirium which resembles the raving of insanity. Anæmia, whether due to a deficiency of red blood corpuscles or to actual loss of blood, is a certain cause of nervousness. Pale and ill-nourished girls present typical cases, yet it is not true that all nervous sufferers are anæmic. When the volume and constitution of the blood become normal, the nervous symptoms usually disappear. The same may be said of nervousness which is caused or complicated by digestional disturbances. In all such cases it is best to attack the physical symptoms first. My friend and associate, Dr. J. Warren Achorn, the well-known stomach specialist of Boston, has succeeded in innumerable instances in controlling severe nervous disorders by re-establishing the equilibrium of digestion and assimilation.

Toxic substances, whether they are retained through defective elimination, or are introduced into the system from without, have a marked effect on our brain and nerve life and upon our states of consciousness. Of these the most important is alcohol. This may be so highly diluted that the action is very slight, but intoxication as the word implies is a poisoning of the higher centers of the brain, which causes a temporary delirium corresponding to the delirium of insanity, and which affects sensibility, locomotion, and speech. The result of so violent a stimulation of the nervous system, especially on one inclined to nervousness, is profoundly depressing. The intoxicated person, as Möbius says, is, for the time being, an invalid.

Not only does he suffer from acute physical and nervous symptoms such as nausea, headache, nervous tremblings, prostration, intense irritability, apathy, etc., but he is far more susceptible than he would otherwise be to other forms of disease and less likely to recover from them.[1]

Acuter forms of alcoholism may cause the diseased condition of the nervous system known as delirium tremens which not infrequently results in death itself, or in permanent insanity, in epilepsy or paralysis. I am speaking here on the effects of alcohol on civilized man; its effect on savages is different. Alcohol makes savages drunk; it does not make them nervous.

Among Byron's trifling and immoral sayings, one for which the world has never forgiven him runs thus: "Man, being reasonable, must get drunk." Offensive as these words are, as we look around the world, the power to become intoxicated seems to constitute one of the striking differences between rational men and irrational brutes. Whither should we go to find a people ignorant of the art of distilling alcohol and of concocting drinks which rob them of their reason? When the barbaric German tribes first came into civilization they were already a beer-drinking people. Their capacity for their national

[1] "I think I am entirely safe in saying that if we could blot out the influence of alcohol, we could save thirty out of every hundred above five years of age now dying from inflammation of the brain and its membranes, twenty-nine out of every hundred now dying from apoplexy, twenty-seven out of every hundred now dying from acute mania, twenty-seven out of every hundred now dying from Bright's disease, and twenty-four out of every hundred now dying from erysipelas, besides all the cases now dying from alcoholism, and all the cases now dying from cirrhosis of the liver." Dr. Andrew H. Smith, *The Influence of Alcohol in the Production of Disease*. New York, 1886.

beverage struck the Romans, who themselves were no mean drinkers, with astonishment. What beer is in Germany, wine is in France, Italy, and Spain, and whisky in Scotland and Ireland. The English, who like ourselves have no one national beverage, welcome with joy the intoxicants of every civilized people. The inhabitants of Kamschatka consume a kind of mushroom which induces a protracted delirium. The descendants of the Incas have their greasy *chica* prepared from corn which has been chewed by mules. The Tartars intoxicate themselves with a fermentation of mutton, rice, and other vegetables, or with their beloved kumiss, made of fermented mare's milk. In the East opium is freely eaten and smoked, a vice which has penetrated every part of the world. In South America coca is the favorite narcotic, which of late years in the form of cocaine has become popular with all nations. If there is a people on earth so primitive as not to have learned how to poison itself with alcohol or narcotics, civilization no sooner finds that people than it teaches them these deadly arts.

What is the reason why the whole human race with scarce an exception has so willingly yielded itself to the dangerous pleasures of alcoholic and narcotic poisoning? Undoubtedly because of their effects. There is nothing which man dreads so much as the dulness and monotony of a barren existence. A life of suffering is hardly so dreadful as a life of ennui. Now in intoxication man finds the longed-for escape from a monotonous existence, and the more barren life is of vital interest, the greater the temptation to this relief. Especially noticeable is this cause in our western states and territories, where men regard a prolonged debauch almost in the light of an innocent recreation, a refuge from the deadly monotony of their daily lives. Intoxication is a form of delirium in which all the forces of the nervous system are temporarily exalted. Of course, the reaction of profound depression follows quickly on the heels of enjoyment, but this is a consideration few men have strength enough to weigh, or if they do take it into account they dismiss it as a lesser evil. We rightly think that intoxication degrades a man, but that is not what the drunkard thinks, at least when he is drunk. Drunken men are almost always optimists: nothing troubles them. Listening to their conversation one would suppose them to be kings and princes, superior to their fellows, able to do what they will. The first effect of alcoholic intoxication seems to be an exaltation of self-consciousness, an elevation of feeling, a sense of importance which in a sober man would be foolish egotism. This feeling may rise to madness and give birth to crime, in fact the larger proportion of all crimes is directly inspired by alcohol. The forces of the mind, goaded to unwonted activity, break their uniting bond and fall into a wild whirl of anarchy, in which thoughts and emotions, joy and sorrow, good and evil, stretch out their hands to one another in a furious dance, and the whole soul is given to unbridled license, not, however, untroubled by remorse.

As intoxication becomes profounder its effects are more overwhelming. The whole mind and body, with the exception of the medulla oblongata, become drunk together. The muscles relax and cease to obey the will. The senses are obscured and the mind cut off from its usual means of communication with the external world, and madly stimulated is plunged into a sea of gloomy and delirious thought. The will vainly struggles to preserve its autonomy against the overwhelming flood of physiological disturbances which threaten to engulf it on every side. The flashes of intelligence grow faint and intermittent. Then they cease, and night, spiritual night, the night of death, throws its sable pall over all. That physical death does not instantly follow is due to the fact that in the strange dispensation of things, the palsied hand is no longer able to carry to the lips the poison which would next overthrow that watchful guardian which presides over the beating heart and the function of respiration. Were some kind friend to perform this office, the drunkard's troubles would end then and there. That such a state is sinful, degrading to manhood, destructive to soul and body, goes without saying. Only a man of the lowest instincts can find pleasure in so brutal an indulgence. We may lose ourselves thus once and find ourselves again, yet not as before. The soul lost in the darkness of flesh and sin does not bring all its spirituality back with it, nor does the brain recover quickly from so gross an injury. On the other hand, the nervous system is wonderfully plastic, it learns its lessons quickly and retains its habits with fatal tenacity. The man who has been intoxicated only once is not without danger of becoming a drunkard.

> "From drinking fiery poison in a den,
> Crowded with tawdry girls and squalid men,
> Who hoarsely laugh and brawl and curse and fight,
> I wake from day-dreams to this real night."[1]

[1] James Thomson.

The effects of narcotic poisoning differ radically from those of alcohol and vary with the substances employed. The subjective effect of opium differs widely in different persons and races and in different stages of its habitual use. The Chinese, for example, regard the use of opium very much as we do the use of tobacco, *i.e.*, as mildly deleterious. At first, according to the accounts of educated white men who have carefully observed their sensations, there is a sense of well-being; not, however, the expansive and boisterous happiness of alcoholism, which demands outward expression, but rather an inward state of untroubled peace which the Chinese call "a flame which burns far from the wind." The subject of opium or of morphia is for the time being calmly happy, for the sorrows of life cannot penetrate the veil behind which he slumbers. He is not bored by his environment, for a fine, intense organic cerebral activity supplies him with an unending series of mental images. No fancy is so bold, no pencil so accomplished, as to be able to depict the visions which rise out of the chaos of his brain and which display themselves to his closed eyes. Alcohol draws men together. Its votaries must have companions to laugh with, to drink with, to talk with. The victim of opium goes his way alone for the reason that no other human being can accompany him. No other eye can see what he sees, no other heart can know what he enjoys and suffers.

The effects of the habitual use of opium and morphia is even more injurious to the brain and nervous system than the use of alcohol, and the habit also is more difficult to control. The moral effect of opium is the erection of a veil between its victim and the world. At first this veil is of such diaphanous texture as to be scarcely perceptible. A man dimly feels that his relations with the world have undergone a change, a change for the better, he thinks, since now he has a refuge from every ill of life. Only when he attempts to rend this slight tissue of illusions does he discover that it is composed of finest steel. His inner life may be a Heaven, or it may be a Hell; the fact remains that he cannot escape from it. The veil between him and the world thickens. He looks out on life as one sees a light through an alabaster vase. He feels the world as one feels a piece of glass through a silk glove. In time his thoughts are apt to become of a darker complexion, and his moral vision is wholly obscured. The only truth to him is what he experiences on his mysterious journeys to the land of nothingness. The one thing needful in life is the means of prolonging his slumber. To obtain this he would betray his best friend, rob the fatherless, make dominoes of his parents' bones. For the thing which he dreads most is awakening. So every tie which binds the opium-eater to his fellow men gives way. The victim of opium has but one tie — that which binds him to his drug. If alcohol drowns the soul, opium immures it. Its votaries continue to live in their prison, but it is a life which dreams of death.[1]

"From wandering through many a solemn scene,
  Of opium vision with a heart serene,
  And intellect miraculously bright,
  I wake from day-dreams to this real night."
— *James Thomson.*

[1] These two statements are based in part on the fine and discriminating description of the phenomena of alcoholism and of the opium habit of Paolo Mantegazza. *Physiology of Pleasure*, chap. 19.

No etiology of nervousness would be complete which did not call attention to the extraordinary prevalence of nervous disorders on this continent, and which did not deal specifically with the problem of American nervousness. So far as nervousness is to be regarded as the disease of civilization, it is to be expected that America, in which the processes of civilization are most accelerated, should be the land in which this disease would most plainly reveal itself. Fortunately for us, however, our peculiar national tendency to nervousness is in the direction of the lighter functional neuroses. The severer organic forms of nervous disease are by no means unusual, but there is nothing to show that they are more prevalent in America than in other civilized countries, nor do the milder nervous disorders tend to pass into severer organic nervous diseases.

The causes and symptoms of American nervousness have been treated comprehensively by Dr. George M. Beard. His book [1] is now old, but it remains the best popular treatise on the subject with which I am acquainted. Dr. Beard, as we have already seen, regards nervousness as a direct outcome of modern civilization. He emphatically asserts that without civilization there can be no nervousness, and that neither bad habits, climate, race, nor environment can make nervous disease possible and common except when reinforced by brain-work, worry, and an indoor life. He recognizes the hereditary factor in nervous disorders, but he does not give it sufficient weight. Seventy-five years ago, Dr. Beard affirms, ner-

[1] *American Nervousness, Its Causes and Consequences*, Putnam, New York, 1881.

vousness was unknown to America and to the world. Today (1881) there are more than fifty thousand cases in this country alone. (If Dr. Beard were writing now he would have to multiply these figures by ten.) What is the cause of this unexampled spread of a new disease? In attempting to answer this question, Dr. Beard enumerates many of the characteristics of American nervousness, and then states what he believes to be their causes. Among the former he mentions the fine organization so characteristic of the native-born American, which is marked by fine soft hair, delicate skin, nicely chiseled features, small bones, and which is frequently accompanied by a slight physical and muscular system. This, as he observes, accompanies the true nervous temperament. Such a constitution can only be produced by a high form of civilization, and in Dr. Beard's opinion it protects us from ordinary fevers and inflammatory diseases. Among other physical indications of nervous weakness Beard notices the fragility of American teeth, an early baldness of American men, increasing sensitiveness to pain and to heat and cold, and digestional weakness. Irregularities of teeth, like their decay, are the product primarily of civilization, and secondarily of climate. The only races which have poor teeth are those that clean them. I submit, however, that as long as American women are distinguished by their long and abundant hair, nervousness can hardly be regarded as the cause of baldness in our men. Dr. Beard also calls attention to the growing disability of American women to sustain the burdens of the marriage relation and to perform the functions of maternity. In speaking of the increasing sensitiveness of the digestive organs, Dr. Beard calls attention to the fact that a generation or two ago pork and Indian meal formed the chief staples of life in America, as they are still in many parts of the South and West. This diet could no longer be tolerated by people who live in cities. "In America pork, like the Indian, flees before civilization." Americans eat better and more carefully prepared foods than any other people in the world and suffer most from indigestion. The first of these propositions is, I think, open to question. The well-to-do and intelligent in America, who after all form but an insignificant fraction of our whole population, unquestionably live better than any class of the same numerical strength in other lands. But when we pass into the homes of the poor and uneducated, we find ignorance of the simplest principles of dietetics, a vast amount of waste, and the ruin of good food by bad cooking. Moreover, as regards our public eating houses, apart from the fine hotels of our larger cities, there is no other country in the civilized world where it is so difficult to obtain a decent meal as it is in America.

Dr. Beard comments very interestingly on our increased susceptibility to alcohol and narcotics and also to drugs and medicines. "Among Americans of the higher order, those who live indoors, drinking is a lost art. A European coming to America sees a sight which no other civilized nation can show him — greater than Niagara — an immense body of intelligent people voluntarily and habitually abstaining from alcoholic liquors, females almost universally so, and males temperate if not totally abstinent. There is, perhaps, no single fact in sociology more instructive and far-reaching than this, and this is but the fraction of the general and sweeping fact that the heightened sensitiveness of Americans forces them to abstain entirely, or use in incredible and amusing moderation, not only the stronger alcoholic liquors, whether pure or impure, but also the milder wines, ales, and beers, and even tea and coffee." This is not altogether the impression of our habits which intelligent visitors from abroad have received on visiting America, nor does this statement coincide with the fact that a vaster quantity of malt and spirituous liquors is manufactured and sold in America than in any other country on earth. In all human probability this is drunk by some one. No doubt the Germans and Irish to whom Dr. Beard assigns the whole amount get their share, but it is improbable that they consume it all. Still Dr. Beard is unquestionably right in his assertion that a growing susceptibility to the effects of alcohol is characteristic of the higher type of American and that this is a sign of nervous weakness. It is also certain that climate has a marked effect on man's craving for alcohol and on his ability to endure it. Englishmen, Scotchmen, and Germans visiting this country have frequently commented upon the fact that they neither desired nor could endure their usual quantity of stimulating liquor.[1] The large daily ration of whisky of which the Scotch and Irish partake apparently with impunity at home would be destructive to them in this country. The same may be said of tea and coffee, and of tobacco. Their effects on persons of nervous temperament in this country are unquestionably injurious. As

[1] See *e.g.* Charles Kingsley's first letter from America.

Beard puts it, "Our fathers could smoke, our mothers could smoke, but their children must ofttimes be cautious, and chewing is very rapidly going out of custom, and will soon, like snuff-taking, become a historic curiosity while cigars give way to cigarettes."

Dr. Beard, speaking as a physician of experience, also asserts that Americans are far more sensitive to the action of medicines than other peoples, and that this sensitiveness is increasing. While fonder of drugs than any other people, they are least able to endure them. This is shown among other instances in the effect of cathartic remedies which are administered in constantly decreasing doses. "Where two or three powerful pills were formerly required for a strong cathartic effect, now one or two, perhaps half a pill, suffices." Physicians who have both hospital and private practice constantly observe how temperament modifies physiological action of drugs. Coarse and phlegmatic natures can endure far more powerful medicines than the nervous and sensitive. This is brought home to those of our people who come under the care of foreign physicians, whether in England or on the continent, and they have learned by bitter experience that they cannot tolerate the powerful medicines which those physicians are accustomed to administer. A friend of mine, a delicate and sensitive woman, almost lost her life as a result of taking sixty grains of phenacetine which were prescribed for her as a single dose by a celebrated German physician. Among other symptoms of American nervousness, Dr. Beard cites the wide-spread prevalence of hay-fever and catarrh, the tendency to abbreviate speech, and the high-pitched American voice and our nasal intonation.

The causes of American nervousness Dr. Beard finds in the high pressure of American life, re-enforced by the stimulating and depressing effects of our climate. The latter cause in itself could never produce nervousness, since the American Indians, who were far more exposed to climatic changes than ourselves, are among the least nervous of mankind. Working in conjunction with our intense mental activity, our indoor life, and with all the nervous tension to which we are exposed, climate unquestionably is an important factor in the creation of nervous diseases and disorders. The influence of climate and environment together is shown in the fact that a new and distinct type of humanity has been evolved in the course of a few hundred years on these shores, a type that differs perceptibly from its English prototype. The American is taller, sparer, less ruddy than the Englishman. Both American men and women are less inclined to become corpulent with advancing years, partly because they eat less and drink less.[1] The moist skin of our English ancestors in our climate has become dry, their curly hair straight and silken. Especially does the American differ from the Englishman in excess of nervous energy and in the rapidity of his mental operations. This is shown especially in our rapidity of speech and in our great facility in public speaking.

The characteristics of our climate which have done most to accentuate our tendency to nervousness in Beard's opinion are its extreme dryness, the immense variation of its summer and winter temperatures, and its rapid

[1] Dr. Mitchell comments on this fact and ascribes it chiefly to climatic causes. *Fat and Blood*, p. 21.

fluctuations. I am, however, by no means sure of the correctness of the first of these causes. No part of this country suffers so much from nervousness in all its forms as New England, whose climate can hardly be called dry, but on the other hand the very dry climate of Colorado, Montana, Arizona, and Wyoming has already developed a very marked tendency to nervousness. Beard's observations on the effects of extreme heat and cold and of rapid changes of temperature are very interesting. He reminds us of the powerfully stimulating effect on the system obtained by the alternation of ice and hot water and by the Turkish bath. This intense stimulation, however, soon gives rise to exhaustion. The American is stimulated to greater activity by his climate, but its permanent effect is to exhaust him. Foreigners visiting this country have frequently observed this. They feel more energetic but they tire sooner than at home.[1] "The inhabitants of the northern and eastern portions of the United States are subjected to severer and more sudden and frequent alternations of heat and cold than the inhabitants of any other civilized country. Our climate is a union of the tropics and the poles: half the year we freeze, the other half roast, and at all seasons a day of painful cold is liable to be followed by a day of painful warmth.... Apart from the direct effect of these conditions on the nervous system, they confine us too much to our houses. During a large part of the year, either because it is too warm or too cold, we are disinclined to go abroad or to take much exercise. The extreme cold compels us to maintain a temperature in our houses

[1] See *e.g.* Kingsley's, "Letters from America."

which Europeans find oppressive and intolerable. The effect of the degrees of our climate is to accelerate all the vital changes of our organism, with the result that we actually live faster than other peoples and wear out earlier." As one travels south in this country one sees nervousness steadily diminish. Boston, as a city, is more nervous than New York, New York more nervous than Philadelphia and Baltimore, and further south the tendency to nervousness is not wide-spread. This is probably due partly to inherited tendencies in regard to the conduct of life, partly to the effect of a warm and too enervating climate in relaxing the restless activities of man. As the conditions of Northern life are introduced into the South, they can hardly fail to be followed by increasing nervousness.

In general it is to be remembered that the functional nervousness we have been describing has no perceptible affect upon longevity. Americans suffer more than any other people from these disorders, but they excel all nations but the Jews in the average length of life. This is shown particularly in the longevity of brain-workers which here as elsewhere exceeds that of manual laborers and indeed the longevity of any other class. Dr. Beard's discussion of this subject forms the ablest and most interesting chapter of his book. As an offset to the deleterious influences of our civilization, we see many healthful influences at work to check and neutralize the effects of over-exertion. I allude here to such tendencies as longer vacations for all, general relaxation of all interests during the heated term, the disposition of well-to-do families to live in the country for the larger portion of the year, a renewed love of out-of-door life and sport, the athletic spirit cultivated by our colleges, and physical activity and prowess of our young women. These tendencies, if they persist for a generation, cannot fail to be productive of great good. By this means, and by the cultivation of the spiritual life, we may escape from the flood of nervous disorders which threatens to overwhelm us.

CHAPTER VIII

THE NERVOUS SYSTEM IN HEALTH AND DISEASE

THE cellular theory has been one of the most stimulating movements in modern science. This theory considers all living organisms, whether animals or plants, as composed of an immense number of independent, yet interacting, units, called cells. A cell may be defined as a microscopic, anatomical unit, limited by a membrane or wall and containing a semi-liquid substance called protoplasm. Within this protoplasm lies the most vital portion of the cell, from the standpoint of heredity and energy, known as the nucleus. This protoplasm has been defined by Huxley as "the physical basis of life." Cells can be seen and studied by means of the higher powers of the microscope. Simple as they may seem, yet their complexity is marvelous, and the rôle played by them in development, inheritance, disease, and physiological function is of the highest importance. In the middle of the nineteenth century, Virchow, the great German pathologist, applied the cell theory to the disease processes of living beings, and so fruitful has this concept been, that medicine has uninterruptedly advanced along these lines. The various bacteria are really very minute cells. Plants and trees are composed of millions of identical cells, but it is in living animals that we find the greatest diversity of cell-forms, and of special functions of individual groups of cells. Each organ has its special cells; the liver cells secrete bile; the cells of the stomach secrete gastric juice, etc. The list might be indefinitely extended. But it is in the central nervous system that the cell has reached its highest development in form and function. A great variety of cells can be found in the various portions of the brain and spinal cord, and these, with their interlacing network of fibers, each an offshoot from an individual cell, form a complexity of nerve tracts that is positively bewildering even to the trained neurologist. During recent years the anatomy and physiology of the central nervous system has attracted an immense amount of attention. To take an entire library on nerve anatomy, physiology, and pathology, with all the technicalities, and to condense this material within the limits of a single chapter, is a formidable task. We must therefore ask the indulgence of our readers for all sins of omission that this chapter may contain. Everything in the living animal organism, muscular movement, secretion, excretion, breathing, the heart-beat, even consciousness itself, is dependent on the central nervous system. Thus the nervous system may be called the master tissue. To the ultimate units of this master tissue, the nerve cell itself, we will first direct our attention.

A. *The Normal Nerve Cell.* In Figs. 1 and 2 are represented normal nerve cells from the brain and spinal cord. One of these (Fig. 1) is known as a pyramidal cell from its shape; the other (Fig. 2) is an anterior horn cell from the spinal cord. In Fig. 3 is another pyramidal nerve cell, but a different variety of stain has been used. Nerve cells vary in shape and size, from $\frac{1}{250}$ to $\frac{1}{3000}$

NERVOUS SYSTEM IN HEALTH AND DISEASE 181

of an inch in diameter. Their number is enormous, the figures amounting to hundreds of millions. When stained by one of the aniline dyes (methylene blue), a normal nerve cell shows the following characteristics. In the center of the cell there is an oval, light area, within which lies a round, dark body. This light area is known as the nucleus; the dark body within is called the nucleolus. Outside the nucleus and within the cell body are a number of irregularly shaped granules, arranged rather concentrically and called the Nissl bodies, after a dis-

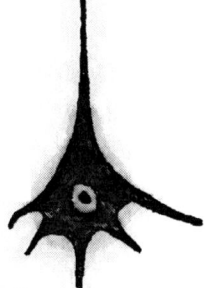

FIG. 1.—Normal nerve cell from the brain (Nissl Stain).

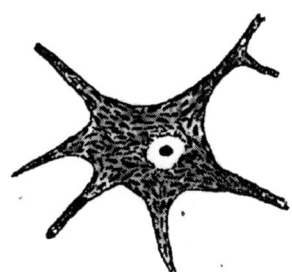

FIG. 2.—Normal nerve cell from spinal cord (Nissl Stain).

tinguished German neurologist. Running through each nerve cell and passing into the various processes of the cell are a large number of fine thread-like structures, called neuro-fibrils (not shown in the illustration). These neuro-fibrils are perhaps the conducting substance of the nervous system.

Two varieties of processes come from the cell body. One of these, called the dendrites, divides and sub-divides in an antler-like fashion, and thus spreads over a considerable territory. The other, called the axis-cylinder, is smooth, but instead of being grouped around the cell like the dendrite, it runs out a considerable distance, varying from the smallest fraction of an inch to the length of the spinal cord. A nerve cell can have many dendrites, but it can have only one axis-cylinder. Upon the dendrites may be seen minute buds or swellings called gemmules (see Fig. 3). The entire cell, with its axis-cylinder, dendrites, gemmules, etc., is known as a neurone. Each neurone is an independent anatomical and physiological unit, but they all interlace and connect with one another in a most complex and bewildering manner (see Fig. 4). Every neurone, in spite of its independence, acts in conjunction with several other neurones, and wide communications are possible by means of the dendrites and axis-cylinders. The supporting tissue of the neurones is known as the neuroglia. The axis-cylinder is composed of three layers; an inner layer of fine fibers, a middle protecting layer arranged in segments and known as the medullary sheath, and an outer thin membrane called the neurilemma. The nerve cells make up the gray matter of the brain and spinal cord; the white matter is composed of the axis-cylinders. Nerve impulses are carried to the cell by the dendrites and away from the cell by the axis-cylinder.

FIG. 3.—Normal nerve cell from the brain (Golgi Stain).

FIG. 4.—Section through the brain showing layers of nerve cells and their connections (Golgi Stain).

NERVOUS SYSTEM IN HEALTH AND DISEASE 183

The grouping of the axis-cylinders makes up the central nervous pathways and the nerves themselves, which either communicate with central cells in the brain or cord (point of origin), or with the skin or various organs of the body (point of distribution). Like all cells of the body, the nutrition of the nerve cell is dependent on its blood supply.

B. *The Diseased Nerve Cell.* In organic diseases of the nervous system marked changes are found, not only in the nerve cell, but also in the nerve fibers. Figures 5 and 6 show very common appearances of diseased nerve

FIG. 5.—Diseased nerve cell from the brain (Nissl Stain).

FIG. 6.—Diseased nerve cell from spinal cord (Nissl Stain).

cells in the brain and spinal cord, such as is pre-eminently found in chronic alcoholism and alcoholic neuritis. Observe that the nucleus is no longer central, but is pushed to one side, while the Nissl bodies have almost completely disappeared and are replaced by a fine dust-like substance. Fig. 7 A shows the appearance of a nerve cell when its blood supply is cut off, the dendrites and gemmules having in great part disappeared. In Fig. 7 B is shown the destructive effect of ricin poisoning.[1] Note

[1] Ricin is an alkaloid found in the seeds of the castor oil plant.

the spindle-shaped swellings on the dendrites and the complete disappearance of the gemmules. The above are only a few of the changes that can take place in various diseases. In senile dementia, general paralysis, locomotor ataxia, hemorrhage or softening of the brain or spinal cord, not only are the cells diseased, but the nerve fibers likewise suffer destruction. Fever of any kind has an especially deleterious effect upon the nerve cell, and this accounts for the delirium of fever. Alcohol, morphine or cocaine, the bites of certain venomous snakes or spiders, in tetanus or lockjaw, and in certain forms of melancholia, marked changes are found in the nerve cell. Chronic alcoholism, leading to alcoholic insanity or dementia or to alcoholic neuritis, is particularly prone to injure the nerve cell. One man's drink flies to his head, another to his heels, but both the incoherent speech and the staggering gait of the intoxicated individual are due to the influence of alcohol on the central nervous system. In certain severe states of exhaustion and fatigue, the tired nerve cell becomes shrunken and diminished in size. When a nerve fiber is cut or diseased, its connected cell shows a characteristic change (Figs. 5 and 6). Now in all functional nervous diseases, such as the various forms of neurasthenia, hysteria, and psychasthenia, the nerve cells appear absolutely normal. In these diseases we are dealing, not with any anatomical

FIG. 7.—Diseased nerve cells from brain (Golgi Stain).
A. Cell from which blood supply has been cut off.
B. Cell showing effect of ricin poisoning.

changes in the cell, but with a disordered function of the cell, a change in its physiology.

C. *Nerve Physiology.* We have briefly reviewed the anatomy of the nerve cell and its fibers in health and disease. Before taking up the general features of consciousness and cerebral localization, it will be necessary to consider some essential facts of nerve physiology. Nerve tissue possesses two fundamental characteristics. One of these is nerve conduction, whereby motion, sensation, and reflex action become possible; the other chief function of nerve tissue is the storing up of impressions and reproducing them in the same order. This latter forms what is known as associative memory. The brain is the organ of mind or of consciousness, while the spinal cord may be called the organ of reflex action. Of course this is true only within certain limits, as the various functions are not isolated phenomena, but there exists a considerable overlapping. It is generally believed, however, that the spinal cord possesses no consciousness.

The reproduction of impressions is due to the peculiar characteristics of the protoplasm of the nerve cell, which in many ways acts like the cylinder of a phonograph. Nerve conduction takes place in the axis-cylinder and this axis-cylinder resembles a copper wire through which a current of electricity is transmitted. The medullary sheath surrounding the axis-cylinder acts like an insulating substance, in the same way as an electric wire is insulated with gutta percha. If the protoplasm of the nerve cell is diseased, it cannot store up impressions and therefore cannot reproduce them. Under these conditions, either a loss of memory or amnesia results, or there is a state of mental enfeeblement or dementia. When the axis-cylinder is cut or diseased, conduction becomes impossible, and there results loss of motion (paralysis), or loss of sensation (anæsthesia), or loss of reflex action.

Certain nerves and their endings in the internal organs have an isolated function of their own. The olfactory nerve, for instance, can only react to odors; the auditory nerve to air vibrations which are appreciated as sound in the central nervous system; the optic nerve and the retina can only react to the ether waves which become sensations of light. The optic nerve cannot react to sound vibrations nor the auditory nerve to ether waves. In other words, we cannot *see* sound, nor *hear* light. Simple as this may seem, yet this absolute reaction of a nerve to a fixed stimulus forms one of the most fundamental facts in modern neurology, what is known as the doctrine of the specific energies of nerves.

If the finger touches a sharp point or a hot object, it is drawn quickly away. There is a sensation of burning or of pain. Both sensation and motion have taken place. But if the nerves in the arm had been previously cut, thus paralyzing the arm and abolishing sensation, no pain or burning would have been felt, neither would the strongest effort of the will have sufficed to have drawn the arm away. What does this mean? It means that the feeling of pain does not reside in the fine nerve filaments of the finger or in the large nerve trunks of the arm, but in the brain itself. The nerves merely conduct the physical stimulus of a sharp point or a hot object to the brain and there it is felt as pain. It is the brain, on feeling the painful sensation, that *wills* that the arm be drawn away. This impulse is conducted from the brain to the spinal cord and down the nerves of the arm. A short but appreciable and easily measurable length of time is needed for this act, before the pain is felt in the central nervous system, appreciated in consciousness, transformed into the idea that the arm must be pulled away to prevent further injury, the reaction chosen and the arm quickly moved. The act appears simple, but in reality it is quite complex. It takes time. It is really a movement of protection, a reflex action. This choice of reaction in the brain is known as the will.

Nerve conduction can be demonstrated in another way. If one of the large leg muscles of a frog with its attached nerve be excised and an electric current applied to the nerve, the muscle will contract. This can be repeated until the muscle becomes fatigued. In frequently repeated stimulation, the muscular contractions will follow one another very rapidly and a condition called tetanus will result. But if the nerve be cut or the place where the nerve is attached to the muscle (the so-called motor end plate) be poisoned with curare (Indian arrow poison), conduction is interfered with and therefore no muscular contraction can take place.

Reflex actions are very important in studying and diagnosing the organic diseases of the nervous system. What is known as the knee jerk is perhaps the most important reflex from the standpoint of diagnosis. If the patellar tendon just below the knee cap be struck a quick and moderately sharp blow with a rubber hammer, or the finger-tips, there results a contraction of the thigh muscles and the leg is thrown forward. This is the knee jerk. It has nothing to do with consciousness or sensation as when a finger is burnt, but is purely a reflex action. The stimulus from the blow is carried along the nerve trunks of the leg to the spinal cord, there it goes over to the nerve fibers that connect with the muscles, is transformed to a motor impulse which causes the muscles to contract and the kick results. This connection of nerve with spinal cord, and of this latter with the muscles again, forms what is known as the reflex arc. If this arc is interrupted along any portion of its path, in the nerves or in the spinal cord, the knee jerk remains absent. This especially occurs in locomotor ataxia, a disease of the spinal cord.

Other nerves, such as those which control respiration and the heart-beat, seem to act automatically from the brain centers themselves. The nerves which carry sensation are called sensory nerves; those which preside over muscular movements are called motor nerves. Other nerves control the secretion of various juices of the body, such as the saliva or gastric juice. These are called secretory nerves. The so-called trophic nerves govern the nutrition of the tissues.

An example of mixed nerve conduction may be cited. When light falls on the retina, not only is the sensation of light itself produced, but the pupil of the eye narrows in an automatic manner, without the control of the will. Here we seem to be dealing, not only with a sensory reaction (sensation of light), but one which is reflex as well (the contraction of the pupil). The knee reflex can be controlled; the pupillary reflex cannot be controlled.

It has been shown that a nerve transmits impulses by

means of its axis-cylinder much as a copper wire transmits electricity, and also that a certain period of time is required for the passage of the nerve impulse. The popular phrase "quick as thought" has therefore no foundation in fact. Thought is slow when compared to the rate of movement of light (186,000 miles per second) or even sound (1091 feet per second). In man the rate of transmission along nerve fibers is about thirty-three meters (108 feet) per second; in the frog it is about twenty-eight meters (92 feet) per second. By this we see that the reactions to pain or other sensations are not instantaneous as is popularly supposed, but that an appreciable length of time is necessary for stimuli to be appreciated in consciousness as such, and for sensory impulses to be transformed into motor reactions. When something is "willed" this time interval becomes lengthened. The reaction time is greatly increased in old age, where not only the rate of nerve transmission, but the mental processes, become slower.

The storing up of impressions in the central nervous system is based upon the principle that certain molecular changes are produced, which continue after the original stimulus has been removed. Of the simpler examples, the best are those of after images on the retina, or the "feeling" of a day's skating remaining in the limbs long after the exercise has ceased. The highest example of the storing up of external impressions is found in the phenomena of memory.

D. *The Anatomy and Functions of the Nervous System.* The nervous system is composed of the brain, spinal cord, the peripheral and cranial nerves, and the sympathetic nerves. The course of the central pathways in the brain and spinal cord and the ramifications of the peripheral nerves are very complex and bewildering. These central pathways, however, have been followed and mapped out in diseases of the central nervous system, in its embryological development and also in experiments on animals, until now the majority of these are fairly well recognized. The pathways themselves are made up of the axis-cylinders that come from nerve cells. Although these axis-cylinders seem to run in all directions, yet each central pathway is sharply limited, being derived from cells that occupy fixed areas in the brain. Each central pathway is called a system. Now in diseases of the cells or of the brain tissue that contains the cells, these fiber systems undergo degeneration and by means of proper staining methods can be followed along their course. In embryological development, the fiber systems of the brain do not develop or become medullated at the same period, and here also we have a method of following the course of the brain fibers. This last fact is of great importance in the architecture of the nervous system, as was pointed out by the German neurologist Flechsig.

A nervous system is the property of all vertebrates and can be found in a rudimentary form in invertebrates very low in the animal scale, such as the jelly fish. The nervous system has well been called the master tissue, and to it may be applied the quaint description of the heart by William Harvey, the immortal discoverer of the circulation of the blood. "It is the household divinity which, discharging its functions, nourishes, cherishes, quickens the whole body, and is indeed the foundation of life, the source of all action."[1]

The brain is contained within the skullcap in order that its delicate structure may be well protected from injury. Further protection is afforded by three membranes, with which the brain is entirely surrounded. The most external of these membranes, and lying just beneath the inner table of the skull, is called the dura mater. Beneath this is the arachnoid membrane, which is a very fine structure made up almost entirely of interlacing small blood-vessels, and so-called because it resembles a spider's web. Beneath the arachnoid, and covering the entire surface of the brain, dipping down even into its fissures, is the pia mater. The spinal cord lies within the spinal column, which is made up of the individual vertebral bones superimposed upon one another like a pile of checkers. Between each vertebra is a cartilaginous membrane. This not only is protection afforded the spinal cord, but there is also an extreme degree of elasticity, so that the body may be bent in all directions. Like the brain, the spinal cord is surrounded by the same three membranes. The nerve tracts of the spinal cord run lengthwise, and thus connect the brain centers (the cerebrum or hemispheres), and the medulla, with the nerves that go to the muscles.

The brain has several subdivisions. Chief of these are the two hemispheres or the cerebrum, which are connected by a bridge of white substance called the corpus callosum. Within the hemispheres can be found the central motor tracts. The cerebrum itself is divided into lobes, the

[1] William Harvey, *On the Circulation of the Blood*, chap. viii.

frontal, parietal, occipital, temporal, and within one of the great fissures of the brain that separates the parietal from the temporal portions lies another lobe called the Island of Reil. This is not visible externally. Below the cerebrum is the pons Varolii, below this the medulla, and just back of the medulla lies the cerebellum. The medulla contains the centers for respiration and the control of the heart-beat, while the cerebellum presides over equilibrium.

The sympathetic nervous system consists of chains of ganglia, or aggregations of nerve cells, lying on each side of the spinal column. At the base of the brain lie the so-called cranial nerves. Some of these are for the special senses, such as the olfactory nerve for smell, the optic nerve for sight, the auditory nerve for hearing; some supply the motions of the eyeball, and the mimic movements of the face; still others control vital functions, such as swallowing and the heart-beat.

The cerebrum is made up of white and gray matter, the former consisting of nerve fibers, the latter of nerve cells. The gray matter is called the cortex and lies in a folded manner on the surface of the brain, thus greatly increasing its area. Within the spinal cord this order is reversed; it is the white matter that is external and the gray matter within. The prominent raised folds of gray matter in the brain are called convolutions; the grooves between the convolutions are called fissures. In the lower animals, even in the dog and the higher apes, and in cases of lack of brain development, such as idiocy, the cortex is comparatively smooth. In dementia the convolutions are small or atrophied. Thus the area of gray matter and the size of the convolutions can be taken as a measure of intelligence. The brain weighs on the average about 1415 grams (50 ounces) in the adult male, and about 1360 grams (44.5 ounces) in the adult female. In idiots and imbeciles, in dementia and in cases of low intelligence, the weight is much less, sometimes sinking as low as 900 grams (28.1 ounces). In individuals of great intellectual capacity, such as in Daniel Webster or in the naturalist Cuvier, there was a great increase in weight.

Within the spinal cord there is a minute central canal, which expands into several connecting chambers in the brain, known as ventricles. These ventricles act as kind of a drainage system. The activity of the brain depends upon the blood supply, which is quite complex. The arteries of the brain are very ingeniously arranged in a hexagonal shape at the base of the brain. This hexagon of arteries is known as the circle of Willis. If one artery becomes plugged, the circulation can go on through the other branches.

The nerve tracts of the brain are very complex. Some of these control motion, such as the pyramidal tract, others control sensation, while still others, known as the association fibers, seem to be at the basis of intellect and associative memory. In right-handed individuals the intellectual functions are localized on the left side of the brain. This is due to the fact that most of the fiber tracts cross over to the other side. A right-handed person therefore may be said to be left-brained.

The brain is the organ of consciousness or mind; the spinal cord is merely a conducting mechanism for the control of motion and sensation by the higher brain centers. If a pigeon or frog be deprived of its brain, it will live, but its actions will resemble a machine. In other words it will become a reflex automaton, originating nothing, learning nothing. Not a trace of memory can be found. It will show nothing but motor activity. Food put before it will be unnoticed, but if the food be placed in the mouth, it will be swallowed. In man, when the brain is profoundly diseased, as in dementia or idiocy, there can be found some of the phenomena of the brainless animal. When sleep results in a healthy individual, there is a low degree of consciousness, otherwise dreaming could not take place. If there is a hemorrhage in the brain, or the head be struck a severe blow, complete unconsciousness results. All these facts prove that the mechanism of consciousness depends upon the integrity of the brain tissue.

Cerebral localization, or the mapping out of various functions on the surface of the brain, has made amazing strides in the last quarter century. This has been the result partly of autopsies on pathological brain lesions (hemorrhages, tumors, softenings) in man, and partly of excision and electrical stimulation experiments on the cortex of dogs and monkeys. Figure 8 is a diagrammatic representation of the principal areas on the surface of the brain. The area marked *A* controls the movements of the various muscles of the body. Here are localized the large motor cells whose axis-cylinders dip down in a fan-like manner into the white matter of the brain, curve together in the portion known as the internal capsule, and finally, after a more or less devious course, they reach the medulla. Here the fibers from the right side of the brain cross over to the left and vice versa, and then pursue their way down the spinal cord. This system of fibers in the brain and cord is known as the pyramidal tract; the place in the medulla where they cross to the

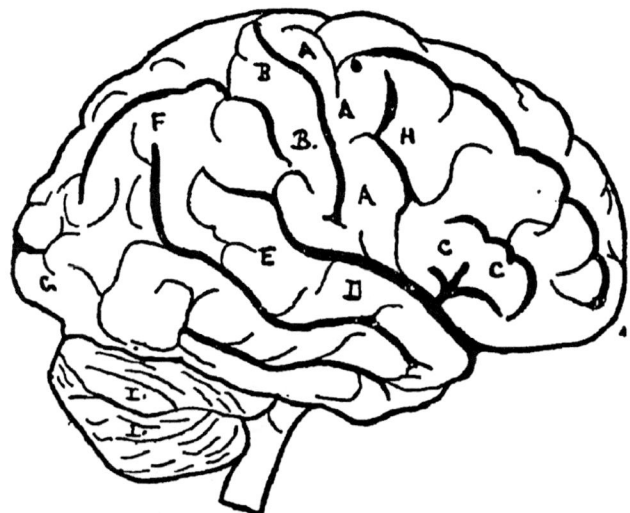

FIG. 8.—Left hemisphere of the human brain, showing the localization of various functions, according to the latest researches.
A. Motor area for movements of limbs, trunk, head, face and eyes.
B. Sensory area for touch, muscular, pain, temperature, and form senses.
C. Motor speech center.
D. Hearing center.
E. Center for auditory memories.
F. Center for visual memories.
G. Visual center.
H. Writing center (?)
I. Center for equilibrium (the cerebellum).
(The centers for smell and taste are at the base of the brain.)

opposite side is called the decussation of the pyramids. A hemorrhage in any portion of the pyramidal tract in the brain causes, therefore, a complete or partial paralysis of the opposite portion of the body. This hemorrhage is accompanied by a sudden loss of consciousness and is known as an apoplectic shock.

The portion behind the motor area, marked *B*, is the cortical center for sensation of all kinds and the recognition of the nature of objects by touch. In the blind deaf-mutes, such as Laura Bridgman or Helen Keller, this center is greatly developed, as their education was entirely along the line of touch sensations. *C* is known as Broca's convolution. It is the center for motor speech and is localized on the left side of the brain. A lesion here causes what is known as motor aphasia, in which the patient becomes dumb or is able to make only a few meaningless sounds, yet can perfectly comprehend what is said. *D* is the hearing center. Disease of this center causes complete deafness. *E* is the center where auditory memories or the memories of the sound of words are stored up. Disease of this portion of the brain causes what is known as sensory aphasia. The patient can talk freely, can hear what is said, but the words are meaningless to him. He hears the words but does not comprehend them; it is as if one spoke in a foreign language of which he was completely ignorant. At *F* the visual memories are stored up. In a lesion here, objects are seen but not recognized; it causes what is known as mind blindness. *G* is the visual center, where all the fibers of the optic nerve terminate. Disease here, on account of the peculiar crossing of the optic nerve, causes a blindness of one half of each eye. *H* is the so-called writing center. In a lesion of this portion of the brain there is inability to write, known as agraphia. *I* is the cerebellum, the center of equilibrium. Diseases of the cerebellum cause the individual to lose all sense of the co-ordination of muscular movements necessary for the equilibrium of the body and therefore he reels like a drunken man. The higher psychical centers for reason, memory, and association seem to be localized in the frontal lobe of the brain, anterior to the motor area (*A*) and above the motor speech center (*C*). In dementia and in idiocy this is the portion that is most profoundly diseased. The mapping-out of these centers in the brain has been of great practical value in the localization of brain tumors and their successful treatment by surgical operation.

As the individual progresses from childhood to adult life, there is an increase in the weight of the brain and in the number of association fibers. In old age the brain atrophies or grows smaller and the nerve cells degenerate. The speech center is highly developed in man, for without speech all abstract reasoning and thought are manifestly impossible. All great thinkers and writers seem to have possessed a large vocabulary, while the language of the savage consists of only a few hundred words. The poet has well said,

> "He gave man speech and speech created thought,
> Which is the measure of the universe."

Unless it has been abused to an irreparable point, so that organic changes occur, the nervous system possesses great recuperative powers. Nervous fatigue is much benefited by sleep, while protracted insomnia or a restless, broken night, has a particularly pernicious effect on the general feeling of well-being, not only in the neurasthenic state, but in perfect health as well. Fatigue may take on a distinctly pathological aspect such as restlessness, muscular twitchings, tremors; various fancies may take possession of the mind which may degenerate into pathological obsessions. As the fatigue increases, there develops that peculiar feeling of incapacity and the disinclination for physical and muscular exercise, symptoms which are very characteristic of the neurasthenic states. The restlessness of school children at the end of a morning or afternoon session, as shown in the movement of the lips, eyebrows, forehead, the picking at the fingers, is due solely to fatigue. Thus we see how necessary it is that fatigue be neutralized by periods of relaxation, either physical exercise or sleep.

Many theories have been proposed to explain sleep, but all of these, when critically examined, are found to have their vulnerable points. The most pertinent interpretation of sleep, from the purely biological standpoint, is that of Claparède,[1] who concludes that sleep is a function of defense, a physiological device, its purpose being to protect the organism against fatigue. Hence the need of sleep is frequently felt before fatigue sets in. This is an admirable mechanism, splendidly fitted to neutralize activity with repose, as it has been shown by Hodge that prolonged activity leading to severe fatigue induces distinct organic changes in the nerve cells, and that after a certain period of rest the cells resume their normal appearance.

[1] Ed Claparède, *A Biological Theory of Sleep*, Archives de Psychologie, IV, 1906.

CHAPTER IX

DISEASES OF THE SUBCONSCIOUS

AROUND the problem of the subconscious is grouped the greater part of the researches and revelations of modern abnormal psychology. The term has been used rather loosely, however, and possesses many meanings for layman and scientist alike. It has proved a convenient talisman with which many of the newer medico-religious movements have conjured; it has become a byword to the layman to explain to his own satisfaction many of the mysterious workings of the mind; even by the psychologist there has been an unfortunate tendency to use the term rather loosely. Before we proceed further it will be well to arrive at a clear understanding of what constitutes the subconscious mind and to define its limitations. The problem is a difficult one, not only because of the varied ideas of different observers, but also because of the extreme complexity of the phenomena presented by subconscious states. Professor Jastrow has recently published a volume on the various aspects of the subconscious, both normal and abnormal,[1] and Dr. Morton Prince's case of Miss Beauchamp in his "Dissociation of a Personality" analyzes in an illuminating manner the changes of personality brought about by subconscious or, as psychologists prefer to call them, dissociated states.

[1] *The Subconscious*, 1906.

On account of the diversity of the views concerning the subconscious, Dr. Prince has recently [1] invited a discussion on the question by several eminent psychologists.

The dominant theories of the subconscious have emanated either from physicians or from psychologists. The former have naturally dealt with the abnormal aspects of the subject; the latter with its normal manifestations. The view-point has been different in each case, whether the subconscious phenomena are studied in the diseased or in the normal individual. The so-called field of consciousness is that portion of our mental life of which one is aware by ordinary introspection. What lies outside or beneath this conscious field is split off or, in psychological terms, dissociated from consciousness. In other words, it is extra-conscious or subconscious. To call this a dissociated portion of consciousness is more accurate and scientific, for then we do not pledge ourselves in placing this extra conscious field in any portion of what we may call the mental space. The stream of thought is made up of consciousness, and consciousness itself is the result of the energy of the central nervous system. By some consciousness is considered the energy itself; by others as running parallel with it. This interaction of the mind on the body, and the body on the mind, forms one of the most important and fascinating fields of physiological psychology. When the nervous system ceases to functionate, consciousness likewise disappears, as in profound sleep or in ether or chloroform narcosis. A sound sleep is dreamless and dreams only occur in the half-waking state. When the nerve cells are diseased, as in the

[1] *Journal of Abnormal Psychology*, vol. ii, Nos. 1 and 2, 1907.

various insanities and in poisoning by such drugs as alcohol or morphine, consciousness becomes distorted and hallucinations or sense deceptions arise. When certain conscious processes go on below the "threshold of consciousness," we are not aware of them and here we have the physiological explanation of unconscious thinking. In other words, we are dealing with subconscious processes. By the "threshold of consciousness" is meant the lowest limit of thought of which we have any perception. If ideas or thoughts are not of sufficient intensity to be perceived by us, they remain below this threshold; they are subconscious or dissociated. This split-off, subconscious, dissociated portion may be a marginal state or a fringe of consciousness in its normal sense, or, if diseased or abnormal, this marginal state grows larger and, as a natural consequence, the dissociated field of consciousness enlarges. This process, of course, narrows the field of normal consciousness, and we shall see later on how important a part this narrowing of the field of consciousness plays in hysteria.

Therefore, the subconscious may mean one of several things:

1. Any portion of consciousness outside the field of attention.

2. Ideas split off from the main stream of consciousness.

3. Split-off personalities.

4. Forgotten experiences, *i.e.*, experiences and memories out of mind.

5. A great tank of consciousness exists within us, but we are conscious of only a portion of it (the subliminal self).

6. Unconscious brain action or thinking.

It would lead us too far into technicalities to discuss the complex theories given above, of which only the simplest outlines are indicated. One fundamental idea seems to underlie them all, however, namely, that certain portions of consciousness are or may become detached from the main stream. These portions have all the attributes of our entire conscious stream of thought, and the difference in interpretation becomes either purely psychological or purely physiological. The psychological interpretation is the one usually accepted to-day. A lack of feeling, of "awareness," on the part of the individual is the distinguishing characteristic of these subconscious or dissociated states. For our purpose, however, it will be best to consider the subconscious as consisting of dissociated states, memories, emotions, and personalities; in fact, any portion of mental activity in its entirety, split off from the main stream of consciousness. These dissociated states have a mental activity and independence in every way analogous to our normal conscious states. Sometimes only ideas are dissociated, and then the patient is tortured by fixed ideas or obsessions which act as a mental thorn. In other cases, it is the emotions and emotional storms that take place, as shown by attacks of irritability, excitement, depression, or even convulsions. Sometimes certain memories are dissociated and then we have the condition known as amnesia. Entire groups of thought may be split off and in these cases the phenomena of automatic writing or crystal gazing may take place. Finally, in the most highly developed forms the personality itself, with its thoughts, memories, emotions, complete in themselves, may become completely dissociated, and it is here that we have the wonderful phenomena of double or multiple personality.

Before we enter into a discussion of abnormal subconscious phenomena, it will be well to inquire briefly into the question — Do subconscious states exist normally or are they always abnormal? Dr. Prince says:[1] "The ease with which the mind in perfectly healthy persons can be dissociated and the dissociated states synthetized . . . shows that subconscious synthetized states are not always evidences of disease." Janet strongly maintains the pathological nature of subconscious states, but experimental evidence shows that the process may be purely a normal one.

Before proceeding further, therefore, it will be necessary to give a few examples of the normal subconscious working. In every-day language, this is known as "absent-mindedness." People speak of doing things *unconsciously*, when in reality they mean *subconsciously*. A woman in opening eggs throws the yolk away and proceeds to beat the shells; another discards the inside of a banana and eats the skin; a third, in working, stirs with the poker of the stove instead of a spoon. The perennial joke of the professor inquiring for himself at his own house is another example of absent-mindedness or dissociation of consciousness. These are very simple examples. Far more complex, but in reality having the same underlying mechanism, is the following. When one is

[1] Address delivered before the Section on Abnormal Psychology at the St. Louis Congress of Arts and Sciences — *The Psychological Review*, March–May, 1905.

intently absorbed in the contents of an interesting book one becomes totally oblivious to passing sights and sounds. This is what occurs in hypnosis. But is this real oblivion, is consciousness totally blotted out, or is it merely narrowed upon one topic and has it reached a state of dissociation? Let us see. While a person is reading, the telephone bell rings or some one asks a question. He apparently pays no attention to it. Yet it is really perceived, but perceived by the subconscious or dissociated self. A few minutes later he comes to himself, suddenly starts out of his day dream or reverie, shakes himself together, answers the telephone without knowing why, or gives an intelligent reply to something he knows not what. When the bell rang or the question was asked, his consciousness was dissociated; when he answered the bell or replied to the question, the consciousness had become synthetized or reassociated. The fact that an intelligent reaction *did* take place is proof that he subconsciously perceived the stimulus which brought forth the reaction. Now the disease hysteria, the phenomena of hypnosis or of multiple personality, of amnesia, are merely more or less protracted forms of this absent-mindedness. The underlying principle of all absent-mindedness is dissociation. The striking points of all are these — that the gaps in memory or personality or thought are not real gaps at all, but merely chips of consciousness carrying memories or ideas that have floated off from the main stream of conscious thought. In other words, they are subconscious, dissociated. These subconscious fragments of consciousness in their own narrow way act like the full content of the stream of thought.

Take a still more complex condition from the abnormal standpoint. In the case of Miss Beauchamp (*The Dissociation of a Personality*), one of the personalities who called herself "Sally" was wont to do all sorts of pranks, of which the original Miss B. knew nothing. On one occasion Sally smoked a cigarette, and when the Sally personality changed to Miss B. there was no recollection of the act. But when Miss B. was asked to gaze into a crystal, she saw therein a vision of herself smoking a cigarette. She was naturally horrified at seeing herself at an act of which she had absolutely no recollection. Now what had happened? Sally was one of the dissociated personalities and although she knew the acts of Miss B., yet Miss B. knew nothing of Sally. The crystal gazing had produced in Miss B. a state of abstraction or absent-mindedness, and in consequence there arose a reversion to the Sally personality with all her acts. Miss B. by this means was able to penetrate to regions that her conscious, waking memory was unable to reach. The dissociation had disappeared and with it came the vision of Sally's behavior. On another occasion Sally destroyed some bank notes belonging to Miss B., and the latter was astonished to see herself, in the crystal vision, in the act of tearing the bank notes into fragments. In reality we are dealing in both these episodes with subconscious hallucinations. Miss B. was the unfortunate victim of her subconscious behavior of which she knew nothing and consequently was unable to understand her conduct in the Sally personality. We have thus indicated and explained, as clearly as the nature of the subject will allow, what is meant by the subconscious in all its degrees, from the most simple manifestations of every-day life to the complex phenomena of multiple personality. In an interesting little volume, Freud has shown how great an influence is exerted by the subconscious on our every-day life.[1] According to him all dreams originate in our subconscious mental life, while certain familiar daily events, the forgetting of proper names, the slips of the tongue, etc., are also examples of this mental dissociation. Thus there are no gaps between the normal and abnormal subconscious workings; the phenomena shade almost imperceptibly into one another.

We are now prepared to briefly discuss the abnormal manifestations of mental dissociation, or what we shall call the diseases of the subconscious. We have given examples and explanations of the normal workings of the subconscious, all of them taken from the happenings of every-day life with one exception, and this was introduced in order to complete the series of subconscious phenomena from the simple to the complex. It now remains to point out the principal aspects of the abnormal workings of the subconscious, their causes and the indications for a rational scientific treatment. For it is the diseases of the subconscious that in all ages have offered the most baffling problems to physicians. The many-sided disease, hysteria, is dependent upon a dissociation of consciousness; the phenomena of hypnosis can be utilized as powerful therapeutic and experimental factors; neurasthenia is the curse of modern civilization; and lately there has arisen the conception of psychasthenia, as indicating the peculiar mental state accompanying obsessions and fixed

[1] *Zur Psychopathologie des Alltagslebens*, Berlin, 1904.

ideas. The cases of multiple personality and of amnesia (a systematized loss of memory) are dependent upon dissociations of consciousness, and the cure of these conditions by proper methods is one of the triumphs of purely psychological principles. These are all diseases or artifacts or abnormal aspects of the subconscious. The very mention of their names at once indicates their importance.

Hypnosis is not really a disease of the subconscious, but is rather an artificially induced state of absent-mindedness. It is so important that a separate chapter will be devoted to its consideration. The most important of all the diseases of dissociation or of the subconscious is that protean malady called hysteria. Many-sided it really is, for in no nervous disease are the symptoms so diverse. Hysteria can simulate almost anything from the paralysis of brain disease to complete loss of voice (aphonia). Two of the most distinguished investigators, Prince in America and Janet in France, look upon hysteria as a dissociation of the personality. Dr. Prince [1] says: "Hysteria is a manifestation of disintegration, and the neurasthenic state, one of the stigmata of hysteria, is pathologically a type of dissociation of the personality." According to Janet,[2] "Hysteria is a form of mental depression characterized by the retraction of the field of personal consciousness and a tendency to the dissociation and emancipation of the systems of ideas and functions that constitute personality." These are purely psychological definitions and are based on sound experimental evidence. Clinically this dissocia-

[1] Morton Prince, "Hysteria from the Point of View of Dissociated Personality," *Journal Abnormal Psychology*, vol. i, No. 4, October, 1906.   [2] Pierre Janet, *The Major Symptoms of Hysteria*, 1907.

tion is manifested in many different ways. There may be a paralysis of one or more limbs, losses of sensation in various parts of the body may arise (hysterical anæsthesia), the memory for certain periods may disappear (amnesia), complex acts of somnambulism may take place, the voice may become suddenly lost (aphonia), there may be convulsions, phantom tumors may suddenly appear, and finally there may be disturbances of vision, from an extreme narrowing of the visual field to complete blindness. But these symptoms when carefully studied are found to have their peculiarities, and the chief of these is their inconsistency. It is this inconsistency which gives the appearance of simulation to many of the acts and symptoms of the hysterical. The paralysis and anæsthesia may show anatomical impossibilities, the right arm or the left leg or *vice versa* may be paralyzed; the patient may be able to move the legs in bed without a trace of muscular weakness and yet be totally unable to walk; the anæsthesia does not follow the distribution of any nerve; the patient may be unable to feel a painful sensation over an area resembling a glove or stocking, or it may be sharply limited to one side of the body, even the tongue being involved. The peculiarities that hold for one group of symptoms hold for all the others, so there is no need to enumerate them all. The hysteric who has lost the voice will scream on a sudden emotion; if tests show almost complete blindness, yet obstacles are intelligently avoided. What is the meaning of all these symptoms? An account of a few experiments is necessary to illustrate the psychology of hysteria more clearly. Take an hysteric who has lost all sensation in the right hand.

Blindfold the patient, prick or pinch the hand, the patient asserts that he feels absolutely nothing. Repeat the experiment and pinch or prick the hand a definite number of times, then ask the patient to tell you the first number that comes into his mind, and it will be found that this number will correspond to the times the hand has been pinched or pricked. Repeat the experiment any number of times and under all variations and the result will be the same. What does this mean? It means that the patient subconsciously perceived what was done to him and how many times. In other words, there is not a real anæsthesia, such as would follow if a nerve were cut or diseased, but a subconscious anæsthesia, a psychic one. The feeling of the limb is only split off, dissociated, but is clearly perceived by the subconscious self. It is this inability to call up the idea of a motion of a limb or its feeling, or the failure of the faculty of recollection, that causes the paralyses, the anæsthesias, the amnesias. What is true of one symptom or group of symptoms in hysteria is true of all. They are merely dissociations. One peculiarity of the hysterical symptoms is their sudden appearance and disappearance. Hysterical phantom tumors resemble a real tumor, but get well without surgical operation. The sudden onset of blindness, and its just as sudden recovery after months or years, is usually hysterical. The paralyses of years' duration that recover under the stress of a strong emotion, or even in a single night, are always hysterical.

These motor and sensory dissociations are the result of a morbid auto-suggestion. The hysteric is above all highly suggestible. That is why he can be so easily hypnotized and why the symptoms will disappear in hypnosis. Sometimes painful ideas of a disagreeable nature are suppressed during the day, to appear again at night in sleep-walking or somnambulism, as in the case of Lady Macbeth. In one of Janet's cases the young woman obstinately refused to eat, because she immediately vomited any food or drink. Furthermore, she was insensible all over the body. When this young woman was hypnotized, in the hypnotic state the insensibility of the body disappeared, the vomiting ceased and she accepted food and drink. The only way in which this patient could be nourished was by placing her in the hypnotic state, otherwise death would have resulted by starvation. One of our cases was an hysterical boy, who suffered from convulsions and one-half of his body was anæsthetic, even the tongue and mucous membrane of the mouth being involved. Furthermore, he had attacks of hysterical paralyses and contractures involving the left arm and leg. All these paralyses, contractures, and insensibility of the body could be made to appear or disappear at will, by mere waking suggestion. Ultimately, as a result of suggestion, all the hysterical symptoms, even the convulsions, disappeared.

An example of crystal gazing has already been given. In automatic writing the hand unconsciously produces weird drawings, words, sentences, anecdotes, often scraps of knowledge written in some outlandish tongue. There is nothing supernormal in these productions, the hand merely writes previous knowledge and experiences, which in some way have become dissociated. The content of the writing may represent a mechanical repetition of the dissociated knowledge, or there may be considerable elaboration or even fabrication. In these subconscious ideas we see the resurrection of some forgotten knowledge. In most cases the subject is in a state of deep abstraction during the process, the movement of the hand is unperceived, and there is no memory of what has been written. In reviewing a series of automatic writings by Mrs. A. W. Verrall [1] it was stated that there was nothing to show that the content of the writings either did not represent the previous knowledge and experiences of the subject or was not a pure fabrication. The source of this knowledge, however, in most instances, had been long forgotten, in reality had become subconscious, but later was reproduced in a condition of abstraction.

The best example in which the automatic writing was a purely subconscious fabrication is found in Flournoy's study of Mlle. Heléne Smith.[2] In the Martian Cycle of Mlle. Smith the subject made drawings of an alleged Martian landscape, a Martian alphabet was produced, and finally a large number of rather fragmentary Martian texts. This "subliminal astronomy" Flournoy traces back to his subject's interest some years previously in the Martian canals, although he admits that the original elements have been recombined and molded in a very original fashion. In Hyslop's case of Mrs. Smead,[3]

[1] *On a Series of Automatic Writings*, by Mrs. A. W. Verrall. *Proceedings of the Society for Psychical Research*, part liii, vol. xx, October, 1906, pp. 432 + x. (See review in *Journal Abnormal Psychology*, December, 1906, pp. 226–229).

[2] See Flournoy's interesting book, *From India to the Planet Mars*, 1901.

[3] James H. Hyslop, "Apparent Subconscious Fabrication," *Journal Abnormal Psychology*, vol. i, No. 5, December, 1906.

there were also alleged communications of life on the planet Mars, and later a hieroglyphic language was developed.

The amnesias or systematized losses of memory are of great theoretical and practical importance. Sometimes this loss is for a few days only; sometimes it compresses an entire period of life. But in the functional amnesias, as distinct from those dependent on organic brain disease, the memory is really not lost, it is dissociated merely; it exists in its entirety in the subconscious. By proper psychological devices, the subconscious memories can be synthetized with the normal consciousness and thus the memories for the lost period can be permanently restored. These losses of memory occur frequently in hysteria and in alcoholism, but are occasionally found in those who are neither hysteric nor alcoholic. Accounts are occasionally published of a person suddenly disappearing, foul play is suspected, and for weeks or months the person will be unheard of. Suddenly, in some strange, remote place, this person will suddenly come to himself, will wonder how he reached there and will find that he has been passing under another name. The entire past for several months will be a blank. Now it is of the utmost importance sometimes, for social and therapeutic reasons, that this blank period should be restored. It is not a real blank, however, for the memories of the lost period are merely dissociated, subconscious. Now these lost memories can be fully and permanently restored, and, in fact, this has been successfully accomplished. In one case, following a blow on the head, a man of wide learning became like a child in intellect; another wandered to a distant city without any recollection of the act; in still another, an educated woman, after several exciting episodes, went into a deep stupor, and on awakening it was found that all memory of her previous life had been obliterated.[1]

Modern researches have established that neurasthenia and psychasthenia are merely diseases of the subconscious. All the symptoms of neurasthenia can be referred to a dissociation, — the fatigue, headaches, dizziness, heart and gastric symptoms, the mental state and the fleeting pains. This dissociation probably originates in an exhaustion of the brain. Occasionally the neurasthenic state is merely a symptom of hysteria.

Sometimes, however, after the strong emotional shock of a railway accident, with its harassing experiences, there develops a peculiar group of symptoms, partly hysterical, partly neurasthenic in nature, known as the traumatic neuroses. The injury may be slight or severe, in fact the development of the symptoms, or their intensity, seems to bear no relation to the severity of the injury. The ultimate cause, therefore, of these traumatic neuroses seems to be the very sudden emotional disturbance. Much of the litigation in our courts is based on this particular form of nervous disease.

Psychasthenia can also be interpreted psychologically. It is a disease of the mental level, and when the mental

[1] For details see William James' *Psychology*, vol. i, pp. 391-393 (case of Rev. Ansel Bourne). Boris Sidis, *Multiple Personality*, 1905. Isador H. Coriat, "The Experimental Synthesis of the Dissociated Memories in Alcoholic Amnesia," *Journal Abnormal Psychology*, vol. i, No. 3, August, 1906. Isador H. Coriat, "The Lowell Case of Amnesia," *Journal Abnormal Psychology*, vol. ii, No. 3, August, September, 1907.

level sinks below a certain point we have the phenomena of psychasthenia. It is to the great credit of Janet, that he succeeded in unifying many diverse symptoms which had previously been described separately, and established that psychasthenia is really the mental state accompanying obsessions and fixed ideas. It has many features common to epilepsy, hysteria, and neurasthenia. There are depressions, various obsessions, often a feeling of unreality and peculiar crises and convulsive attacks. The obsessions or fixed ideas may be those of crime, disgrace of self or body; frequently absurd ideas of violence arise. The patient may become agitated, perplexed, over-scrupulous, ask many peculiar questions, develop all sorts of fears, such as a fear of open places (agoraphobia), a fear of contamination by dirt (mysophobia), etc. In addition there are frequently attacks of intense anxiety and the mental condition shows a marked indecision.

There is another point. Attacks closely resembling epilepsy are sometimes observed, which are not real epilepsy at all, but only outwardly resembling it. Neither have they any relation to hysteria or psychasthenia. On close study it will be found that these attacks have a subconscious origin. They do not yield to the usual treatment for epilepsy, but some form of psychotherapy is very beneficial and in most cases curative.

We have left for the end the subject of multiple personality. The subject is so large and complex, however, that only the barest outlines can be indicated. All cases of multiple personality are accompanied by amnesia or loss of memory, and much that was stated about the latter will be found to be true of the former. In fact, there may be a transition from one to the other. Those who are interested in the subject will do well to read Dr. Prince's narrative of Miss Beauchamp in his *Dissociation of a Personality*.[1] The final synthesis of Miss Beauchamp's several personalities into one healthy self furnishes a splendid example of the efficiency of purely psychological methods in bringing about a cure. These methods were based upon the modern theories of the subconscious. In this patient, an intelligent young woman of twenty-three, there was presented at first nothing but the symptoms of ordinary neurasthenia. One by one, however, four distinct personalities appeared, and in their unfolding a complex drama was enacted. The various personalities are analyzed with great skill. One of these, designated by the name of "Sally," played all sorts of pranks and tricks, of which the other personalities were ignorant. Examples have already been given in the paragraphs on crystal gazing. The origin of the dissociation was due to a strong emotional shock. Each personality was an organized, subconscious self, and each acted according to its own memories, moods, and intelligence. Each shifted and replaced the other from time to time, although "Sally" was the most successful in this shifting and seemed to take an impish delight in remaining "on top of the heap." The case is a perfect mine of abnormal psychological phenomena, ecstasy and sudden religious conversion, alterations of character, losses of memory, hysterical and neurasthenic symptoms, automatic writing and crystal vision; in fact, nearly all the manifestations of a subconscious mental

---

[1] Longmans, Green & Co., 1906.

life. In the end, the original Miss Beauchamp was reconstructed.

There is one more curious fact of the subconscious that merits notice. In amnesia, the lost memories reappear in sleep, but are looked upon by the patient as pure imaginative creations, as dreams. In one of Janet's cases, the patient talked in her sleep and pronounced names of which she knew nothing in her waking state; the dreams of two of the personalities of Miss Beauchamp were alike and each remembered them as her own; in the Lowell case of amnesia the patient's dreams were those of experiences that occurred in her former life, but of which she had no memory on awakening except as a dream.

Now what causes these dissociations? Exhaustion may fail to synthetize the consciousness; certain emotional shocks may split the personality; alcohol may cause extensive losses of memory; fixed ideas may exist subconsciously and act as a constant psychic irritation by turning the mind topsy-turvy. Even convulsions resembling real epilepsy may occur. When these functional conditions once occur, they can recur a second time more easily. The ideas break through on slight provocation and then we have the hysterical attack or the loss of memory or the change of personality.

What can science do for these diseases of the subconscious? Everything, but by psychological methods exclusively, not by drugs. If certain diseases are caused by a dissociation of consciousness, it naturally follows that a state of healthy-mindedness can only be secured by a reassociation, a synthesis of this split consciousness.

Figuratively, we must "tap the subconscious" and synthetize the dissociated portion with the main stream. This can be accomplished by many psychological devices: psychic re-education; utilization of reserve energy; suggestions given in hypnosis or in states of deep abstraction, etc. These must be frequently repeated, for it is a well-known law that a state of dissociation once established can more easily take place again. By these methods there follows a re-association, a synthesis of the dissociated state. The attention becomes strengthened, the subconscious field again enters consciousness and is perceived, whereas before it lay outside of consciousness and consequently was not perceived. Thus memories of lost periods may be restored, multiple personalities may be blended into one healthy personality, hysterical symptoms may be made to disappear and fixed ideas may be permanently destroyed. Certain hidden emotional states may be brought to light and curious disease manifestations of otherwise obscure origin, such as paralyses and convulsions, may be permanently benefited.[1]

[1] For pertinent examples, see the following papers: Boris Sidis and Morton Prince, "A contribution to the Pathology of Hysteria based upon an Experimental Study of a Case of Hemianæsthesia with Clonic Convulsive Attacks Simulating Jacksonian Epilepsy," *Boston Medical and Surgical Journal*, June 23, 1904. Isador H. Coriat, "Nocturnal Paralysis," *Boston Medical and Surgical Journal*, July 11, 1907.

CHAPTER X

THE NATURE OF HYPNOTISM

THE words *hypnotism* and *hypnosis* were first suggested by Braid of Manchester in 1843, although many of the phenomena had been recognized from remote antiquity. The words are derived from a Greek root signifying sleep, in spite of the fact that there is a distinct difference between hypnotic and natural sleep, and furthermore that some hypnotic states do not resemble sleep at all, being rather conditions of intense abstraction or absent-mindedness. Hypnosis, however, designates a group of very complex phenomena, whose analysis is not fully completed, but whose importance for therapeutic and psychological purposes is daily becoming more manifest. Hypnosis is as old as the human race, but it is only within the last twenty-five years that it has been scientifically investigated and its nature understood. Animals, too, may be hypnotized and in them may be observed some of the phenomena that occur in human beings. Max Verworn, has given us a very pertinent account of hypnosis in animals and has illustrated it by some interesting photographs.[1] "It may suffice to recall a few well-known phenomena. The ancient experiments of the Egyptian

---

[1] General Physiology, *An Outline of the Science of Life*, pp. 494–496. See figures 151 (guinea pig) and 245 (asp and fowl), for illustrations of hypnosis in animals.

snake charmers, which Moses and Aaron performed before the Egyptian Pharaoh more than three thousand years ago, belong to this category (*i.e.*, hypnosis in animals). By slight pressure in the neck region, it is possible to make a wildly excited, hissing, erect asp (hooded snake) suddenly motionless, so that the dangerous creature can be put into any desired position without fear of its fatal bite. The well-known experiment of Father Kircher depends upon the same causes. If any excited fowl be seized suddenly with a firm grip and laid carefully upon its back, after a few brief attempts to escape it lies motionless. Guinea pigs, rabbits, frogs, lizards, crabs, and numerous other animals behave similarly." According to Verworn, the hypnosis of human beings depends upon the same physiological mechanism, that is, an inhibition of the will.

Like all new movements in medicine, hypnosis was compelled to pass through an era of skepticism before it became firmly rooted as one of the most important methods of treatment and investigation possessed by medical science. In fact hypnosis, or some other form of psychotherapy, is the only rational treatment of the functional as distinguished from the organic nervous diseases. Hypnosis is quite popularly known, but its unfortunate use by traveling charlatans and mountebanks for public exhibition purposes has made it the subject of wide-spread misconception, fear, and even ridicule. Even from the trained physician, the word hypnotism proposed as a therapeutic agent for some functional disorder of the nervous system causes the patient almost instinctively to shrink when the term is mentioned, to ask what it means, if it will make them unconscious, destroy their will power and even their personality. When an explanation is given and the treatment begun, there still remains at first the conscious or unconscious resistance. If this short chapter helps to dispel the popular illusion and ignorance and places hypnotism on the sound scientific basis to which it rightfully belongs, its purpose will not have been in vain. The beginning of the scientific investigation of hypnotism occupied a position analogous to the kite in the hands of Franklin or the dead frog in Galvani's laboratory. But as from these arose modern electro physics and electro chemistry, so hypnotism evolved until it developed into one of the important features of modern abnormal psychology.

But we know to-day that we are dealing with one of the most valuable and penetrating therapeutic and experimental agents. Stripped of all its mystery, hypnotism stands out as one of the triumphs of modern science, whose laws are fairly well known and whose mechanism is far removed from the occult. From the standpoint of therapeutics, many of the functional disorders of the nervous system, particularly that protean disease called hysteria, have been greatly ameliorated and in many cases absolutely cured by hypnotic suggestion. On the other hand, experimental hypnosis has enabled us to penetrate deeply into the workings of consciousness, especially the baffling states of double personality and subconscious phenomena.

The historical development of hypnosis forms one of the most interesting chapters in modern medicine and it is to this history that we will briefly direct our attention. Here we have a very pertinent example of the evolution from mysticism in medicine to sound scientific theory. The French have been and are to this day among the foremost students of hypnotism, for it was in France that the beginnings of scientific hypnotism arose. The history of hypnotism may be conveniently divided into three periods: that of Mesmerism from 1780 to 1788; that of Magnetism from 1820 to 1850, and finally the period of the scientific study of hypnotism beginning in 1875 and continuing up to the present time. In 1780 Friedrich Anton Mesmer, a physician and a student of the occult, first made his appearance. He claimed miraculous powers and clothed his procedures with picturesque and mystic effects. Indeed, to the public, many of his cures appeared miraculous, on account of their ignorance of what constituted suggestion. Mesmer believed in an external, invisible fluid, which was able to penetrate all portions of the body, especially the central nervous system. He thought this fluid could influence and modify in various ways all psychical and physiological reactions. So great was public interest in these phenomena, that the French Government appointed a commission of savants, one of whom was Benjamin Franklin, to investigate the claims of Mesmer. In their report they verified the results, but attributed them to purely physiological causes. Soon after, owing to some unfortunate failures with prominent patients, Mesmer's influence rapidly declined. Except for some sporadic investigators, the subject of hypnotism remained unnoticed and almost forgotten until the so-called "magnetism" began to attract attention in 1820. It would exceed the scope and purpose of this chapter to trace its development in subsequent years. It must suffice to state that gradually the old "magnetism" gave way to the more modern and, so far as we can see, the scientific theory of hypnosis. This may be summed up in a few words, namely, that all the phenomena of the hypnotic sleep are purely the results of suggestion. At first it was believed that hypnosis was due to somatic causes, the fatigue of fixation and attention (Braid), or to the various physical, peripheral stimuli, such as fixation, stroking the forehead, manipulation of the eyelids (Charcot and his school). It was finally due to Liébeault, Bernheim, and the so-called Nancy school, that the fundamental importance played by suggestion was first realized.

Since then hypnotism has attracted the serious attention of all scientific physicians. Among the French investigators may be mentioned Gilles de la Tourette, Charcot, Liébeault, Bernheim, Janet; in England, Braid and Bramwell; in Switzerland, Forel; in Germany and Austria, Moll and Krafft-Ebing; in Sweden, Wetterstrand, and finally, in America, William James, Morton Prince, and Boris Sidis.

Hypnosis, therefore, stripping it of all mysticism, may be defined as an intense form of artificial abstraction (absent-mindedness) brought on by suggestion. This artificial abstraction either narrows or dissociates the consciousness, and to this splitting of consciousness many of the phenomena and therapeutic effects of hypnotism are due. Experimentally, it constitutes one of the methods for "tapping" the subconscious, analogous to the hypnoidal state, or to the state of experimental abstraction or distraction. The three marked characteristics of the hypnotic sleep are amnesia (complete loss of memory), suggestibility, and subconscious phenomena. Whether one or all of these appear, depends partly on the susceptibility of the patient and partly on the depth of the hypnosis induced. The amnesia, of course, comprises only the period occupied by the hypnotic sleep. Instead of a complete amnesia there may be only a slight haziness of memory or even a perfectly clear recollection of the hypnotic state. These, however, do not influence the condition of heightened suggestibility that accompanies all depths of hypnosis. Of course, if the suggestions are not remembered they cannot be antagonized or modified; in other words, when there is complete amnesia the suggestions are dissociated or become subconscious. The suggestibility is likewise subject to variations, dependent on the temperament of the patient and the depth of the hypnosis induced. There may be an intense reaction to hypnotic or post-hypnotic influences with a clock-like precision, or many séances may be necessary to secure the required result. The subconscious phenomena are variable and form a gradually increasing complexity from mere automatisms to complete dissociation of the personality or memory, forming what is known as double or multiple personality.

In a popular book like this, it has been thought desirable to omit technical terms as much as possible, but a few of these are so expressive that some definitions become necessary, in order to avoid repetitions in the future. A short explanation of what constitutes hypnosis has already been given. This will be elaborated upon later, when we shall also briefly discuss the difference between hypnotic and natural sleep. The word "hypnotist" does not require a definition. By some writers this is considered synonymous with dictator. By suggestion we mean the dictation of certain commands or the giving of certain orders and their acceptance to a person either in a state of light hypnosis or in a deep hypnotic sleep. According to the nature of the case, the commands given in hypnosis are to be carried out while in that state, or, as is more frequently the plan, they are given in such a manner that they will react after the person has been awakened from the hypnotic sleep. These latter are known as post-hypnotic suggestions and in this peculiarity lies the great value of hypnotism. Suggestions are usually given verbally by spoken words or by placing the hypnotized person in a certain position, thus calling forth a more complex suggestion through the association of ideas. Auto-hypnosis or auto-suggestion is the mental state produced by the person's mind reacting on itself, either consciously, unconsciously, or subconsciously. Of course, from the very nature of the process, it possesses far less therapeutic value than suggestions given in hypnosis by a second party.

Thus we have seen that the fundamental characteristic of the hypnotic state is the altered condition of consciousness, whereby the normal suggestibility is heightened or greatly intensified. It can be produced by mere verbal suggestion, by various mechanical devices, such as staring at a bright object or listening to a monotonous sound stimulus, thus fatiguing the sense organs and brain by a narrowing of consciousness upon one point. In all hypnotized persons there is a rapport or connection between the hypnotizer and the person hypnotized. This is of

THE NATURE OF HYPNOTISM

great importance, as it enables suggestions to be mentally assimilated and to be carried out as post-hypnotic phenomena. It is this connection that constitutes the great difference between hypnotic and normal sleep. Auto-hypnosis or auto-suggestion, the reaction of the mind upon itself, is interesting from the historic standpoint, as this constitutes the ecstatic state of the Hindu Mystics. The intense abstraction in these cases is produced by the firm fixation of the eyes upon the umbilicus and constantly repeating the sacred syllable Om. From the scientific standpoint, however, the only rational method of inducing hypnosis is through suggestion, by means of the dictation of others, although auto-suggestion is of limited value in the milder types of functional disorders.

According to the best authenticated statistics and also as the result of personal experience, one can safely assume that from 80 per cent to 96 per cent of all persons are hypnotizable. These figures are not exaggerated, if we consider how many of the human race are suggestible in the waking condition. Some of the French investigators claim that only cases of hysteria can be successfully hypnotized, and this has led one writer to state that the hysterics are the frogs of experimental psychology. However, personal experience and the experience of others leads us to decidedly dissent from this view. We have hypnotized many persons who were certainly not suffering from hysteria. Every mentally healthy person is hypnotizable, especially the strong-willed, contrary to the popular belief. Children, on account of their credulity, are very suggestible and, therefore, very easily hypnotized. Idiots and the insane are very difficult, if not impossible, to hypnotize. Waking suggestion differs in many respects from hypnotic suggestion. In the hypnotized subject there is an annihilation or a lowering of the will power and of the conscious resistance, and therefore the reaction to the commands can be dissociated or split off from the command itself. In the waking subject, however, this waking resistance consciously or unconsciously takes place. Suggestions can act in any depth of hypnosis, with this difference, however, that in the lighter grades a more frequent hypnotization becomes necessary. Therefore, in hypnosis there is a state of over-credulity produced by the heightened suggestibility, whereas in the waking state this over-credulousness, at least in adult individuals, may be antagonized or neutralized by counter suggestions. In children, however, mere waking suggestion is often sufficient for therapeutic purposes. Post-hypnotic suggestions act powerfully because of this increased suggestibility in the hypnotic state. For this reason, these suggestions, if remembered, are usually not antagonized. If not remembered, or in other words, if there is an amnesia, they are completely dissociated from the waking consciousness and therefore antagonism or counter-suggestions are impossible. Therefore, as will be easily gathered from the above, when the hypnosis is deep and an amnesia supervenes, in other words, where there arises a state of hypnotic somnambulism, suggestions are more penetrating and effective. When the hypnosis is light and there is no amnesia, the same result can only be secured by more frequent séances.

Before we proceed further to discuss the therapeutic

value of hypnotism, it is necessary to inquire into two important questions: first, the relation between ordinary sleep and hypnotic sleep; and second, the various physical and mental phenomena of the hypnotic state.

Sleep has been defined as the resting time of consciousness, but it is rather a partially conscious mental state and not a complete annihilation. A sound sleep is dreamless just like a complete anæsthesia, and dreams only appear in the half-waking state or at the end of an ether or chloroform anæsthesia. Not only does the imagination run riot in dreams, but also slight external stimuli, such as the position of the bedclothes or the exposure of certain parts of the body, are important factors in making up "such stuff as dreams are made of." Deep hypnosis resembles outwardly normal sleep, — it is somnambulistic and there is amnesia or loss of memory on awakening. There is one important difference, however, — the hypnotic subject is suggestible to a high degree, either in the hypnotic state itself or as a reaction on awakening, the so-called post-hypnotic suggestion. There is a kind of mental connection between the hypnotized person and the hypnotist; in other words, the subject is *en rapport* with his hypnotic dictator. In deep natural sleep there is no suggestibility or psychic connection, although in the half-waking, or what is technically known as the hypnagogic state, there is a mental condition closely analogous to the true hypnotic sleep. In this half-waking state, catalepsy or fixation of the limbs into any desired position may be brought about, — the limbs may be manipulated as if made of wax, and peculiar somatic sensations may arise, such as transitory paralysis or numbness, startings of the body and sensations of falling. Hypnotic consciousness and dream consciousness have many points in common, such as hallucinations, peculiar sensations, and dissociations of the personality. No wonder the savage looks upon the dream as a departure of the soul from the body during sleep. Dreams also may be projected into the waking life and cause hysterical symptoms. In a young woman under our care, following a dream of falling down a hill, there developed on awakening a partial hysterical paralysis of the limbs. Forel says,[1] "Normal sleep, like hypnosis, is a condition of heightened suggestibility—*i.e.*, a dissociated condition — only as a rule the condition of exhaustion of the brain is added and the connection with the hypnotist is wanting." Bechterew, however, takes an opposite view,[2] and believes that hypnosis is nothing but a modification of normal sleep, although he is compelled to admit that ordinary normal sleep in most people reaches such a depth that the influence of suggestion is impossible. The more we study the question, the more we are led to believe that hypnotic sleep, natural sleep, and the sleep from narcosis of ether or chloroform are different phenomena. Hypnosis is purely a psychical state; natural sleep is dependent on changes in the circulation and chemistry of the body, while the narcosis of ether and chloroform is caused by the chemical action of these drugs upon the nerve cells of the brain.

The artificial stages that have been proposed to desig-

---

[1] *Hypnotism and Psychotherapy*, p. 97.
[2] W. v. Bechterew, "What is Hypnosis?"—*Journal Abnormal Psychology*, vol. i, No. 1, April, 1906.

nate the various depths of hypnosis are of limited value, and this only for purposes of description. This can be easily seen when it is stated that the variations of the hypnotic sleep shade imperceptibly into one another and therefore there is a decided overlapping of types. The only variations in the intensity of hypnosis comprise an almost imperceptible series of changes from light drowsiness, in which the eyes can be opened only with difficulty or not at all, to a deep somnambulism. Recollection may vary from a clear retention or a slight haziness of memory to a complete loss of memory for the hypnotic séance. Of course in all the stages there is an increased suggestibility. When there is an amnesia from the suggestions on awakening, these suggestions are completely dissociated from the consciousness, and therefore cannot be antagonized, corrected, or minimized. When there is a deep somnambulism with amnesia on awakening, the various happenings of the amnesic period can be recalled perfectly in the next hypnosis, according to well-known psychological laws. For descriptive purposes, Forel has given us the best and simplest classification of the degrees of hypnosis. This classification is a vast improvement over the more complex one of Charcot and Bernheim. According to him there are three transitions:

1. Somnolence or sleepiness, in which the influenced person can resist suggestion and open his eyes.

2. Light sleep, in which the eyes cannot be opened, and obedience to suggestions is obligatory, but there is no loss of memory on awakening.

3. Deep sleep or somnambulism, with amnesia and fine post-hypnotic effects.

The various psychic and physiological accompaniments of hypnosis are of great interest as they serve to elucidate many of the suggestive phenomena. Of first importance is what is known as catalepsy, that is, the eyes cannot be opened on command, the limbs can be placed in a strained position or molded like wax and kept in this uncomfortable position for a much longer period than in the waking state, without any signs of fatigue. Anæsthesia or insensibility to pain may also take place. Hallucinations[1] of the various senses (sight, hearing, touch, smell, taste) may be experimentally produced. The disturbances of memory, consciousness, and will have already been described. The breathing usually becomes deeper and the pulse rate increased. From the purely mental standpoint, fixed ideas, obsessions, abnormal impulsions and habits, tendencies to alcoholism and to various drugs, on account of the great proneness to suggestion in the hypnotic state, may be greatly ameliorated or completely removed. Herein lies the great therapeutic value of hypnotic suggestion. When hypnotic suggestion is used for medical treatment, it is impossible and in fact highly impracticable to keep the patient continually in hypnosis. Left to himself, the hypnotized subject will either awaken spontaneously or there will be a gradual transition to a natural sleep. Both of these are incompatible with suggestion. Fortunately, however, there is another phenomenon, which is perhaps the most important in the whole range of psychotherapy. This is what is known as post-hypnotic suggestion, whereby suggestions given in hypnosis are carried into and obeyed in the waking

---

[1] An hallucination may be defined as a false perception.

state. The carrying-out of suggestions in the waking state, whether given in this state *per se*, by command, persuasion, or argument, or whether preceded by the hypnotic state, furnishes the keystone of suggestive therapeutics in the modern scientific sense.

In any degree of hypnosis there is increased suggestibility and an uncritical and unantagonized acceptance of all commands and requests. These suggestions are given in such a manner that they will act, not in the hypnotic state itself, but are projected into the future as it were, into the waking condition. Sometimes these suggestions are remembered dimly or clearly; sometimes there is complete oblivion for the suggestions (amnesia), according to the depth of the hypnosis. In either case, if the suggestions are repeated a sufficient number of times in a series of hypnotic séances, if an insistence on the impossibility of failure be added; in other words, to use a slang phrase, the suggestions are "rubbed in," in the end they will be found to be successful. They have become unified with the personality. In post-hypnotic suggestion there is a condition of absolute obedience or automatism. For instance, if we hypnotize a patient and tell him that at a certain hour the next day he will write a letter, on awakening he may or may not retain a memory of the command. In either case it will not trouble him until the exact hour arrives, when he will feel literally impelled to write the letter without knowing the reason therefor. The suggestion has been there all the time, only it is split off, dissociated, in psychological language, from his waking consciousness. If we hypnotize another patient for the treatment of chronic alcoholism and suggest that he will no longer drink, that he will not only lose the craving for alcohol, but develop a positive distaste for it, this too will be effective when the patient awakens. Of course, in the treatment of drug habits, a number of hypnotic séances are necessary, in order to cure the old habit, to change the current of the patient's thoughts and to strengthen the will power. Another patient may be the victim of fixed ideas or obsessions, and these too in time will yield to post-hypnotic suggestion. The above are not mere fictions, but stern realities that can be found in the practice of anyone who has utilized hypnotic suggestion for therapeutic purposes. The relation of post-hypnotic suggestion to crime would exceed both the limits and the purpose of this chapter.

The dangers of hypnosis have been greatly exaggerated. In fact, in the hands of a properly qualified and trained physician there is absolutely no danger. Personally, we have never seen hypnosis act harmfully. There is no weakening of the will power as is popularly supposed. If the subject be given a few suggestions directed against headache, eye-strain, and dizziness just before being awakened, and if the awakening be gradually accomplished, there are absolutely no bad after effects. The subject will feel the same as if he had awakened from a natural sleep. A patient that has once been hypnotized, however, can be more easily hypnotized subsequently, but any illegal use of this fact in the hands of a disqualified individual can be easily guarded against by suggesting that only a physician will be able to hypnotize him in the future and that only for the purpose of medical treatment.

We must here emphatically denounce as inhuman and barbaric the hypnotizing of persons for purposes of public exhibition by traveling charlatans. Here the real moral danger of hypnosis lies, for hypnosis is not a plaything, but a sound psychological procedure which should be used only for therapeutic purposes or for the analysis of certain abnormal mental states. If a hypnotized patient be left to himself, there will either be a transition into a natural sleep or he will awaken spontaneously after a certain length of time. As the hypnotic state is brought about by suggestion, so suggestion can terminate it at any time.

As to-day the theory of suggestion is the only accepted one, it may be stated at the outset that the various mechanical methods of hypnotizing are merely devices. The basis of all these is suggestion. Of course, no one method is universal in its application; it varies with the individual and the nature of the disease. Various investigators seem, however, to have a personal preference for certain methods, but this is more the result of habit and individual training than of any special virtue in a particular method.

CHAPTER XI

THE THERAPEUTIC VALUE OF HYPNOTISM

We have now reached the most important part of our subject, and that is, the therapeutic use of hypnotic suggestion. Janet says (Lowell Lectures) that "there is no physiological function which is exempt from modification by hypnotic influence, if not complete control by it." This is true only within certain limits, for hypnosis must not be looked upon as a panacea for all the physical and psychical ills that flesh is heir to. While its field of action is limited, yet within that field it is absolute master. Since it has been found that hypnosis is practically only effective in those diseases designated as functional as distinguished from the organic type, the first perquisite is a thorough and careful examination of the patient by a competent medical man. This examination should comprise a minute study of the disease, its origin and symptoms; it should be determined if the disease is organic or functional, and if the latter, are there any organic complications into which physical therapy must enter? These are facts of the highest importance, for without these a serious and even a fatal mistake might be made if we attempted to treat an organic disease by hypnosis where it would require surgery or some specific drug. It is into these errors that the various irregular sects and practitioners of suggestive therapeutics, mind cure, and mental healing have fallen. They disregard the physical and mental examination and look upon disease as purely imaginary, as an error of mortal mind. What surgery was in the hands of the barber surgeons of the Middle Ages, so to-day psychotherapy in the hands of the mind curists occupies an analogous position. Their errors fill our hospitals and clinics and add to the number of obituary notices. We only hear of their few successes; of their many mistakes they preserve a wise silence. But with a proper medical examination such errors are reduced to a minimum, and although it narrows the field of hypnotic therapy, yet it greatly increases its efficiency. This examination is just as important for the patient as for the physician. Now in what functional diseases has hypnosis been most effective and what are its results? To this we will briefly turn.

The medical aspects of hypnotism are of great practical importance and, as previously stated, the basis of all hypnotic therapy is found in the increased suggestibility of the hypnotic state and in the phenomena of post-hypnotic suggestion. Hypnosis is most efficacious in the so-called functional nervous diseases. Hysteria with its manifold symptoms is very amenable to hypnotic treatment. Hysterical symptoms all tend to disappear in the hypnotic sleep, a fact which speaks emphatically for the soundness of the modern theories of hysteria. By this we mean that hysteria is a mental disease whose symptoms are due to a dissociation or splitting of the personality. In the hypnotic state the splitting disappears and the hysteric individual remains well while in this condition. On being awakened the symptoms tend to recur, but by repeated hypnotizing there is established a psychic re-education through the suggestions, and ultimately a cure results. Hysterical paralysis and convulsions, losses of sensation (anæsthesia) or of memory (amnesia), losses of the voice (aphonia), the various digestive and motor disturbances of hysteria, yield to hypnotic treatment. Many of the sudden recoveries of persons who have been paralyzed for years are cases of pure hysteria. If the paralysis were of an organic nature, that is, caused by a hemorrhage or softening of the brain or spinal cord, such a recovery could not occur. In one case of hysteria with convulsions the attacks disappeared under hypnotic suggestion; in another case of hysteria with peculiar wandering acts, and a complete loss of memory for the same, these memories were recovered in the hypnotic state and remained permanent on awakening. In still another case of hysterical paralysis of an arm, suggestion brought about a rapid recovery. As hysteria with all its symptoms is due to a dissociation of the personality, so hypnotic suggestion can synthetize this dissociation and bring about a cure.

Another field where hypnosis yields brilliant results is in the various sexual aberrations. There is perhaps nothing in the whole range of nervous diseases which tends to make the individual so miserable, as the unfortunate victims of these aberrations are usually persons of high intelligence and culture. In these cases hypnosis must be repeated a great many times until the abnormal state is firmly and perfectly replaced by healthier associations and habits of thought. As a rule, most of these patients are difficult to hypnotize.

These sexual aberrations or psychopathies are very wide in their range and of great medical and forensic interest. They comprise such vices as masturbation, the condition known as sexual neurasthenia, sexual hyperexcitability, the various acts of active or passive cruelty or violence with lust (masochism and sadism), the association of sexual ideas with certain portions of the female person or with certain articles of female attire (fetichism), and finally the development of a homosexual tendency and a contrary sexual instinct. Sometimes these unfortunate individuals are led to crime, such as lust-murder, or the larceny of articles of female attire. Many of the petty thievings of women's gloves or handkerchiefs, or the so-called "hair clippers" which sporadically create excitement in our large cities, are in reality sexual psychopaths. Krafft-Ebing has given us a masterly description of these sexual aberrations, while Schrenck-Notzing has shown how much suggestive therapeutics in the form of hypnosis can do for these diseases. Our own observations on the value of hypnotic therapy in the sexual psychopathies have been in harmony with the authorities cited above.

The most prevalent nervous disease of modern times is neurasthenia or nervous exhaustion. This disease, more than any other, taxes all the patience and ingenuity of the physician. Most of the unfortunate victims of this disease are chronic sufferers. Perhaps no human malady has had so many lines of treatment suggested for its cure. Rest and isolation seem to have been the most successful; drug treatment has been weighed in the balance and found wanting; electricity has but a limited value.

Neurasthenia like hysteria has many symptoms, but the principal complaints of the patient are the rapid exhaustion, the sleeplessness, the various fleeting pains, gastric distress, palpitation of the heart, headache, and dizziness. One or several or all of these may be present, in various grades of intensity. Many chemical and physical theories have been proposed to explain neurasthenia, but the latest researches seem to show that we are dealing with a disease of the subconscious, a dissociation of the personality. Much can be accomplished in the way of treatment by waking suggestion and a system of psychic re-education, which comprises persuasion and a rational explanation of the symptoms to the patient. In fact, surprising results have been secured by these psychotherapeutic conversations, within recent years. If we approach neurasthenia from the sound, psychological standpoint, much can be accomplished by hypnotic suggestion. The fatigue can be made to disappear, the cardiac symptoms to vanish, and by this system of psychic re-education, the patient can be taught to pay less attention to himself, to become less introspective. Continual mental analysis is the worst thing that can befall a neurasthenic, and once this demon of analysis has taken possession of the mind it can plunge one into the lowest depths of psychic misery and torture. This is why neurasthenics are so miserable; they are too self-analytical and introspective. This self-analysis can lead to something else, namely, the condition known as hypochondriasis, wherein the patient is continually examining his fleeting bodily pains and finally comes to believe that he is suffering from a severe organic disease. He does not for a moment consider that they are purely functional. Palpitation to him means heart disease; headache, brain tumor; gastric symptoms, an incurable affection of the stomach. Hypnosis can overcome this self-analysis, the bane of all neurasthenics, perhaps the most important thing that accounts for the chronic nature of the disease. It can direct the thought to healthier channels; it can force the patient to stop thinking of himself, and when this is accomplished, the physical symptoms tend to disappear and the patient is on the road to recovery. Many of the much vaunted and advertised cures of the mental healers, who claim to have successfully treated organic diseases, are merely cases of neurasthenia that have become hypochondriacal, that believed they were ill in body when in reality they were merely sick in mind. Of course, many cases of neurasthenia are associated with poor blood states (anæmia), loss in weight, and other purely somatic disorders. Under these conditions, it becomes necessary to combine rational, medical treatment with the purely psychic procedures.

What is known as psychasthenia, which is really a name for the complex mental state accompanying fixed ideas and obsessions, is rather more difficult to treat by hypnosis. Many of the symptoms resemble neurasthenia, but the fixed ideas predominate, the mental torture is greater, crises of intense anxiety may arise and there is often a feeling of unreality. Like neurasthenia and hysteria, its basis is purely psychic, what is known as a disturbance in the mental level, a lowering of the psychological tension. By persistence, however, these obsessions or fixed ideas which torture the mind of the patient; by reason of his appreciation of their absurdity, can be finally annihilated. For instance, one psychasthenic was tortured by the fear of stammering, another was possessed of the fixed idea that his throat was closing up and therefore he must continually swallow to keep the passage open. Both of these practically recovered under hypnotic treatment.

Many functional aches and pains, sleeplessness, the recurrence of distressing dreams, drug habits, such as chronic alcoholism, stammering, constipation, irregular menstruation without organic complications, the various pernicious habits of childhood such as bed-wetting, yield brilliant results by hypnosis. Many forms of sleeplessness or insomnia are caused by the patient acquiring a fixed idea that he cannot sleep. This fixed idea usually reaches its greatest intensity at bedtime and so keeps the patient awake. Hypnotism destroys this fixed idea and sleep follows, without the danger of acquiring a drug habit. When the insomnia is purely symptomatic, however, as occurs in many forms of mental diseases, a different line of treatment is indicated,— baths, drugs, rest in bed, etc. In one patient this fixed idea that he would be unable to sleep brought on an intense insomnia and caused several months of severe mental torture. Light hypnosis after a short time effected complete recovery.

The dangers of prolonged insomnia are manifold. It can lead to intense psychic pain, to despair bordering on suicide, to loss in weight, extreme restlessness, sense deceptions, and finally even mental diseases (exhaustion psychoses) may arise. An interesting research on the experimental effects of loss of sleep has been carried out by

Prof. G. T. W. Patrick and Dr. J. Allen Gilbert.[1] Subjects were kept awake for about ninety hours and at six-hour intervals a series of pyschological tests were made. In one subject, the experiments were discontinued, as hallucinations of sight arose; he saw innumerable insects running on the floor and ceiling of the laboratory.

The hypnotic treatment of cocainism and morphinism has not been very successful. Such cases are best isolated in a sanatorium and the drug gradually withdrawn. The absolute unreliability of the cocaine or morphine habitué, the intense craving for the drug, the fearful depression, pains, restlessness, hallucinations, weakness and often collapse which accompanies its withdrawal, show how important is careful nursing and constant watchfulness on the part of the physician. These can only be secured in an institution, where the patient is placed in a new environment and carefully protected from securing the drug surreptitiously. In fact the deceit practised by these patients, which is due to the moral obliquity caused by the drug itself, is almost incredible.

Hypnotism has yielded good results in chronic alcoholism. The patient can remain at his work or business, can live with his family and prolonged sanatorium residence becomes unnecessary. Hypnosis strengthens the will power of the chronic alcoholic and creates a profound distaste for liquor. These two factors exert the strongest influence in preventing a recurrence of the habit. Medical and physical treatment, however, may be necessary in conjunction with the hypnotism, as chronic

---

[1] "The Effects of the Loss of Sleep," *Psychological Review*, vol. iii, pp. 469–483, September, 1896.

alcoholic indulgence has a particularly pernicious influence on the nervous system, the arteries, and the digestive organs. On the nervous system, there may result degeneration of the nerves (polyneuritis), various forms of alcoholic insanity (delirium tremens, paranoia, a state resembling general paralysis, alcoholic dementia); thickening of the arteries (arterio sclerosis) may take place and lead to apoplexy or degeneration of the heart muscle, and finally Bright's disease, chronic affections of the stomach, and cirrhosis of the liver. Of course, the effects on the nervous system are the most severe, degeneration of the peripheral nerves, diseases of the brain and spinal cord, insanity, peculiar disorders of memory (alcoholic amnesia). The specific effect of alcohol on the nerve cell itself has already been discussed. The effect of even moderate doses of alcohol is very unfavorable; the attention is lowered, the mental aptitude, especially for arithmetical calculations, is considerably reduced, and association time becomes lengthened. These effects can last for more than twenty-four hours after the last dose. On physical exercise, contrary to the popular opinion, heavy work is not made lighter and fatigue more rapidly supervenes. It is true that alcohol increases the facilitation of muscular movements at first, but there is a decided lessening of the power of muscular work and of the quantity of work performed, on account of this rapid fatigue. Kraepelin, who has conducted exhaustive experiments on the psychical action of alcohol, concludes that it cannot be classed among the harmless condiments.[1]

[1] For special articles see A. Forel, "The Alcohol Question," *American Journal of Insanity*, No. 2, 1900. Kraepelin and Kurz, "The persisting

Alcoholism or inebriety is a disease, and the chief factors in its production are heredity and environment. Alcohol is used for its effect upon the nervous system and seldom for the taste of liquor alone. The numerous advertised specifics for alcoholism are useless as each patient and each case is a law unto itself and requires individual study and treatment.

It has been generally conceded that, of all methods of treatment, for chronic alcoholism, without organic complication or severe mental disease, hypnotic suggestion is the most successful. The alcoholic as a rule is easily hypnotized, except when the subject is intoxicated, on account of the exciting effect of alcohol on the brain. The desire for drink should be totally destroyed, the will power strengthened, and new associations built up. There should be no tapering down; total abstinence from the start is the key-note of success. This procedure is without danger, although some medical or physical treatment may be necessary in the beginning in addition to the hypnosis. The length of time that liquor has been used is no contra-indication to treatment by hypnotic suggestion. In fact several of our cases were alcoholics of years standing, and yet all completely recovered by hypnosis.

By many, chronic alcoholism and dipsomania are believed to be identical, but from a medical standpoint there

---

influence of slight chronic alcoholic intoxication," *Psychologische Arbeiten*, vol. iii, p. 2 and 3, 1900. Ach, "The Influence of Certain Drugs on Attention," *Ibid*. Kraepelin, "Recent Investigations Concerning the Psychical Action of Alcohol," *Münch. Med. Wochenschrift*, Oct. 3, 1899. I. H. Coriat, "The Mental Disturbances of Alcoholic Neuritis," *American Journal of Insanity*, vol. lxii, No. 4, April, 1906.

is a distinct difference. The chronic alcoholic is the steady tippler, the man who consumes a certain number of glasses of liquor daily, with perhaps an occasional spree. In dipsomania, however, the tendency to drink to excess is periodic. The individual for months remains a total abstainer, in fact he may have a positive disgust for liquor and a keen appreciation of the moral degradation of the drunkard. Then suddenly he begins to be restless and depressed, may be troubled with dizziness, leaves his home and business, wanders around to various low resorts for days or weeks, all the time drinking all kinds of liquor in a perfectly bestial manner. Rather suddenly he ceases drinking, the restlessness and depression disappear, and he returns to his work with a sense of shame, and usually with either a very hazy memory or a complete amnesia for his behavior and wanderings. Then he remains sober until the next attack. The peculiar periodicity of the disease and the associated mental condition has led many to consider dipsomania as a form of epilepsy.

We have secured good results by hypnosis in the bed-wetting and habit spasms of children when all other treatment had failed. Here the hypnosis was combined with a psychic or motor re-education of the child. One case of bed-wetting which had existed for a number of years, and another of facial habit spasm from which the patient suffered since a small child, yielded to these methods. Of course we must be careful to see that organic complications are absent. Hypnotism has also been used to some extent as a part of suggestive pedagogy, in the training of incorrigible children and of their vicious habits.

The conditions and diseases mentioned are only a few in which hypnotic suggestion is indicated. An enumeration of all the diseases to which hypnotic therapy has been applied by various investigators would make a formidable list. But they have all one characteristic in common. None of these possess any anatomical basis so far as known. We are dealing with purely functional disturbances, the tissue itself as tissue being unaffected. Most of these diseases are of a chronic nature, but patience and perseverance will enable one to succeed. Prolonged treatment is usually necessary, although of course a shorter time is required for the more acute conditions. The patient's nervous system must be remolded, as it were, along new lines, and this takes time. The use of hypnosis in disease may well be designated as a system of psychic re-education or training.

However, there are a few other important points which we wish especially to emphasize. Even in the purely functional nervous diseases hypnotic suggestion sometimes fails, either because of the chronic nature of the disease and the formation of new habits of thought, or perhaps because of our ignorance of certain fundamental psychological laws. Hypnotic suggestion is but one of the many methods of psychotherapy. It is not applicable to or indicated in all functional nervous diseases, for psychotherapeutic methods must vary with the disease and with the individual. In any method of psychotherapy or psychic re-education, other lines of treatment are frequently necessary in conjunction with the purely psychic procedures — drugs, baths, systematic exercises, motor re-education, diet, etc.

Hypnosis has but a limited value in insanity. Before the organic brain diseases, such as senile dementia or general paralysis, it is helpless. Here, other lines of treatment are necessary. In the mild depressions and slight delusional states, however, psychotherapeutic conversations, without going to the depth of hypnotic sleep, are sometimes beneficial. Delirium due to drugs or fever requires, of course, appropriate medical treatment. Krafft-Ebing says: "Successful treatment by hypnotic suggestion can only be expected in functional psychoses, and, too, in patients who are aware that they are sick and who lend themselves to hypnosis." Of course, the entire subject has its theoretical and practical limitations. A person may suffer from a mental disease of a mild type or a severe nervous disease with mental symptoms, without the necessity of going to an insane hospital. It is in these milder affections that hypnotic suggestion is useful.

CHAPTER XII

PSYCHIC AND MOTOR RE-EDUCATION

There is one aspect of psychotherapeutics which has received but a limited degree of attention, and yet when this phase of the problem is more clearly understood, we can hope for further advances along these lines. We refer to what may be termed the psychological mechanism of psychotherapeutics. Certain beneficial results *can* be produced by means of the various forms of suggestion, but *how* these results are produced offers at present a wide field for speculation. When we understand *how* suggestion from *without* can cure an hysterical paralysis which the hysteric is unable to control by suggestion from *within* (auto-suggestion), or *how* a fixed idea or a phobia can be eliminated from consciousness, we have advanced towards a final solution of the problem. To state that in hypnosis or in certain states of abstraction or distraction there arises a condition of hyper-suggestibility, is to leave a portion of the question unanswered.

On ultimate analysis it appears that psychotherapeutic procedures are either substitution, suppression, inhibition, elimination, analytical or educational. In certain morbid psychopathic or neuropathic states we attempt to substitute a healthier emotional complex for the existing diseased condition. In still others, inhibition or suppression is the proper line of treatment. Sometimes, when the symptoms are caused by the voluntary suppression of some emotion or emotional episode, a full confession on the part of the patient will relieve the mental tension. By analytical we mean an inquiry into the origin and nature of the mental or nervous state, by means of special technical methods, thus laying bare the essential mechanism of the particular disorder. This is especially difficult when we are dealing with dissociations of consciousness, such as psycho-epileptic attacks or recurrent sub-conscious ideas, automatisms or motor states. With the exception of psychic re-education, all of the above subjects have been discussed more or less extensively, but these educational methods are so important that a more extended account of their principles seemed necessary.

In many cases the patient has become the victim of a faulty habit of thinking and has thus built up a series of abnormal associations. These abnormal tendencies have not only served to give the disease an indefinite continuance, but the unhealthy auto-suggestion has created artificial symptoms. Thus a vicious circle is continually being formed. It is just in these severe and chronic cases that another method of suggestive treatment is indicated, what is known as psychic re-education. Psychic re-education may be briefly defined as a system of mental gymnastics or rather a systematized method of applying suggestion, whatever particular method is used. Of course all psychotherapy is mental re-education, but the term is best limited to those methods which attempt the mental reconstruction of the patient.

Education forms certain habits and these habits become "set" in our nervous system. One of the peculiarities of the nervous system is that it is plastic in nature. This plasticity decreases with old age and therefore re-education is more difficult in the old than in the young, or in the chronic than in the more acute diseased conditions. Thus we see that the principles on which psychic and motor re-education are based, are physiological principles. We are dealing with the dynamics of living matter. Living matter, and this applies particularly to the substance of which the nervous system is composed, is distinctly plastic in character. It is thus able to store up stimuli and impressions in the same manner that the retina stores up colors and reproduces them as after images. The frequent repetition of stimuli makes a firmer impression on this plastic nerve substance and this summation of stimuli finally produces so firm an organization that it can be obliterated only with difficulty. Even a minimal stimulus if applied for a sufficiently prolonged period can leave its traces on the nervous system. In an analogous manner, constant suggestions, applied judiciously, at first simple in nature, but gradually increasing in complexity, can remold the plastic nervous system, whether in health or in disease. The repetition of bad movements, or constant auto-suggestion along unhealthy lines of thought, may at first seem foreign to the organism, but by the constant repetition and summation of these stimuli, a habit becomes established, either of morbid consciousness or of abnormal motility. What at first was accomplished consciously and with effort, now becomes an automatic action. A person will develop a peculiar mannerism as an act of defense towards some external stimulus; for instance, he may twist his head in a peculiar manner to avoid contact with the roughened edge of a collar. At first this is a so-called reaction of defense, but by constant repetition this normal movement may degenerate into a pathological habit spasm. The individual has broken down the line of normal resistance in his nervous system: the movement has become thoughtless, automatic. The treatment of such a condition consists in leading the individual back to his normal state by means of carefully co-ordinated muscular exercises and by an increasing, conscious inhibition of the abnormal muscular movements. It is a discipline in will power as well as in motor training. This is motor re-education, a form of psychotherapy which is also of great value in hysterical paralysis and in the inco-ordinated muscular movements of locomotor ataxia.

The evolution of many psychic conditions (fixed ideas, phobias, obsessions, hypochondriacal, neurasthenic and hysterical states) has frequently a closely related mechanism. Many of these are association neuroses or the results of habits of expectation and apprehension. We are really dealing with recurrent mental or nervous conditions. The mechanism may also work in an opposite direction. Constant repetition along normal lines of thinking or motor activity may react in a favorable manner on the nervous system, for the function makes the organ, just as much as the organ makes the function. Thus the training of the will is an important factor in psychic re-education, for the will is nothing but a selective action or reaction to certain ideas. By constant repetition, this selection can be directed into almost any channels.

This is the basis of psychic and motor re-education, and educational methods are so successful because the nervous system is a plastic and not a rigid tissue. We can educate ourselves to good habits of thinking, feeling, and doing as well as to bad. Thus we have seen the physiological principles of psychic and motor re-education and are now prepared to consider the more practical aspects of the question.

Psychic re-education is a combination of mental therapeutics and physiological hygiene. Educational treatment is complex, requires considerable time to carry out properly, and taxes all our patience and ingenuity, because of the individual variations of even similar diseases. It would exceed the scope of this chapter to consider all these points in detail, as they involve technicalities into which we cannot enter here. We must be careful, however, to maintain a neutral attitude, for in some cases suggestion is necessary: in others, only educational methods are of value. A rational psychotherapy is an individual problem and must be modified according to the personality of the patient and the character of the disease. To treat all functional disorders blindly by the same methods spells failure.

A few details taken from actual cases will perhaps make these principles of psychic re-education clearer. It is in the chronic neurasthenic and hysterical states that these methods of mental gymnastics have been most successfully utilized. In many cases of neurasthenia, particularly those of long duration, rest, isolation and over-feeding during the prevalence of the more acute stage, have been used with little benefit. So long as such theories of auto-intoxication or of visceral ptosis were promulgated to explain the neurasthenic symptom-complex, and treatment was instituted along the lines suggested by these theories, just so long did therapeutics fail to accomplish the desired result — the cure of the patient. We do not mean to affirm that in certain acute exhaustive states of the nervous system rest is not beneficial, but we do claim that in those cases where the fatigue is not a real fatigue, but only a habit fatigue, we are very apt to create artificial symptoms. If we interpret neurasthenia as a disintegration of the personality, our efforts at cure must be directed along educational lines, to synthetize the dissociated states of consciousness. Of course appropriate methods of hygiene and direct suggestion will have to be combined with our educational procedures in order to suppress individual symptoms. The neurasthenic is the victim of an apprehension and an expectation which has reached the permanency of a fixed idea, and thus there arises an emotional complex, associated with feelings of anxiety and depression and not with those of health and well-being. Constant, morbid auto-suggestion has served to lend to these feelings an indefinite continuance and to make them worse. Here we have a habit neurosis, a constantly recurring mental state. Not only is the method of thinking at fault, but also the reaction to surroundings. The patient yields to every slight sensation of fatigue and to every fleeting pain. The object of the educational method in neurasthenia is to train the patient to healthier habits of thought and to substitute for the morbid emotional complex a feeling of pleasure and of energy in all the acts and reactions of every-day life. The process is naturally a slow one analogous to all educational methods, but "as use doth breed a habit in a man," so constant application can direct the mind into healthier channels. As an athlete is compelled to go through a certain method of training before his muscles become fit for the competitive contest, or the beginner in piano playing requires long practice to arrive at any degree of proficiency, so the faulty neurasthenic habit of thought requires a long course of mental gymnastics to transform it to a normal mode of activity. This is the secret of the psychic re-education of neurasthenia and, once this mental reconstruction of the patient is established, recovery follows as a natural consequence.

How is this psychic re-education carried out in these severe functional nervous states? Without entering into technical details, we may say that the best plan is to attack the diseased condition from various standpoints, thus bringing a number of forces to bear upon the patient. In the nature of things, this is more effective than any single line of treatment. First we must be sincere with the patient and instruct him in the nature of the disease and its individual symptoms, and thus free his mind from any popular medical misconceptions and fallacies. Next, the individual symptoms themselves must be suppressed by various therapeutic agents and corrected from this explanatory point of view and a healthier emotional state must be substituted for the existing abnormal one. The reaction to surroundings should be modified by an insistence on a changed daily routine and finally over-feeding and isolation may be necessary. So we see that the educational method comprises not merely mental therapeutics, but every therapeutic agent must be utilized to effect the complete mental reconstruction of the patient. It is really a summation of stimuli, the individual forces of which should harmonize with the most recent developments in scientific medicine.

Psychic training has its analogue in the physical sphere, namely motor re-education. As in the functional neuroses, the psychotherapeutic action of educational methods acts like a real force in reconstructing the mental attitude of the patient, so the motor educational methods can harmonize muscular inco-ordination. It is a training in motility when this motility acts in an abnormal manner. Before we pass to this aspect of the question, however, a few words are necessary as to the mechanism of co-ordinated movements.

We have already had one example of the disharmony of muscular activity in the development of habit spasms. The movements of the body as a whole or in part are produced by the muscles which are attached to the bony skeleton. All muscular movement is produced by the contraction of individual muscular fibers. These movements are under the direct control of the nervous system. Muscles are seldom or never contracted individually: all muscular movements are actions of groups of muscles. When we will a muscular contraction, the intended movement is for a common physiological purpose, such as locomotion, sitting down, climbing stairs, or the carrying of food to the mouth. A number of muscles must be thrown into activity in order to produce these complicated movements. In the healthy, adult human being only harmonious muscular movements take place. For the production of muscular activity, the nervous system acts either as a conducting apparatus, chiefly by means of the spinal cord, or a selective idea of a co-ordinated muscular movement takes place in the brain. This selective idea is known as "willing" a movement. All normal muscular activity is co-ordinated or directed towards a specific end. When the conducting apparatus in the spinal cord is at fault, for instance as in the disease known as locomotor ataxia, or when the idea of a muscular movement is lost or suppressed, as in hysterical paralysis, the machinery of co-ordinated movements may then be said to be out of gear. The execution of voluntary movements then becomes faulty, ill-balanced, awkward: it cannot be directed towards a definite end. Locomotion is entirely lost or is so disordered that it resembles the gait of a drunken man or of a normal person attempting to walk on the ice. Liquids cannot be carried to the mouth without spilling, while the finer movements of the fingers, as in writing, become impossible. The list might be indefinitely extended to comprise any variety of motor activity of which the human adult is capable. Vision is very important for normal muscular activity and this is why the blind walk awkwardly or letters are poorly formed when we attempt to write with the eyes closed.

The study of the normal and abnormal movements has recently received a strong impetus by the taking of instantaneous photographs and projecting these upon a screen, as in biograph pictures. The film of course can be stopped at any desired point and thus a complicated movement can be studied at leisure in any of its stages.

This method has been applied to the gait in locomotor ataxia, paralysis, habit spasms, and epileptic convulsions.

We have seen that co-ordinated muscular activity in normal individuals is adapted to specific, intended actions, and these actions are the result of education and practice. This is true of only voluntary movements which are under the control of the will. Involuntary muscular movements, such as breathing and the heart-beat, are innervated by the lower brain centers and therefore automatic in action. This is an admirable mechanism, as these activities are necessary for the preservation and continuance of life, and if under voluntary control would not only demand an amount of conscious thought incompatible with any other activity of every-day life, but would also cease during sleep.

The newly born infant cannot perform any co-ordinate muscular movements It is unable to walk, can carry objects to the mouth only in an awkward manner, and even harmonious movements of the eyeball are absent, so that when a young child hears any unusual noise, it turns its entire head in the direction of the sound. Thus we see how even in the normal human being, the co-ordination of ordinary muscular movements has to be learned, in fact is educational. This is even more true of skilled actions. It is a training of the nervous system, and an action like learning to walk, performed at first with difficulty, finally becomes purely automatic. It is unnecessary for normal adults to think *how* to walk: they can perform other actions while walking and there is no need to observe the movements of the limbs. In the child, on the contrary, learning to walk is a distinctly conscious process, slowly and awkwardly performed. Distract this child from these conscious activities, or if he ceases to observe his limbs for a moment, he falls. When an adult is acquiring a skilled movement, like piano playing, skating, or bicycle riding, a new type of muscular co-ordination is needed. The beginner in skating or in bicycle riding resembles the child that is learning to walk. It is a conscious process and a visual perception of all the movements is necessary. By practice, a less and less conscious effort is needed, and finally it becomes entirely automatic. Thus again we see how the learning of co-ordinated muscular activity, whether the ordinary movements in the child or the skilled movements in the adult, has a purely physiological basis, depending upon the plasticity of the nerve substance. Now certain diseases of the nervous system are associated with this awkward muscular activity known as ataxia, which is in a way a reversion to the motor disharmony of the child. In learning any skilled movements (and all muscular co-ordination is in the highest sense skilled), we are all inco-ordinate or ataxic at first. Constant repetition, however, makes the movements less and less awkward, until finally they are executed with a minimum of effort and with absolute accuracy. This is the principle of motor re-education, the treatment of the various types of muscular inco-ordination by systematic and graduated exercises.

These methods of treatment by motor re-education are particularly applicable to such organic nervous diseases as locomotor ataxia and the ataxias of childhood, to such functional disorders as the various tics or habit spasms and to certain hysterical disturbances. In tabes (locomotor ataxia) there is a degeneration of certain portions of the spinal cord. One of the most prominent symptoms of this degeneration, in fact the symptom from which the disease derives its name, is muscular inco-ordination or ataxia. This effects the arms and legs, more particularly the latter, depending, of course, upon the portion of the spinal cord that is diseased. When the arms are involved, the finer skilled movements of the fingers and hands become impossible. If the legs are affected, locomotion is extremely difficult and ill-balanced. In the educational treatment of tabes, we do not influence the degenerated portions of the spinal cord, but we merely train other parts of the nervous system to take on those activities which the diseased spinal cord is incapable of carrying out. The plan of treatment is dependent upon the results of the neurological examination, but the motor exercises are carefully graduated, extremely simple in character at first and gradually increasing in complexity. Fatigue must be especially avoided. After a course of treatment, it is surprising to see the stumbling, ill-balanced ataxic walking with perfect confidence and steadiness.

In some forms of hysteria, the patient suffers from a peculiar group of symptoms. He is perfectly able to move the legs when lying down, there is no sign of muscular weakness or paralysis, but all attempts at walking are unsuccessful. Here is a purely functional disorder and not an absolute loss of nerve tissue as in tabes. The patient has lost or suppressed the mental images of the co-ordinated movements necessary for locomotion. His nervous system or tissue is intact; the most careful examination will fail to reveal any organic lesion of the brain or spinal cord. The object of the educational treatment is to substitute a new system of the mental images of locomotion by carefully graduated exercises. Here we are dealing with motor plus psychic re-education, as the therapeutic action of confidence is a strong factor in these cases and this confidence increases in power as the normal motor activities become established.

The various tics or habit spasms are infinite in variety, as these pathological muscular movements may result from any of the normal muscular activities of which the body is capable. As indicated previously, these may result from reactions of defense or may arise almost spontaneously in a neuropathic individual. In all these cases, therefore, the mental or nervous condition of the patient must be made the subject of a careful analysis. The educational treatment of tics is a systematized motor and volitional discipline. Its object is not only a training of the affected muscles to perform their normal functions, but also an inhibition of abnormal muscular movements. All these can be accomplished by appropriate exercises.

CHAPTER XIII

THE GENERAL PRINCIPLES OF PSYCHOTHERAPY

THE chief object of this volume is to present to the reader an epitome of one of the most important tendencies in modern medicine — namely, the treatment of certain functional nervous disorders by means of suggestion. Technically, this is known as psychotherapy. As a great deal on the subject had been scattered through the chapters of this book, it seemed desirable to unify the various statements and to present a short account of the general principles of psychotherapy. While psychotherapy is by no means a new method of treatment, but has been employed by physicians in one form or another from the earliest dawn of medicine, yet its scientific and rational application has been the work of only recent years. Formerly much empiricism prevailed in this field, at least so long as psychology was looked upon as one of the occult sciences and a branch of a more or less unpractical metaphysics. But with the advent of physiological psychology, of sound experiment instead of hazy generalizations, with the modern advances in the study of hysteria and the various aspects of the dissociations of consciousness, it was soon perceived that a rational psychic treatment was indicated in purely psychic disorders. Therefore all the diagnostic criteria of modern neurology and psychiatry were brought to bear upon the study of functional nervous disorders, and the result has been not only new and sound conceptions, but rational psychologic indications for treatment.

In order to free the reader's mind from any *a priori* misconceptions, it will be well to state in the beginning, that while psychotherapy in some form or another is the rational treatment for functional nervous disorders, yet it is not indicated in all, neither are all functional disorders amenable to psychotherapy. It is rather in the severe cases which do not yield to ordinary physical methods and in certain types of pure dissociations of consciousness that psychotherapeutic treatment is indicated. We cannot reiterate too frequently that a thorough neurological, psychiatric, or general medical examination is absolutely necessary before the institution of any form of psychic treatment, not only to rule out any organic disease or distinctly organic complications of a seemingly pure functional disorder, but also to obtain an intelligent comprehension of the case. Only in this way can grave errors be averted and the patient saved much unnecessary loss of time if other lines of treatment are indicated. For instance, in one case of a middle-aged man, there was a complaint of some vague gastric disorder in association with ill-defined neurasthenic symptoms. A chemical examination of the stomach contents revealed a beginning cancer of the stomach. Immediate operation was advised, and while it is yet too early to ascertain a definite outcome, yet the chances of cure are much greater than if the patient's valuable time had been wasted by a wholly ineffectual psychic treatment. Another case will show an exactly opposite state of affairs. The patient was a young man who for years had been treated for an organic disease of the stomach, by means of drugs and special diet. He did not improve, however, and finally a careful neurological examination revealed that the symptoms referable to the stomach were not only functional in nature, but that these symptoms were only a portion of a severe functional nervous disease. In fact the patient was a sufferer from hysteria. Careful psychic treatment directed towards hysteria brought about a disappearance of the gastric symptoms and finally a cure. The above are merely two cases out of many that could be cited.

Pyschotherapeutic methods vary, the object of some is purely therapeutic, of others distinctly analytical, to penetrate into the origin of certain disturbances and lay bare the essential emotional complex. Suggestions may be given in the waking, half-waking, or hypnotic state; psychic or motor re-education may be necessary in diseases of long duration, where habits of thought or of activity have become distinctly abnormal. Isolation is indicated in certain hysterical states, while persuasion or a rational, sincere explanation will often appeal to the more intelligent class of patients. Ignoring and purposeful neglect are sometimes of value in the hysteria of children. The principle of reserve energy[1] has opened up new vistas in psychotherapy. To all of these, of course, treatment by physical agents is frequently necessary — rest, baths, electricity, massage, diet, drugs. Nor must

---

[1] William James, "The Energies of Men," *Philosophical Review*, 1907. Boris Sidis, "Studies in Psychopathology," *Boston Medical and Surgical Journal*, March 14 to April 11, 1907.

we forget one factor of the highest importance, — the individuality of the physician.

It would exceed the scope and purpose of this book to discuss the above methods in detail, as most of these are not only far too technical to admit of intelligent comprehension by the lay reader, but all presuppose a thorough medical examination. A rational psychotherapy can only be developed on the basis of a rational psychopathology.

The nature and value of hypnosis have already been discussed. In many cases, however, hypnosis is unnecessary; in fact, it is only used when other lines of treatment fail. Frequently in the psychoneuroses, a rational explanation and analysis of the patient's condition will go far toward relieving many distressing symptoms, especially if the patient, as is too frequently the case, has been the victim of some popular medical misconception or superstition. Recently the application of these pyschotherapeutic conversations in the management and treatment of certain paranoic states, or in limited types of delusion formation, has attracted considerable notice. Of course, for a sound, psychotherapeutic treatment, the psychogenesis of these states must be carefully analyzed, and this presupposes a knowledge of mental diseases that is not possessed by any of the pseudo-scientific cults of mental healing. For the principles of psychic re-education, the reader is referred to two papers by Prince and Coriat.[1] The results in this series were most gratify-

[1] Morton Prince and Isador Coriat, "The Educational Treatment of the Psycho-Neuroses," *Journal Abnormal Psychology*, vol. ii, No. 4, October–November, 1907. Isador H. Coriat, "Some Further Studies on Nocturnal Paralysis," *Boston Medical and Surgical Journal*, December 5, 1907.

ing considering that the cases were of years' duration and had resisted all other methods of treatment. Here were treated and cured convulsive attacks of purely functional origin, the peculiar types of nocturnal paralysis, nocturnal enuresis, psychasthenic states, and functional gastric disorders. Of course, in some of these cases psychic treatment was combined with physiological hygiene, but the general principles of treatment were carried along the line of the correction of faulty habits of thought, instruction of the patient into the nature of his disease, and the suppression of individual symptoms by various suggestive measures.

Motor re-education has been of value in the various tics and habit spasms of adult life and childhood. These conditions are sometimes mistaken for chorea, but are really functional motor disturbances, in many cases the result of a faulty motor education. Isolation methods have been of great value, particularly in hysteria or neurasthenia, and recently Dubois of Berne has written a popular book on the purely psychic treatment of certain psychoneuroses.[1]

A question of great importance now arises — what particular form of psychic treatment shall be used? To this we reply — that the method of treatment is absolutely dependent on the results of the medical examination, particularly, the origin and nature of the particular nervous disease. Also, it is frequently the case, that even in

[1] L. F. Barker, "Some Experience with the Simpler Methods of Psychotherapy and Re-education," *American Journal of the Medical Sciences*, October, 1906. J. Camus and P. Pagniez, *Isolement et Psychothérapie*, Paris, 1904. Paul Dubois, *The Psychic Treatment of Nervous Disorders*, 1905.

purely functional disorders, medical treatment is necessary in combination with psychotherapy, and sometimes, in a functional disorder, physical therapy alone is indicated. The outline of the treatment, like the diagnosis of the condition, should be in the hands of a competent physician.

CHAPTER XIV

FEAR AND WORRY

FEAR is one of our most elemental and primitive emotions. Indeed the biologist assures us that along with Surprise it was the first to be developed, as the feeling of the Ludicrous was the last. Fear is common to all forms of animal existence, even the lowest. Darwin says that the earth-worm knows fear and darts into its burrow like a rabbit when alarmed. This universality of fear has come about through the working of the law of natural selection which prescribes that only those creatures survive that best adjust themselves to their environment. Without fear no organism could survive, for no organism could relate itself to the hostile forces in its environment. The animal that feared rightly increased its chances of survival, whereas the animal that feared wrongly weakened the forces that made for self-preservation. Within limits, then, fear as a primary instinct has been and is eminently useful. It is the cry of alarm raised by the senses which act as the guardians of the body; and at the signal, in virtue of the nervous automatism, the organism is put in a position of defense. Yet this is only half the truth. If it is an advantage to the animal organism, it is also a disadvantage. For example, it has been observed that many birds, though scarcely wounded by small shot, fall to the ground as though struck by lightning, panting, with wide-open eyes. Then again it often happens that the fear which prompts efforts to escape a threatened danger turns out to fail of its purpose. We know also that in human life fear, beyond a certain point, becomes an intolerable curse. It excites to activity, and at the same time tends to paralyze this very activity. At best, it would appear to be a clumsy device of Nature to preserve the species.

Man inherits fear from his sub-human ancestry. The new-born babe fears. Every mother and every nurse knows the instinctive fear of falling shown by the infant on her knee. In this tendency and in the babe's power of clutch, the biologist sees a survival of the time when man was an arboreal animal and when he put his young to sleep on the branches of trees or on ledges of rock. "The fear," says Mosso, "which children have of dogs and cats, before they have learnt why they are to be feared, is a consequence of heredity; even later, when they have gained some experience, they are overcome with fear at the sight of sucking pups or kittens, which would be ridiculous if it were not an innate aversion."[1] We are born, then, to a heritage of fear. Some dreads we outgrow; to others we are in lifelong bondage. Fear in man has a wider field than in the animal, just as man's nature is higher and more complicated than the animal's. Man is a being of "such large discourse, looking before and after," and to the fears of the sense he adds those of conscience and imagination. It is true that optimistic voices would reassure us with the glad news that science is gradually abolishing fears and that before its steady

[1] *Fear* (English translation), p. 231.

advance the dark shadows that scare the soul will flee away. But such a boast is of the vainest. Science does not change the amount of fear; she but redistributes it. The fears of superstition and ignorance vanish before her presence, only however to be replaced by those of truth and knowledge. If we fear ghosts and demons less, we fear microbes and bacteria more. Witches and warlocks no longer affright us, but tuberculosis and cancer cannot be laughed away. And if science can do something to combat pathological fears, she has no healing word for the dreads that originate in the moral and spiritual nature, the self-fear that debases life, the specter of guilt that will not down.

Who can classify the fears of man or woman? They are as multitudinous as are their desires. Perhaps what a woman fears most is wrinkles and so she has resource to cosmetics, and rouge-pots and "beauty-doctors" in vain attempts to ward off the enemy, forgetting the hygiene of the soul that alone makes winsome the "human face divine." The professional man or the business man fears failure. Now up to a certain point this fear is a good; it is an incentive to action. Beyond this point it is an evil and works only harm. So, too, with the public speaker. He fears his hearers and so is nervous; only thus does he bend them to his will. But let him be overnervous, the spell is broken, his speech evokes pity, or contempt, and his effort is a failure. Hence the man of business or of art should not let his fears conquer his judgment; he must by self-discipline turn them into a steadying and solemnizing influence which may act as a re-enforcement to his active powers. Men are bound to fear, but the fear should stimulate, not enslave. It is significant that, as Starbuck has shown, fear as a motive in conversion is fifteen times as great as hope. It would seem, then, that we must distinguish between fears that are normal and fears that are abnormal. Normal fears, that is, fears which are common to all healthy minds, may and often do become abnormal, and are then symptomatic of a disordered nervous state. But there are also fears which have no counterpart in healthy minds. Where the line is to be drawn between normal and abnormal dreads, who can say?

Stanley Hall in his remarkable "Study of Fears" wisely remarks: "There is no one without fear, and those few who so emphatically disclaim all fear, and the psychologists who tabulate the percentage of fearless people, are thinking of shock or panic or acute fright, or special physical dread, but not of the subtler forms, like fear of God, of dishonor, failure of their highest purposes, for themselves or others. Not only does everyone fear, but all should fear. The pedagogic problem is not to eliminate fear, but to gauge it to the power of proper reaction. Fears that paralyze some brains are a good tonic for others. In some form and degree, all need it always. . . . Without the fear apparatus in us, what a wealth of motive would be lost! Aristotle's conception of education, as learning to fear in due proportion those things worthy of being feared, would not serve badly as a definitive also of courage."[1] Men are bound to fear, but they should not merely fear. The good man in the presence of a moral temptation is afraid and by his fear wins the

[1] *American Journal of Psychology*, vol. viii, p. 242.

victory; the fool, not knowing that there is anything to fear, falls struck through with a dart. To enumerate the fears that afflict otherwise healthy minds would be a tedious task. Fear of lightning is said to be the most common, yet its groundless character is proved by the insignificant percentage of deaths caused by lightning. Fear of darkness is the standing misery of childhood, especially of imaginative and delicately organized childhood. A well-known novelist describes the sufferings from this cause of her hero's boyhood. "Every night brought its own distinct horror. The black dormitory was full of murderous visions that he dared not look upon. Only the blanket lay between him and the wolves, the blood-stained daggers held by a severed hand in the air, the bat-like old women measuring drops of poison into a cup. Awful indeed is the war of a child with darkness, when imagination is at its height, and reason is scarcely born in him. . . . Even now, as he harked back to this period, he could not recall it without a shudder. 'Childhood a happy time! What do they mean who say so?'"[1]

Some fears persist through youth into adult life. They seem to root themselves so deeply in the memory that even the greatest vicissitudes, the most revolutionary changes in experience, leave them untouched. "Every ugly thing told to the child, every shock, every fright given him, will remain like minute splinters in the flesh, to torture him all his life long. An old soldier, when I asked what his greatest fears had been, answered me thus: 'I have only had one, but it pursues me still. I am nearly

[1] M. E. Coleridge: *The Fiery Dawn*, p. 77.

seventy years old, I have looked death in the face I do not know how many times, I have never lost heart in any danger, but when I pass a little old church in the shades of the forest, or a deserted chapel in the mountains, I always remember a neglected oratory in my native village, and I shiver and look around, as though seeking the corpse of a murdered man which I once saw carried into it when a child, and with which an old servant wanted to shut me up to make me good.'"[1]

How may this fear of the dark be cured or at least mitigated? Not certainly by coercion or scolding. Such measures only aggravate the trouble. First of all, the child should not be allowed to hear or to read stories or legends of an exciting character. All morbidity of imagination should be checked and the mind strengthened and developed by simple, practical, scientific reading. With the growth and maturing of the body many of these childish fears gradually disappear. Hence the need for open-air exercise, nutritious food, and the avoidance of an over-stimulation of the brain by too much mental work. Finally, a few reassuring suggestions administered in a firm voice to the child when he is in a half-waking, half-sleeping state, will be found to be of the greatest value. Happily the child-mind is most amenable to suggestion.

A very wide-spread fear, especially in adolescence, is fear of disease. This secret and intense dread often causes nervous disorders so that, as Stanley Hall says, if the mind can cure the diseases it can make in adolescence, it can do much. Perhaps the greatest cause of this fear

[1] Mosso, *Fear*, p. 226.

is too much attention to passing sensations. A slight palpitation of the heart is so magnified by attention being fixed on it that the subject begins to fear he is developing *angina pectoris*. A student has, perhaps, overworked his brain, or has, from one cause or another, fallen into a neurasthenic state, with its concomitant depression, lack of volitional power, psychic pains in the head and so forth, and becomes seized with the idea that he is about to lose his reason. This dread, of course, only deepens his morbidity, though observation goes to prove that the dread is rarely justified. The sufferer should reassure himself by the reflection that this, like all other morbid fears, is the symptom merely of a nervous state, is mental in character and can therefore be suppressed by the manipulation of thought. The rule, then, is: *Morbid thoughts can be driven out only by other and healthy ones.* Substitute for the fear the thought of some duty not yet achieved, or the thought of the Divine presence which is near us alike in our going out and in our coming in. Cultivate that condition of mind which, conscious of God's fatherly regard, feels safe in His hands, and is willing to meet good or evil as He wills it. In a word, re-educate yourself, morally and spiritually. Summon the forces of your nature against this debasing fear, and through prayer, through obedience to law moral and law physiological, through concentration on some enterprise that carries you beyond your petty interests, win back the gift of self-control which is the secret of every life worth living.

Of all the fears that visit middle age, one of the most frequently encountered is fear of poverty. There are amiable writers who spend much ink in proving that poverty is no evil. Indeed, if we are to believe these optimistic souls, poverty so far from being an ill to be avoided is rather a blessing to be prized. There is a grain of truth at the bottom of their contention. And this grain is that there are evils worse than poverty. The woman who sells her soul for diamonds and thereby places dishonorable ease above honorable poverty, commits, it is agreed, both a sin and a blunder. Yet if poverty, as Juvenal says, makes us ridiculous, if it means dependence, loss of friendship, forfeiture of established position, physical discomfort, suppression of intellectual desires, frustration of worthy ambitions, lack of self-respect and the respect of one's neighbors — and poverty beyond a certain point means all this — then it must be esteemed an evil, though we cannot agree with Christian Science in regarding it as a moral offense. A whiff of Dr. Samuel Johnson's robust common-sense suffices to dissipate the sophistries of those who think otherwise: "Sir, all the arguments which are brought to represent poverty as no evil show it to be evidently a great evil. You never find people laboring to convince you that you may live very happily upon a plentiful fortune." Let it be granted, then, that in the hierarchy of mischiefs that vex humanity, poverty has a place, though the place is not so high as many think, what are we to do? Are we to let this fact breed a morbid fear which will curse our lives, make hard the heart, shut our ears to the cry of distress, and degrade the whole man into a self-centered, grasping money-grubber? Then shall we become poor indeed. That the fear is often the mark of an unhealthy mind cannot be questioned. Said a very intelligent man to the writer: "I am haunted with the fear that I will end my days in the poor-house. The thought fills me with an unutterable depression, and makes work impossible." And yet the man who so spoke had over one hundred thousand dollars invested in "gilt-edged securities." A healthy fear of indigence will lead to prudence, industry, thrift, to such measures as will secure one's personal independence. Having done honest work, making the while such provision as is possible for old age or sickness or for those dependent upon us, let us in faith leave the rest to Providence before whom a sparrow's fall is not without regard, and let us comfort ourselves with the witness of ancient piety: "I once was young and now am old; and never yet have I seen the righteous forsaken or his seed begging bread."

There is one fear which is absolutely universal: it is the fear of death. In the strict sense, one must be human in order to feel it. Originating as a blind instinct unconscious of its end in our animal ancestry, it has deepened and widened with the growth of mind and imagination until to-day it seems the master evil of the world. The animal knows pain and fears it: man, alone able to project himself into the future, knows the deep mystery of death, from which he draws back, but into which he must pass. Around this mystery have gathered the superstitious fears of ages bred of an undisciplined imagination, and even Christian theology cannot be acquitted of adding the spiritual pangs with which generations have gone down into the grave. Sad is the reflection that there are millions obsessed with an intense and secret fear of death which takes the zest out of existence, and makes the heavens gray. They cannot take hold of life with both hands, for the fear of death inhibits them.

Now when we analyze this fear, we find that it consists of several elements. (1) The instinctive or animal shrinking from death. This in a certain measure is normal; without it the race would soon disappear. It is a mark of our animal nature, and as such is necessary for the preservation of the individual. As animals, then, we rightly shrink from dissolution; but as human beings, called to organize our life on a moral basis, it is our prerogative to subordinate this fear to ethical ends. And as a matter of fact, we know that mighty as is this organic instinct, "there is no passion," as Lord Bacon remarks, "in the mind of man so weak but it mates and masters the fear of death; and therefore death is no such terrible enemy when a man hath so many attendants about him that can win the combat for him."[1] (2) Associated with this instinctive repugnance is horror at the physical accompaniments of death. The closed eyes, the stilled heart, the rigid form, and then the gloomy pageant of the funeral, the burial in the pent-up prison of the grave, the slow decay of the body, "the changes wrought on form and face" — all these lay hold of the imagination and fill it at times with unutterable misery. And yet a little reflection shows that we are here simply the victims of an illusion. We imagine ourselves undergoing these experiences which exist, however, only for the living. "Nothing, if we truly realize it, is less real than the grave. We should be no more concerned with the after fate of

[1] Essay, *Of Death*.

our discarded bodies than with that of the hair which the hair-cutter has cut off. The sooner they are resolved into their primitive elements the better. The imagination should never be suffered to dwell upon their decay." [1]

(3) Fear of pain in the hour of death. We speak of the "last agony." And the phrase has helped to perpetuate the idea that apart from the symptoms of a given disease, there is some mysterious pain in the act of dying. But as a normal and natural event, our end is probably as painless as our beginning. Medical science assures us that no special misery is felt by the dying. Nature administers her own anæsthetic and the end is, as a rule, peace. Professor Osler in his Ingersoll lecture on "Immortality" says: "I have careful records of about five hundred death-beds, studied particularly with reference to the modes of death, and the sensations of the dying. The latter alone concern us here. Ninety suffered bodily pain or distress of one sort or another." Here it will be noted that though one sixth or so of the observed cases suffered physical pain, this pain was not connected with the act of dying but with the disease which ended in death. Another distinguished student of medicine writes: "I would have the reader take the word of one who has witnessed many and various deaths that the term 'death-agony' does not correspond to any fact. The immediate cause of death, in all but very exceptional cases, such as accident, is the poisoning of the nervous centers by carbonic gas, which accumulates in the blood owing to the failure of the arrangements for its removal. Normal death, if the phrase be permitted, is a painless occurrence,

[1] Lecky, *The Map of Life*, pp. 350, 351.

usually preceded by a gradual loss of consciousness, entailing no more suffering than going to sleep, which it most closely resembles, literally as well as poetically."[1]

The truth is that unworthy fear of death is banished when we sink deep into our minds the thought that death is as much a part of the divine order of the world as life, and that therefore for all God's creatures it means not evil but good. The approach of the end may work grief and pain in the beholders, but to the dying, apart from accident or other abnormal forms of death, it is received not with resentment but with acquiescence and in the majority of instances with relief. We do not dislike the interruption of consciousness which we call sleep. No more will we resent that deeper interruption which we call death. Until our hour comes, faith in the Divine goodness, combined with an active love of service to our fellowmen, with a sinking of our own petty personality in the interests of the larger world to which we belong, will slowly but surely emancipate us from this as from all other degrading fears. He who knows how to live will know how to die.

There is a type of fear which may take hold even of the healthy mind, though it is often also the sign of a pathological state of the nervous system. It is the type to which the term "Worry" is applied. It is almost unnecessary to describe it: the futile regret over past mistakes, past follies and past sins, the miserable forecasting of the future, the constantly bearing with us, not only the real sorrows of the present but the imaginary sorrows of what might have been or what may yet be. These are the cursed forces that lay hold upon the soul,

[1] Saleeby, *Worry*, pp. 250, 251.

shake it to its center, while the cross currents of thought are flowing to and fro without aim and without an end, and life threatens "to grow into one tissue of impossibilities." "Worry," says Dr. Beard,[1] "is the one great shortener of life under civilization; and of all forms of worry the financial is the most frequent and for ordinary minds the most distressing. Merchants now make, always have made, and probably always will make, most of the money of the world; but business is attended with so much risk and uncertainty and consequent anxiety that merchants die sooner than physicians and lawyers." The philosophers would comfort us with the reflection that to worry is the sole prerogative of man. The animal does not worry. Shelley envies the skylark his power of giving himself up to the joy of the moment and contrasts therewith his own faculty of sorrow:

"We look before and after
And pine for what is not,
And our sincerest laughter
With some pain is fraught."[2]

This power to look before and after is the expression of man's self-consciousness of his ability to identify himself under all the changes of the past, present, and future. As a man rises in the scale of personality, he is the more prone to live in the past and in the future; to be content with the present alone is the mark of the animal mind. Thus worry is the shadow cast by man's moral and intellectual greatness and, as Pascal says, "the grandeur of man is also his misery." Important as is this reflection, it carries us but a little way, for the insistent question is,

[1] *American Nervousness*, p. 202.   [2] *To a Skylark*.

How can we conserve our ethical and rational character and yet not worry? Now it is here that psychology rightly claims to help us, and religion will help us even more. As springing out of the fundamental postulate of the profound unity of mind and body, psychology warns against the influence of fatigue on the nervous sytsem. Often worry is the result of overwork and oftener still of ill-regulated work. Loss of power of memory, blunting of the sense perceptions, lessening of the inhibiting or checking energy of the will, instability and weakness of attention — these are the results of a sort of blood poisoning by the chemical products of overwork or wrongly-worked brain. These morbid states may grow to a certain point, and they then issue in neurasthenia, the almost invariable concomitant of which is extreme fatigue. Another hint which psychology offers us is the value of a wide circle of interests, if we would win the virtue of endurance and suffer with patience "the slings and arrows of outrageous fortune." It is sadly significant that our asylum populations are mainly recruited from the classes whose lives are spent in narrow monotonous surroundings. Hence the fixed ideas, the obsessions and generally the all-absorbing egotism of insanity. With a good store of valuable and permanent interests one is well safeguarded against the attacks of worry. For if he is shut out from one channel of activity, he can work out his salvation in other directions. All his fortunes are not staked on one throw of the dice. Further, the root of the worrier's misery is lack of self-control. His greatest need, therefore, is moral re-education with a view to the co-ordination of his powers and the concentration of them on some worthy end. It is true that the emotions are not under the direct control of the will. Nevertheless, indirectly we can suppress or modify them by selecting the things to which we will give attention and the things selected will excite the appropriate emotion.

But it is in religion that we find the most powerful antidote to worry. Dr. Saleeby has pointed out that the two greatest religions the world has ever seen, Buddhism and Christianity, are essentially anti-worrying religions, though reaching the goal indeed by very different routes.[1] Buddhism says, "Worry is an inevitable accompaniment of life. In order to get rid of it you must destroy the desire to live, and the goal of all being is Nirvana. It means absolute acquiescence; the end of worry because the end of life." Christianity, on the contrary, says, "The great need is not less, but a more abundant life. Worry is something that may be transcended, and the power by which you transcend it is trust in God and the service of man." Christ, because of His faith in the omnipotence of goodness, could utter his great saying, the standing rebuke to the distracted spirit, "Be not therefore anxious for the morrow, for the morrow will be anxious for the things of itself. Sufficient unto the day is the evil thereof." It is not a theologian but our leading American psychologist, Professor James, who says, "The sovereign cure for worry is religious faith. The turbulent billows of the fretful surface leave the deep parts of the ocean undisturbed, and to him who has a hold of vaster and more permanent realities, the hourly vicissitudes of his personal destiny seem relatively insignificant things."[2]

[1] *Op. cit.*, p. 203. [2] *Talks with Teachers on Psychology.*

CHAPTER XV

ABNORMAL FEARS

WE now pass on to speak of abnormal fears.[1] These are evidences or symptoms of an unhealthy psychical state. They are especially associated with neurasthenia and psychasthenia. Neurasthenic differ from psychasthenic fears in being milder, not so deeply rooted in the mental organism and more amenable, therefore, to psychical treatment. When these fears assume a precise and systematized form, they are technically called "phobias."[2] To enumerate them were impossible; for a phobia may attach itself to almost any object or idea. Among the more common are "monophobia," fear of being alone; "claustrophobia," fear of narrow places; "agoraphobia," fear of broad or open places; "ereutophobia," fear of blushing; "triskaidekaphobia," fear of the number 13; "mysophobia," fear of dirt or microbes; "nosophobia," fear of disease. Janet classifies all phobias or systematized dreads under four heads: —

1. The phobias of the body, — which arise in connection with psychic pain felt on the movement of any of the limbs. The body is in every respect healthy, yet the sufferer is conscious of intense agony: it may be in the

---

[1] In the following paragraphs the writer is especially indebted to Janet, *Les Obsessions et La Psychasthenie*, and Freud, *Neurosenlehre*.
[2] From the Greek *Phobos*, fear.

teeth or in the skin, ear, eyes — in brief, in any part of the organism. One sufferer is afraid to walk; another is afraid to sit down because he has the feeling that on doing so he is elevated in the air; a third is afraid to eat because he conceives it to be painful. Janet tells of a woman who from remorse refused nourishment and had a horror of eating. This trouble was cured, recurred, and once more was cured. On the third attack the trouble assumed an opposite form: the patient eats well, but has a fear that her sickness is coming back; that she is prevented from eating by this fear, and that thus she is on the way to death from starvation. The result is that she eats with anxiety from the fear of having the fear of eating.

2. The phobias of objects. These are produced by the perception of certain objects. As the emotion is dreaded by the patient, there results a fear of the object which is the occasion of it. One trembles at the sight of a dog; another fears to look at the stars; a third is terrified at the thought of being polluted with microbes. Dr. Weir Mitchell tells of a sufferer on whom an experiment was tried. A cat was secretly imprisoned in a cupboard. The patient came into the room a little later. The cat was neither heard nor seen, nor did the patient know that there was such an animal in the house. Nevertheless, after a few minutes, he showed the greatest fear, was conscious that a cat was near at hand, and as a result could not be persuaded to remain in the room. Dr. Weir Mitchell admits that he has found no satisfactory explanation of this incident. Readers of John Bunyan's "Grace Abounding" will remember that in his uncon-

verted days he took great pleasure in ringing the bells of the parish church at Elstow. Then, under the goad of a morbid conscience, he felt it to be wrong. The result was that he contracted a phobia, a terrible fear of seeing or hearing bells.

3. Phobias of situation. These may develop in connection with the patient's perception of a physical or moral situation in which he happens to find himself. For example, in a broad or open space the patient feels himself isolated; he has a sense of vacancy all around him. The fear amounts to a terror such as would be produced by toppling over a precipice. A classical example of this type of fear is the case of Pascal who was obsessed throughout his life by the feeling that an abyss stretched on his left hand beneath him.[1] What gives rise in the sufferer to overpowering anxiety is the feeling of being alone without any moral or physical support. The opposite to agoraphobia is claustrophobia, fear of narrow spaces. Under this head would come fear of entering a carriage or a railroad car, fear of being in a church, a fear by the way which appears to be very widespread, or fear of entering a tunnel. The sensation is most painful; it is as though one were traveling along a corridor which was becoming more and more narrow. Or again there is monophobia, the fear of being alone and separated from people. Perhaps the fear arises from the perception not of a physical but of a moral situation. Here we have a typical example in the fear of blushing,

[1] This fact throws light on the references in his *Thoughts* to the dreadfulness of astronomical space. "I behold those terrible spaces of the universe which encompass me."

ereutophobia. This very fear is itself the cause of blushing. So painful is this misery at times that the sufferer will avoid society, give up his professional work and become a misanthrope. Another example is "dysmorphobia" or fear of bodily disfigurement. A woman, for example, is afraid that her hair is falling out, or that she is losing her teeth, though both hair and teeth are quite as sound as they ought to be.

4. Phobias of ideas. These arise in consequence of an abstract idea which presents itself to the mind of the patient. For example, a psychasthenic imagines that he has outraged religion by, it may be, bringing the thought of the Deity into connection with something trivial or debasing. There follows upon this obsession a phobia of blasphemy or he may have a hypochondriacal idea out of which spring all sorts of morbid imaginings about death, especially the fear of being buried alive.

Many of these and allied fears are so absurd, so fantastically whimsical, the product, one might suppose, of a sort of inverted genius, that only one accustomed to deal with such sufferers can bear their condition with patience. It cannot be too forcibly impressed upon the minds of friends and relatives that the unhappy victims of these psychical miseries ought to be pitied and helped, not scolded or blamed.

Perhaps the story of one who has suffered from these strange and painful emotions will be more helpful and instructive than any abstract discussion. Some twelve years ago, alone in his office one Saturday afternoon, the patient had been taking account of his financial situation. He had weathered the panic of '93, but he was still "playing a losing game," and he "must keep up the smile," as he says; for pride forbade letting go and starting anew. Sitting thus at his long office table, the table slowly rose in the air, he with it, and both began to revolve to the right, increasing in speed. He clung to the edge of the table and the mental cyclone continued for some minutes. Finally, the man and table came to rest, and shaking with fear, he made his way to the office of a physician friend; from there he went home in a carriage. Following upon this came eye trouble, throat trouble, stomach trouble, insomnia, one vanishing as another appeared, like moving pictures, but the one abiding thing was fear, culminating in panics, or what the patient terms "Bull Runs." This began with hesitation to go out of town alone; then to go to his office alone; then to stay at his office alone; and finally to be alone anywhere at any time. Indeed, sometimes he was conscious of a panic if his wife went out for an hour, notwithstanding the presence of a servant in the house, a telephone in the hall, and the family physician only two blocks away. We will now let the patient describe his phobias in his own words, and we do so with all the greater readiness as his account is singularly intelligent and shows incidentally that these abnormal feelings are possible to men otherwise of more than ordinary mental power. "I think to begin with the pride that kept me going was after all fear of criticism. As I lost faith in my own powers, my fear of the eyes, thoughts, and words of others increased proportionately. For example, the fear in taking a street-car was not primarily fear that anything serious would happen to me, but that something would happen which would result in a scene — fear that I should make a spectacle of myself. I think the beginning of every panic was either some slight physical disturbance, a pain, a dizziness, or something of that sort; or else a matter of environment or association would suggest a panic. To illustrate this: in going to a specific place which could be reached by two equidistant routes, if I had had a panic going by one route, I might go with ease by the other path at another time; but a retracing of the path in which a panic had overtaken me would result in a second panic at almost the identical point in the road where the first panic had occurred. I have found I can go further and more easily when the means of locomotion are under my own control, that is, walking or riding a bicycle, or driving in a carriage under my direction as contrasted with a railway-car, a trolley, or even a carriage under the control of another. I resolve to go to my office on my wheel — an easy, delightful ride. At the end of three or four blocks I begin to get scared; another block, I am breathing hard and my heart is pounding, but I pedal on; another block, and I am shaking. I call myself a fool and a coward. I ransack the vocabulary of abuse wherewith to rouse some sense of manhood, and I keep on pedaling; another block, and things get hazy, but I grit my teeth and I vow I will go on if I drop dead on the street. Then comes the 'Bull Run.' The next thing of which I am conscious is the fact that I am riding back towards home as though a demon were at my heels. It is much the same in a street-car or in an elevator. I have often walked up eight flights because I was unable to take any one of the four high-speed elevators at my command, but I think I could have run any one of those elevators myself all day with perfect composure. The chief permanent effect of these panics is a deepening of my self-distrust. The immediate but passing effect is utter exhaustion and incapacity for work." It is pleasant to be able to say that this gifted but unhappy man is on the road to recovery.

Let us now ask by what methods can this type of suffering be relieved and cured. Space will permit only the briefest outline. (1) Hypnotic suggestion. According to some French investigators, it is possible to produce the hypnotic state only in patients who are suffering from hysteria. Basing his idea on such a theory, Janet states in the work on which we have so largely drawn, as well as in his later Harvard lectures on "The Major Symptoms of Hysteria," that it is impossible to hypnotize the psychasthenic. If hypnosis, as Janet affirms, is an artificially produced hysteric state and therefore can only be induced in those suffering from hysteria, this remark is quite true, but if we take the more probable view that the hypnotic state is merely an artificially produced mental condition allied to the absent-mindedness of every-day life, then we must take exception to his statement. Any one who has had any experience in psychotherapeutic work can easily recall case after case of psychasthenia without any hysterical manifestations and conforming in every detail to Janet's conception of the disorder in which hypnosis was produced as a therapeutic measure.[1] (2) Still more important than hypnotic suggestion is re-education. The function of the real must be restored, and this

[1] For illustrations, see Bramwell, *Hypnotism, its History, Practice and Theory*, pp. 238–256.

is done by creating a happy emotion. A happy emotion increases our vitality. The more vitality we have, the more conscious are we of our reality. The happy emotions can be produced by demonstrating the true character of the disorder to the sufferer and by showing how curable it is. The result is, the psychological tension is relieved. (3) Work is a valuable therapeutic agent. Physical exercise, especially such exercise as requires great attention, exerts a most beneficial influence on the disorder. Cataloguing, clay-modeling, gymnastic exercises are of the greatest value. (4) Finally, the religious instinct should be appealed to. A sense of the ideal presence of God should be aroused. The sufferer's faith that, though apparently alone, he is really not alone, that about him is an Unseen Presence, will often avail to ward off an emotional crisis.

CHAPTER XVI

FAITH AND ITS THERAPEUTIC POWER

THERE is perhaps no subject connected with religion about which there is so much confusion of thought as the question of faith. This confusion arises from a variety of causes. The word is used so vaguely that the mind loses itself in the attempt to grasp its real significance. Sometimes faith is confounded with credulity or superstition and made to mean belief without any evidence why we should believe or even belief against all accessible evidence, as in the famous definition of the little boy that "faith is believing a thing when we know it is not true." Again, misapprehension sometimes springs from failure to distinguish between faith as a principle of our nature, which in the religious sphere brings us into contact with spiritual reality, and faith as a body of beliefs formulated in a more or less elaborate creed and accepted by Christian people. As these beliefs are expressed differently in different parts of the Church, it comes about that the Roman Catholic regards his Protestant brother as a man without faith. Once more, the popular mind is bewildered on this subject because faith as a primary instinct of the soul is not open to scientific definition like a fact in the physical world. It is too subtle, too deeply interwoven with the roots of the spiritual life to offer itself to any intellectual analysis. To the question, What is Faith? only a very general answer can be given, such as that of the writer of the Epistle to the Hebrews: "Faith is assurance of things hoped for, a conviction of things not seen." That is, faith makes the invisible world real to us; convinces us that the things of the spirit are not fancies but ultimate realities.

Let us at the outset rid our minds of a very prevalent idea. We often hear men say, "Faith belongs to religion; knowledge is the mark of science; the weakness of religion is its uncertainty; the strength of science is its firm standing on the bed-rock of observation and experiment." Yet as Professor Royce has abundantly shown, the whole structure of science rests upon a body of great faiths, of beliefs which must be trusted but cannot be proved.[1] For example, there is one great belief to which the scientist is passionately attached: the belief, that is to say, that nature is intelligible, that in spite of all appearances to the contrary, nature can be understood, is indeed the embodiment of thought. Such a faith which lies behind all the great scientific advances and discoveries of the modern world must be first accepted and relied on, and in proportion as it is accepted and relied on it evinces its genuineness. If you still insist that the scientific man should prove to you the uniformity of nature or that there is a causal connection between events, he will simply turn upon you with the threat, "If you cannot accept this faith of mine, it is because the spirit of science is not in you." It is therefore no reproach to religion to say that it is based on faith, for if this is a weakness, it is one that it shares with science. But not

[1] *The Religious Aspect of Philosophy*, pp. 291-324.

science only. Our ordinary life is grounded in faith. The greatest rationalist among us who loves to think of himself as viewing all things in the dry light of reason and of being governed by pure logic is in reality under the control of facts and forces which he himself has never tested. When he is overtaken with some sickness, he speedily forgets his rationalism, calls in the doctor and swallows his medicine in faith, and as we now know, the greater his faith, the more potent the medicine. Or again, in some crisis of his fortunes, he commits himself to the guidance of a friend. Doubtless he has a certain knowledge of his friend's character which leads him to an attitude of trust, but still in the last analysis the reason for this trust is that he divines by intuition certain qualities in his friend that are not upon the surface and that do not lend themselves to any logical analysis and argument. He is able to do this in virtue of kindred sympathies in his own nature. If he did not believe in his friend until the friend gave him formal proofs of his trustworthiness, he would be forced to go friendless through life.

Now faith is the same, whether we exercise it in our fellowmen or in God. The difference does not lie in the quality of the faith but in the object to which the faith is directed. Religious faith is simply that trust which the scientist puts in nature and its sequences, which all normally constituted men put in their friends, only now it is extended to the sphere of the unseen where it becomes trust in the goodness of God, in the Divine Love as tʰ law of creation. Just as the scientist believes in the ˙ fect order of nature in spite of experiences to thᵉ trary, or just as the ordinary man believes in his friend against superficial contradictions, so the religious man believes in the goodness of God and in the victory of this goodness in spite of all that seems to tell against it.

Now among the things which seem to tell against faith in the infinite goodness of the Power which this universe discloses are the facts of pain and disease. Ever since man has arisen to self-conscious thought, these phenomena have troubled him, have infected his spirit with doubt, have created the spiritual turmoil out of which have sprung the great theodicies of the world. We may take it that an ultimate solution of the problem of pain is not yet possible. Must faith then believe blindly, that is, irrationally; or can we point to any fact as throwing light upon the Divine attitude toward pain and disease, any fact on which faith can find a firm standing ground from which with untroubled eye it can view the whole problem? We have referred more than once to the so-called healing power of nature. What does this mean? From the standpoint of the physiology of to-day it means that there is a tendency in the tissue itself towards health and normality. This is one of the accepted commonplaces of pathological investigation. But if the order of nature is the expression of the Divine Will it follows that God wills health, that He means his creatures to be healthy, and that He is opposed to pain, disease, abnormality of every kind, just as He is opposed to sin and vice. We now know that in spite of all that can be urged to the contrary, God is on the side of order, of health, mental and physical. Doubtless in the present stage of things there are limitations to the full realization of this gracious Will, but if faith is shut up to the dilemma of denying either the omnipotence or the perfect goodness of God, it will instinctively sacrifice His physical to His moral attributes.

If we regard faith simply as a psychical process or mental attitude, history and experience alike testify that it has healing virtue. Not only does it form an indispensable factor in the various healing cults from those of ancient Egypt and Rome to the mesmerism of the eighteenth century and the Christian Science, the spiritualism and the ecclesiastical pilgrimages to this or that sacred shrine in our own time, but also it may be said to enter into all modern scientific psychotherapy. What indeed is psychotherapy at bottom but an elaborate system of suggestion, and what would suggestion avail were it not met with trust on the part of the sufferer? Faith is as necessary in a psychological clinic as at Lourdes or St. Anne de Beaupré. "Confidence," says Feuchtersleben, "acts like a real force." Hence it is not so much the quality as the strength of the faith that is of vital moment so far as the removal of a given disorder is concerned. The relic of a dead superstition, a bone from the supposed skeleton of a mediæval saint, may achieve as great things in the cure of physical disorders as faith in the living God. How is it that faith as a mere mental state has this power? Modern physiology gives the answer. It tells us that the processes of the body are controlled by the two great nerve systems, the cerebro-spinal and the sympathetic. We perform our conscious acts through the mechanism of the brain; but the involuntary physical processes, such as the circulation of the blood, the complicated process of turning the food we consume into bone and flesh, in a word, all the vital chemistries of the body, are carried on by means of the sympathetic nerve system. Now it is on this system that the emotions have most direct effect. Fear disorganizes and paralyzes the delicate machinery of the nervous organism, and as a result its various functional activities are disturbed or inhibited. On the other hand, faith stimulates and harmonizes them. Well has it been said that "there is no tonic so uplifting and renewing as joy, which sets into active exercise every constructive power of the body." Now faith is a joyous emotion. Any object which excites it profoundly affects the unconscious bodily functions. It sets the body at ease and thus enables its functions to be carried on calmly and normally. Such is the power even of a blind or credulous faith. But its power is limited to the physiological region. There is a realm within which it is worthless. It cannot reconstruct character or summon anew into exercise ethical forces. A superstitious faith may, and does, work physiological blessing. Ethically and spiritually it can achieve only harm. The more deeply personality is involved in any given ailment, the more necessary is it that faith should have an object worthy of man's ethical dignity and one fitted to draw forth in reverence all his moral and spiritual energies. Such an object can be found alone in the supreme Reality, the Father of Spirits.

There are many who feel with Frederick Denison Maurice that the God thus offered to faith seems too often but a dim shadow thrown from our own minds with which no vital contact is possible. But in Christ we see unveiled the glory of God. There have been other great teachers, great reformers, great saints, but in Him the Divine has entered in a unique way into humanity and thus offers itself to the love and faith of men. There are aspects and regions of the Divine nature inaccessible to our limited minds, and hence an element of reverent agnosticism must enter into all our thinking about God, but that aspect of His being which can be apprehended by human faculties is revealed in Jesus as it is revealed nowhere else. He interprets God to us. The shadowy, the abstract, become in Him real and concrete. In His suffering, in His teaching, in His compassionate activity as the healer of the souls and bodies of men, in His entire person as the embodiment of all those qualities which are most divine yet most human — in all this we see God's inmost feeling, His attitude toward the world and toward the individual soul. Trust in such a God draws together the scattered forces of the inner life, unifies the dissociations of consciousness created by guilt and remorse, soothes the wild emotions born of sorrow or despair, and touches the whole man to finer issues of peace and power and holiness. By the sweet constraint of such a faith, the jarred and jangled nerves are restored to harmony. The sense of irremediable ill disappears and hope sheds her light once more upon the darkened mind.

Perhaps nowhere in history can we find the power of faith to heal disorders of a semi-moral and semi-nervous character so strikingly illustrated as in the early centuries of the church's existence. The literature of the ante-Nicene period is permeated with a sense of conquest over sickness, disease, and moral ills of every kind. The primitive Church indeed accepted the current philosophy of disease. It was a wide-spread belief not only among Jews and Christians but generally throughout the Græco-Roman world that demons or malignant spirits caused all sorts of sickness and psychical disorders, indeed in a very real sense ruled the world. This belief was not confined to the uneducated. Even such a man as the highly cultured Celsus, the great critic of Christianity, believed in demoniacal activity. Tertullian (197 A.D.) devotes two chapters of his Apology to a discussion of the nature and influence of these evil powers. "They" (the demons), he says, "inflict on the body diseases and many grievous mishaps and violently visit the man with sudden and extraordinary aberrations. Their wonderful subtlety and tenuity give them access to both parts of man. Spiritual agencies possess great powers. . . . If some hidden blight in the breeze unseasonably hastens forward any fruit or grain in blossom, nips it in the bud, or blasts it in maturity, and if the air infected in some unseen way pours forth its poisonous currents; then by the same obscure contagion the influence of demons and angels brings about the corruption also of the mind with fury and foul madness or with fierce lusts, bringing various errors in their train. . . . They are sorcerers also truly in respect to the cure of diseases, for they first cause the injury and then in order to make it seem like a miracle prescribe remedies which are either new or absolutely opposed to the ordinary methods of treatment, after which they stop causing the injury and are believed to have effected a cure."[1] Harnack sums up well the prevailing mode of thought when he says, "The whole world and

[1] *Apology*, chap. xxii.

the circumambient atmosphere were filled with devils; not merely idolatry, but every phase and form of life was ruled by them. They sat on thrones; they hovered around cradles. The earth was literally a hell, though it was and continued to be a creation of God."[1] Now the early Church believed that Jesus had committed to her weapons wherewith to attack and rout these evil forces and to rescue souls from their grasp. This was no small part of the secret of the rapid growth of the Christian communities. The great masses of the ancient world lay sunken in superstition, held fast by the fanaticism of an unbalanced imagination. In this profound darkness the Church was the one bright spot. "No flight of imagination," says Harnack, "can form any idea of what would have come over the ancient world or the Roman Empire during the third century had it not been for the Church."[2] Gibbon, in his famous fifteenth chapter, mentions as the third cause of the spread of Christianity, "the miraculous powers of the primitive Church," among which he names the expulsion of demons, but he dismisses the whole matter with a scoff as the product of superstition. Wider knowledge now shows that the historian's skepticism was quite unjustified. There is abundant testimony that one of the most important factors in the early propaganda of the Christian faith was an especial power which Christians seemed to have over various psychical disturbances. If this healing was a mere pretense and meant nothing, it is hard to see how it could have induced opponents to embrace the new

---

[1] *Expansion of Christianity*, vol. i, p. 161. (English translation.)
[2] *Ibid.*, p. 158.

religion. Indeed so wide-spread was this healing power of the Christians that the third century witnessed the rise of a special order of men within the Church whose function it was to cast out demons or, as we would now say, to cure nervous disorders. The Apologists again and again refer to this fact as one not open to doubt. Justin Martyr (138–150 A.D.), writing to the Roman emperor of his day, gives the very formula which the exorcist used. He says: "Many of our Christian people have healed a large number of demoniacs throughout the whole world and also in your own city, exorcising them *in the name of Jesus Christ who was crucified under Pontius Pilate*. Yet all other exorcists, magicians, and dealers in drugs failed to heal such people."[1] Irenæus, writing about the year 180 A.D., says: "Those who are the true disciples of Jesus exercise in His name a healing ministry according to the gift which each has received from Him. Some surely drive out demons, so that it frequently happens that those thus purged from demons also believe and become members of the Church."[2] Tertullian challenges his opponents boldly with an appeal to their own experience. "All this dominion of ours and power over them (the demons) derives its force from the naming of Christ . . . so at our touch and at our breath they depart unwillingly and reluctantly at our command out of the bodies of men, and blush with shame in your presence."[3] And again, "What else would deliver you from those secret enemies who are ruining both your mental and physical powers

---

[1] *Apology*, II: 6. Cp. II: 8.
[2] *Adversus Hæreses*, Book II, xxxii. 4.   [3] *Apology*, chap. xxiii.

in every way? I refer to the attacks of the demons whom we expel from you without price or reward."[1] Cyprian, Origen, Athanasius, and other ecclesiastical writers bear similar witness. Even as late as the time of Augustine, we find the belief in the healing power of faith still existent. In his "City of God" he describes various healing wonders of which he was an eye-witness and which were done in the name of Christ.[2] In the course of time, exorcism as a regular function of the Church died out, partly through the abuses to which it gave rise, partly through the secularizing of the Church, with the consequent loss of faith, and partly through the belief that pain, disease, and weakness were the expressions of the Divine Will and were even helpful to the spiritual life. And yet it is significant that throughout later history the appearance of any great religious personality synchronized with an outburst of healing power. Francis of Assisi, Luther, George Fox, and John Wesley were not only great spiritual thinkers, but also by the strength of their faith were able in certain cases to set up a powerful psychical stimulus which resulted in the restoration of health to the sufferers; and wherever there has been a revival of religious life it has been accompanied by a more abundant sense of well-being both in soul and in body.

[1] *Apology*, chap. xxxvii. Compare also chap. xliii; *Ad Scapulam*, 2; *De Testimonio Animæ*, 3; Cyprian, *Ep.* 75; Lactantius, *Instit. Divin.*, II: 16; V: 22; Origen, *Contra Celsum*, I: 25; VII: 4; Athanasius, *De Incarn.*, 48.

[2] Compare Book XXII, 8. Isaac Taylor denies the genuineness of these cures and refers them to wilful imposture on the part of the Church. Modern knowledge, on the contrary, makes them psychologically probable. The Roman Catholic view has won the day as against the older Protestant theory.

We are suffering for the Church's neglect at the present time. Outside her borders mental healing cults are springing up and seek in devious enough ways to supply her lack. The majority of these systems have broken with historical Christianity, and all of them regard academic medicine with distrust, if not with positive contempt. Some of them interpret Scripture in a way which excites the scholar's disgust. Others reject the Bible altogether as a religious authority, and ground themselves on a kind of theosophy baptized with the name of Christian. Nevertheless all these cults heal the sick, dissipate various kinds of miseries, afford moral uplift to the depressed and create an atmosphere of faith, hope, and courage in which achievements are wrought that recall the early springtime of Christianity. But had the Church been loyal to her earlier traditions; had she not lost the heroism of faith, these systems would never have been born. They will serve no mean purpose if they succeed in recalling the Church to the primitive practice and to the realization of the unsuspected riches of the Christian Gospel. A good many physicians, even those who admit the value of psychical treatment in nervous disorders, are still disposed to deny that religious ideas can have any therapeutic value. In so far as these men claim to be scientific, they will admit that in such a matter the only test is experiment, and until they have tried to use the power of religion and have failed they cannot set it aside as valueless. On the basis of our experience, however, we can affirm that religion has a distinct power in certain types of trouble. And it is reasonable to suppose that it will continue to have this power as long as perverted religious ideas form a prominent factor in the causation of the maladies that fill our asylums. Moreover, if, as we contend, religion is an essential element in the normal life of humanity, sound religious ideas must play a considerable rôle in the maintenance of sound mental and nervous health. The Church of to-day has weapons at her disposal which were denied to the Church of the early centuries. In the first place, there are the resources of modern science, and more especially of the science of psychological medicine. We know more about the nature of psychical disorder than did ancient men. In the second place, we have a new sense of the unity of body and spirit and we are no longer hindered and depressed by the somber imagination that peoples the world with demons. We know that God has not committed the humanity He has made to torture and despair. Finally, the history of Christianity fills us with boundless hope. Again and again it has been threatened with extinction and again and again it has burst forth into new activity and revealed unsuspected resources. It looks as if in answer to the materialism of the age, faith, especially faith in God as He has revealed Himself in Christ, should once more prove its power to remove mountains, to lift the burden of despair, to cure the distempered souls of men.

CHAPTER XVII

PRAYER AND ITS THERAPEUTIC VALUE

ONE of our most natural human instincts is prayer. The moral life of man began with prayer, and if the Son of Man find faith upon the earth, it will end in prayer. Prehistoric man used amulets and charms which were simply prayers for protection against the hostile forces with which he felt himself surrounded, and historic man from the first moment of his appearance is engaged in the act of praying. The papyri which are being unearthed from Egyptian graves, the tablets of ancient Babylon, contain much that is superstitious and credulous, but they also contain the speech of men in presence of their Divinity. The first recorded utterance of our own great Aryan people is the magnificent expression of prayer contained in the Vedic hymns. And what is true of the Vedas is also true of the sacred books of all ancient peoples. All the higher religions that exist to-day witness to the belief in prayer. Within a Mohammedan mosque there stood once two ministers of the Christian religion, the one a Roman Catholic, the other a Protestant. Said the Roman Catholic to the Protestant, as they listened to the impressive prayers from the Koran, "Men who pray like this cannot be far from the Kingdom of God."[1] And for modern civilized man at

[1] Dawson, *The Forgotten Secret*, p. 5.

times, at least, prayer is natural. However much we may forget God among the superficial distractions of our mundane lives, and however difficult we may find it to hold real communion with Him, in those hours when we really live, when the heart speaks, when the frozen depths are broken up, we turn to God as naturally as the flower turns to the sun, as a child turns to its mother. A great joy comes to us, and unconsciously our heart goes out to God in thanksgiving for that joy. Grief comes, loneliness and separation, and the God who seemed so far off suddenly comes very near, reveals Himself as our only treasure, our only home. Sudden death comes, and even irreligious men depart commending their souls blindly, perhaps half profanely, into the hands of the God to whom they feel they are going.' These are the expressions of what Tertullian in his famous phrase calls "the soul naturally Christian." The instinctiveness of prayer, the fact that all men from the beginning almost to the present time have prayed and that the great majority of men still pray, is the most powerful argument for prayer, because it is hard to believe that an instinct so universal subserves no purpose in the divine economy of life.

A complete rationale of prayer is impossible. How can one analyze the act wherein the finite mingles with the Infinite? "In prayer," says Jowett, "as in all religion, there is something that it is impossible to describe and that seems to be untrue the moment it is expressed in words."[1] Nevertheless, as far as possible, we ought to try to understand the meaning of prayer and to relate

[1] *Interpretation of Scripture and other Essays*, p. 331.

it to the other elements in our experience. From the dawn of man's spiritual life, God has spoken to man. However man first became aware of a Spirit behind or within this universe, he has been aware of it, and he has felt that in this Infinite Spirit he lives and that on this Spirit his life and salvation depend. Not only has man been conscious of his dependence on a higher Power, but also he has sought to bring himself more and more into harmonious relations with this Power, and his desire goes forth in prayer. In a sense prayer is man's language with God. It is obvious that such a spiritual exercise must have a beneficial reflex effect upon the mind of him who prays. "The man who offers up his petitions with passionate earnestness, with unswerving faith and with a vivid realization of the presence of an Unseen Being, has risen to a condition of mind which is itself eminently favorable both to his own happiness and to the expansion of his moral qualities."[1] The presupposition of prayer is the reality of God. To recognize His reality means to recognize our absolute dependence on Him. To perceive the reality of God and yet never commune with Him involves a profound cleft in the inner life which must end in death; whereas prayer, the expression of our normal relation to God, is a sign of life.[2]

But to the great majority of Christians prayer means something more than this. It is not merely communion with God; it is the offering of certain petitions, the making of certain requests with the expectation that our prayers, as we say, will be answered and our petitions

[1] Lecky, *History of European Morals*, vol. i, p. 36.
[2] Cf. *Realencyklopädie*. Art. *Gebet*.

granted. Now this conception of prayer comes into conflict with the modern idea of nature. We must remember that the early Christian, like his contemporaries, regarded every phenomenon of nature as an independent act of Divine Power; whereas we regard the world as an ordered system of inviolable laws. A true Christian instinct prevents us from praying that God should arrest the law of gravitation or raise the dead or affect the movement of the tides. But outside of these few conspicuous, fixed, and eternal expressions of the will of God, there is a large domain in which things seem to happen more fortuitously and more irregularly, such as the condition of the atmosphere, the growth of the crops, the approach of sickness and death and other dreaded events. Hence many persons who would never dream of annulling the law of gravitation by prayer have found it natural to pray for rain or fair weather as they deemed one or the other desirable, for the victory of their armies or for the fruitfulness of their fields. But modern science has entered these realms one after another, and has shown that even such apparently uncertain things as storms, drought, and the like are equally the result of universal law, which in reality is just as changeless as the law of gravitation. So multitudes of men, believing that prayer can have no effect on the ordering of their lives, have ceased to pray. Like James Thomson, they are ready to say:

"The world rolls on forever like a mill,
It grinds out death and life and good and ill.
It has no purpose, heart, nor word, nor will."

Sir Oliver Lodge reduces the outstanding controversy between science and faith to the question of the efficacy of prayer. "Is prayer to hypothetical and supersensuous beings as senseless and useless as it is unscientific? Or does prayer pierce through the husk and apparently sensuous covering of the universe and reach something living, loving, and helpful beyond?"[1] Admitting fully the inflexibility of natural law, it is a very inadequate reason for ceasing to pray and is really based upon a low conception of religion. The lowest form of religion, which is fetichism, is distinguished by this peculiarity: it believes that by prayer or magic or other necromantic charm it can control the will of the Divinity, and when the god proves himself obdurate, when the rain does not fall or the cow is not cured or the enemy is not conquered, then the god is insulted and his image trailed in the dust. A higher form of religion recognizes the fact that all these things are controlled by a mysterious fate, and does not blame its God for not being able to avert the inevitable. The highest religion, however, sees in everything that happens the expression of the will of God, and while accepting the whole discipline of life as the education of a loving Father, aims at bending man's will to God's and not God's will to the ofttimes blind and misguided desires of man. It does not conceive that there is any *a priori* necessity attaching to natural law, or that it has any independent and coercive power; for an analysis of the idea of law will show that it has no meaning except as the expression of will. The universe then is governed by the Divine Will. It conceives rather that history and experience show that this Will energizes according to certain regular modes or methods, which we have agreed

[1] *Hibbert Journal*, vol. i, p. 61.

to call the laws of nature. But what if there should be a law of prayer amid the mysteries of the universe? Even if you are convinced that no prayer of yours can quiet the storm or augment your fortune, or check the dreaded development of the disease which is taking your loved one from your sight, are there no storms within your own soul which prayer can quell? are there no spiritual treasures more precious than all earthly possessions — peace and reconciliation and pardon, that earnest prayer and communion with God can give you? Even if you have prayed for the preservation of the life of your loved one, and that prayer has not been answered in the sense in which it was offered, is it nothing that by prayer you have reached the joyful conviction that your loved one is safe in God and that in God you will find him again? Tennyson is reported to have said, "The reason why men find it hard to regard prayer in the same light in which it was formerly regarded is that we seem to know more about the unchangeableness of law; but I believe that God reveals himself in each individual soul. Prayer is, to take a mundane simile, like opening a sluice between the great ocean and our little channels when the great sea gathers itself together and flows in at full tide."[1] God is leading us by the very revelation of the laws of nature to a deeper, truer sense of our relation to Him, and so to a deeper and truer conception of the meaning of prayer. We begin our relations with God as children begin their relations with their parents. Our prayers are for the most part mere requests for what we regard as earthly blessings. We importune God for this and

[1] Tennyson, *A Memoir by His Son*, vol. i, p. 324.

that as children importune their parents for everything they want; but a wise father, if it is in his power, gives his child what his wisdom teaches is good for it — the long discipline of education, not the gratification of desires which would corrupt the child's will and place a barrier in the way to its long journey towards perfection. As the child grows older, it appreciates this and its relations to its parents become deeper and holier. It looks to them for love, for strength, for wisdom, for guidance and consolation. Seeing that they have guided it well in innumerable instances in the past, the child has faith in them for the present even if they withhold many things that it desires. This is a parable of the growth of our spiritual relations with God. If we are growing spiritually, our prayers will become more and more spiritual, though this by no means implies that we will ever reach the point where we may not seek an earthly good from God. There is a noble reverence for God and for the conditions of human life in the resolution of Jonathan Edwards: "Resolved, Never to count that a prayer, nor to let that pass as a prayer, nor that as a petition of a prayer, which is so made that I cannot hope that God will answer it."

So far we have almost tacitly assumed that the effect of prayer on the soul of the suppliant is its only real result. This is, however, far from being our view. The prayers of Mohammed, dating from the days when he communed with God in solitude, have changed life for hundreds of millions of our fellow men. Huxley was in the habit of saying that a thought could no more produce a change in our bodies than a steam whistle could run a locomotive. But in view of the wonderful cures effected in certain diseases by strong faith, hope, or suggestion, no experienced physician would endorse this dogmatic statement to-day. Man's will, we now know, has power to co-operate with God's will and to effect results which would not be effected were either factor canceled. The fundamental dogma of modern psychology is the unity of mind and body. It is almost impossible to exaggerate the significance of this fact for our present discussion. It is admitted that, as all the higher religions testify, prayer has a regenerating and uplifting effect on character; but in affecting character it must also affect the nervous system. It does not seem irrational to believe that prayer opens the inner consciousness to the absorption of spiritual energy, by which, as philosophy assures us, the universe is sustained. And this attitude of receptivity toward the highest things in turn affects character and life, and the calmed and purified spirit acts on the nervous organization, restoring its tone and rhythm. Of course the more earnest the prayer, the longer it is continued, the more constantly our soul goes out to God in one direction, the more that prayer is likely to prevail. This is especially true in praying for the sick, especially if the will of the sick man can be aroused to pray for himself. Professor James says, "As regards prayers for the sick, if any medical fact can be considered to stand firm, it is that in certain environments prayer may contribute to recovery and should be encouraged as a therapeutic measure." Under the influence of prayer wonderful recoveries have taken place; whereas it is well known that when men become demoralized and lose faith and hope and the will to live, they frequently die from the slightest causes. Many examples of this latter fact occurred in hospitals during the American Civil War and in times of epidemic. Perhaps the most remarkable example of the power of prayer in sickness is that of Luther and Melanchthon. Prayer, as is well known, rescued Melanchthon from the jaws of death. The cause of Melanchthon's sickness was remorse for the action which he and Luther had taken in giving a modified consent to the bigamist marriage of Philip of Hesse. At Weimar he became so ill that his life was despaired of and Luther was sent for. A contemporary writer describes the scene. "When Luther arrived he found Melanchthon apparently dying; his eyes were sunk, his sense gone, his speech stopped, his hearing closed, his face fallen in and hollow, and as Luther said, '*Facies erat Hippocratica.*' He knew nobody, ate and drank nothing. When Luther saw him thus disfigured, he was frightened above measure and said to his companions, 'God forfend, how has the Devil defaced this Organon!' He then turned forthwith to the window and prayed fervently to God. . . . Hereupon he grasped Philip by the hand: 'Be of good courage, Philip, thou shalt not die; give no place to the spirit of sorrow, and be not thine own murderer, but trust in the Lord, who can slay and make alive again, can wound and bind up, can smite and heal again.' For Luther well knew the burden of his heart and conscience. . . . Then Philip by degrees became more cheerful and let Luther order him something to eat and Luther brought it himself to him, but Philip refused it. Then Luther forced him with these threats, saying, 'Hark,

Philip, thou must eat, or I excommunicate thee.' With these words he was overcome so that he ate a very little and thus by degrees he gained strength again."[1]

Once more — we dare not pray to God to work a miracle, that is, to violate one of those general laws by which He rules the physical world, but on the other hand we must remember that it is difficult at times to decide what does or does not violate the natural order of the world. Wherever we see that the Divine Will has clearly expressed itself, piety suggests that we should not pray that it may be changed. But in a vast majority of diseases, the Divine Will is not unalterably expressed. Men do not die with a regularity and certainty observable, for example, in the phenomena of chemical affinity. If the law of death operated like a law of dynamics, it would fall outside the region where prayer is possible, because to effect it would no longer be the wish of the truly pious man. As a matter of fact, however, it does not so operate. In any given case, death may or may not happen. Why, then, should the desire for the recovery of a sick person be forbidden its expression in prayer to Him who is the Lord of Life and Death? The material world is affected by the spiritual world. Thought and will and emotion are constantly producing changes in things belonging to the region of natural science. Therefore, we ought not to be straitened in our prayers through any nervous fear of infringing upon the laws of nature. Christ lays down the law of prayer: "Whatsoever things ye desire, when ye pray, believe that ye

[1] Seckendorf, *History of Lutheranism*, vol. iii, p. 314; quoted by Richard, *Philip Melanchthon*, p. 272 seq.

receive them, and ye shall have them."[1] This, of course, does not mean that prayer is a species of magic whereby we can gain whatever we may wish, but it does mean that the prayer of faith is a reality and that it can accomplish what seems impossible. Prayer, in the idea of Christ, puts in motion a power which operates with something of the certainty with which a natural energy acts. We cannot set aside as a delusion the experience of high-minded men in all ages who testify that by prayer they have been enabled to rise above physical weakness, to conquer temptation, to face the terrors of shipwreck and earthquake, and to meet with dignity death itself.

The prayer of faith uttered or unexpressed has an immense influence over the functions of organic life. It is significant that a great English newspaper in an article on sleep recommended sufferers from insomnia to betake themselves to prayer. The advice was eminently sound, for in true prayer the mind is in a passive, receptive attitude. It is open to the inflow of the divine forces that bless and heal. Now the great hindrances to sleep are worry, anxiety, remorse, shame, sometimes the fear of not sleeping. Prayer calms and soothes the soul, lifts it into a higher region than the earthly and thus conduces to the state in which sleep becomes possible. Suppose now that our whole waking life were to be lived as Christ's was lived, in an atmosphere of prayer, that is, in a sense of oneness with the Infinite Life, the Soul of our souls, so that we should become channels through which the thought and love of God might have unhindered course. Must not the body so closely connected with the soul feel

[1] Mark xi. 24.

a new uplift and virtue? This is especially true of all nervous disorders, because mind has special relations to the brain and nervous system.

Our view of prayer will be influenced by our conception of the relation in which we stand to God. If we think of Him as some far-off Being, with whom we are only externally connected, the idea of prayer is, to take a homely illustration, like calling up a distant person on a telephone, making known our wishes and then waiting for a return of material goods. This is, of course, hopelessly crude and materialistic. But if we grasp the thought that we are organically related to God, that we exist in Him spiritually somewhat as thoughts exist in the mind, we can see that a strong desire in our soul communicates itself to Him and engages his attention just as a thought in our soul engages ours. The stronger the thought, the more frequently it returns, the more it is likely to be acted upon unless its realization should be injurious. Now, every impulse of the soul affects the whole consciousness, and so, apart from any outward act, has its results within. Therefore it is comforting to think that no strong prayer of ours can be in vain, that it rises in the consciousness of God, and if it is good becomes one of his determining motives. When in prayer we gather up all the forces of the soul in a pure and good desire toward God, we feel the effect of the prayer in character and in life. No man, therefore, has ever truly prayed in vain.[1] The oftener and more fervently we pray,

[1] Erskine of Linlathen, a Scottish lawyer and theologian, speaks of "the awful silence of God." Then he adds: "But it has not always been silence to me. I have had one revelation. After it I did not

the more our prayer accomplishes, though we do not expect God to violate His own gracious will at our bidding. He resists many prayers as we resist many thoughts, and having prayed, let us accept what He deems best to send.

For let us ask what does the truly pious man *desire* when he prays? Doubtless he desires some definite and particular boon either for himself or for another, and for the moment it is this wish that occupies the center of his consciousness. But this is not all. As Hermann says: "A prayer which contains nothing but a strong wish for an earthly blessing and the notion that there is a power which may be moved by urgent request to the fulfilment of the wish, is not genuine prayer. The notion of God here is simply the prolongation of the wish. The man never gets beyond *himself*. His prayer is not really addressed to God, but an attempt to make out of himself what he is not and cannot be."[1] There is another element in the prayer of the truly pious man that forms, so to say, the background of his thought — a desire which at first is not explicit but is nevertheless present and is after all the deepest element in his prayer. He wishes above all things that the Divine Will should be done, because he believes that this Will is perfectly good. His desire for some particular blessing is temporary, while on the contrary, longing for the accomplishment

know anything which I did not know before. But it was a joy for which one might brave any sorrow. I felt the power of love — that God is love — that He loved me, that He had spoken to me, and then after a long pause, that He had broken silence to me." — Cf. Inge: *Studies of English Mystics*, p. 78.

[1] *Realencyk.* Art. *Gebet.*

of the Divine Will is permanent. When the first turbulent emotion has spent itself, the soul falls back upon the eternal will of God and finds blessedness in resignation to this Will. Christ never showed the nobility of His soul more than in His prayer in Gethsemane. He offers his agonizing desire to the Father: "My Father, if it be possible, let this cup pass away from me," and then He recognizes that whether it passes or not, the Father's Will is good — "Nevertheless, not as I will, but as Thou wilt."[1]

So far we have spoken only of prayer in regard to our own personal needs and feelings. A few words must now be said about prayer for the well-being and happiness of others. Whether intercessory prayer can be vindicated by reason or no, it answers at least to the purest and noblest instincts of the heart:

> "Pray for my soul. More things are wrought by prayer
> Than this world dreams of. Wherefore, let thy voice
> Rise like a fountain for me night and day,
> For what are men better than sheep or goats
> That nourish a blind life within the brain,
> If, knowing God, they lift not hands of prayer
> Both for themselves and those who call them friend?"[2]

We know little of the law by which mind acts on mind and of the way in which the mind of man can affect the mind of God, but in view of the fact that telepathy is regarded by many sane and sober men as, if not actually proved, at least exceedingly probable, he would be a rash man who would deny that our emotions and desires expressed in prayer can reach and help the souls of others.

[1] Matthew xxvi. 39. [2] Tennyson: *Morte d'Arthur*, lines 250–256.

According to the view we have taken, when we pray long and earnestly for the moral or physical welfare of another, our soul not only acts on that soul, but our prayer arising in the mind of God directs his will more powerfully and more constantly to the soul for which we pray. It may be said that the will of God is ever acting for the highest happiness of all his creatures. This is true, and yet He may so have ordered the world that our prayer can give a particular direction and energy to His will just as we are able to give a particular direction and concentration to the electrical energy that penetrates all space. Moreover, in praying for the spiritual welfare of another, our prayer cannot conflict with any law of nature. If the person for whom we pray knows that we are constantly praying for him, the effect will be greater, because his spirit will more easily be brought into harmony with the Spirit of God and our spirit. Material blessings wrung from God by prayer may be viewed with suspicion, but no heart can ridicule the souls won to Him by loving desire. If you have prayed long for another and your prayer seems to have accomplished nothing, do not despair, your prayer has certainly accomplished something, and though the resistance is great, it has already yielded and will at last yield altogether. After praying for many years for her erring son Augustine, Monica went at last to see Archbishop Ambrose and told him of her despair. Ambrose comforted her with these words: "Woman, go in peace. The child of such prayers cannot perish." In a little while Monica had the pleasure of giving one of its greatest saints to the Church.

We cannot close this chapter without adding a few words on some too familiar difficulties of prayer. How many sufferers, especially nervous sufferers, have said to us, "I cannot pray, my faith is weak, if, indeed, I have faith at all. It seems impossible for me to command my thoughts, to pray, believing that God can or will answer me." Now it must be remembered that in neurasthenia and other psychic troubles the faculty by which we would commune with God is implicated in the nervous disturbance, is in a morbid state. The sufferer should bear in mind that he is not wholly responsible for this state and that, therefore, God will not demand from him the same amount of faith as he would expect from a normal mind. Therefore, our advice is to be patient with yourself. While using every possible means to regain normal self-control, bear patiently with a temporary eclipse of faith. Wait "until the day break and the shadows flee away." Meantime, the overcharged heart will find relief in brief ejaculatory and pregnant prayers which will win their way.

"A breath that fleets beyond this iron world
And touches Him who made it."

But still more important is the reflection that there is a form of prayer rich in blessing to the nervous and the miserable. This has been long known in the Church as contemplative, or meditative or passive prayer. It consists not in offering some definite request to God, but in sinking the soul in Him, in the union of the finite with the infinite. This practice is as old as religion itself, is found in all the higher contemplative religions as well as among the Quietists and Mystics. It has formed a prominent part of the devotions of the earlier Friends. Passive prayer is possible only when the body is still, placed in such a posture that it is perfectly relaxed and so not able to distract or vex the mind. Then the soul is absorbed in the thought of God, His presence, His power, His peace, so that for the time being all other feelings are obliterated. As Falconi, a Spanish mystic of the seventeenth century, writes: "Establish yourself well in the presence of God; and as it is a faithful truth, that His Divine Majesty fills wholly with His nature, presence, and power, form an interior act of faith, and be strongly persuaded of this important truth. Surrender yourself into His paternal hands, abandon your soul, life, interior and exterior, to His most holy will in order that He may dispose of you according to His good pleasure and service, in time and eternity. That done, remain in peace, repose, and silence; as a person who no more disposes of anything whatever. Do not think voluntarily of anything however good or sublime it may be; and endeavor only to remain in the pure faith of God in general and in the resignation that you have made to His holy will." . . . This kind of prayer "practices the three theological virtues: faith, hope and charity—faith, because it believes God present, hope, because it expects from Him an infinite number of blessings that He is desirous of granting to it, . . . charity, considering that it loves God ardently, that it has wholly resigned itself into His hands."[1] This form of prayer is, as we have said, especially useful for the nervous sufferer; first, because it

[1] Falconi: *The Prayer of Silence* (translated from the French), pp. 7-8.

produces that perfect calm which is so good for agitated minds, and secondly, because it seems to establish some mystical but real connection between the soul and God's spiritual forces. Many remarkable cases of increase of strength, both mental and physical, have been known to follow prayer offered in this way, especially in persons whose minds were so weak that they could not profit by conversation or by any effort to concentrate the mind on anything else.

But even the normal soul often complains of the ineffectiveness of prayer through want of faith. There are many who, as Coleridge says, believe that they believe; but to believe really is to act as if the belief were true. Here comes in the significance of the will, which, as modern psychology teaches, is of central importance in our moral life. What is wrong with these souls is not so much want of faith, as want of will. They believe the doctrines of the Christian faith, but they are unable to commit themselves to them. Now there is only one way in which we can learn to trust, and that is by trusting. Therefore, the duty of the man who feels inert and incapable of rising to the level of his belief is to arouse himself, to appeal to his will, to say to himself again and again until it has become, as it were, his subconscious possession, "Trust in God is rational and right, and therefore trust I will."

XVIII

SUICIDE AND ITS PREVENTION

ONE of the most sinister omens of our time is the alarming growth of self-murder.[1]

Everyday observation appears to confirm the depressing figures of the statisticians. Not a day passes but the newspapers report successful or unsuccessful attempts at self-destruction; the popular novel reflects the prominent place suicide has taken in the modern consciousness; the ever-recurring discussion as to whether and under what circumstances suicide is ever justifiable points in the same direction. Here is a state of matters that must challenge the attention of the philanthropist, the minister of religion, the psychologist, the educator of youth

[1] Taking the period 1826–1890 it has been shown that this crime during these years has increased in Prussia 411 per cent., in France 385 per cent., and in Austria 318 per cent. If we confine our attention to England and America we find that the suicide roll for the entire United States mounts up from 3,932 in 1890 to 6,735 in 1900, and from this point it advances steadily until in 1907 we have the appalling total of 10,782. When all due allowance has been made for increase of population, the figures disclose a sufficiently painful state of affairs. Among those who committed suicide in the United States in 1907 there were no less than 110 persons of distinction, as educators, bankers, capitalists, artists, merchants, manufacturers, corporation officials, clergymen, and physicians. The Registrar General reports 2,205 in England and Wales in 1890, and in 1905 the number swelled to 3,545 — an average annual increase of 85. The rate per 100,000 of the population was in 1890 seven, and in 1905 ten.

and indeed every lover and helper of his kind. We cannot shelve the problem by referring it to the alienist's province on the assumption that suicide is a symptom of insanity. Although we now know that brain-disease, especially melancholia, often leads to suicide, there is no necessary connection between the two so that the suicide must be always diagnosed a madman. For the number of suicides in different countries are in no fixed proportion to the number of the insane. Moreover, insanity is equally common among men and women, whereas there is only one female to every three male suicides.

Perhaps the most pathetic element in the statistics is the increasing prevalence of the malady among children. M. Proal shows that in 1879 out of 5,114 suicides in France thirty-seven were under sixteen years of age, and that in 1902 out of a total of 8,716 the children numbered fifty-nine. Professor Eulenberg of Berlin has counted in twelve years 1152 child-suicides in Germany, while the high schools of Russia alone supply in one year the appalling total of 337. "Fifty years ago," says Strahan, "child-suicide was comparatively rare, but during the last quarter of a century it has steadily increased in all European states, and at the present day is lamentably common in all."[1] This increase of child-suicide has also been pointed out by G. Stanley Hall. The main causes are jealousy, a desire to be revenged on some one who has injured or insulted the youthful suicide, educational overstrain, the failure of the world to meet the claims made upon it. The child commits suicide impul-

[1] *Suicide and Insanity*, p. 174. The statistics are silent as to juvenile suicide in the United States.

sively, never deliberately: the unformed mind, swayed by grief or pain and without any strong realization of the meaning of life and death, is unable to inhibit the suicidal tendency. The blame for the great mass of child-suicide must be put on the environment, moral, social, and physical. Constant ill treatment, improper diet, inadequate sleep, favoritism, harsh punishment, lack of sympathy with and understanding of the child mind—these create a psychic atmosphere in which death seems preferable to life. With the removal of these causes, we may expect to witness a great diminution of this heart-sickening evil.

In young manhood and young womanhood the most frequent cause is disillusion. This is the period of life when hope and imagination run riot. Anything and everything is possible: the limitations of life are not yet realized. When school-time is over and the stern realities of the world have to be faced, the youth undergoes a critical and sifting experience. "Many feel that they are inadequate to the duties of life; some are moreover worried by an evil conscience; weakened in fact or fancy by dissipation; strained, it may be, by having to pass through the stages of religious readjustment of the creed of childhood; find life tedious, monotonous, and disappointing, and are thus inclined to ennui and even melancholy. . . . The mind has been cultivated and the will weakened by inaction, so that when everything depends upon energy it collapses in despair. As the demands of life become complex and severe with advancing culture and civilization, the need of specialization and drudgery, this breaking into the harness of business, profession, and the conventions of society seems unreal or cruel fate, against which the soul rebels. All these conditions are copiously illustrated in the lives of adolescent suicides, and rare is the earnest soul who has not at this stage at least coquetted with thoughts of self-inflicted death."[1] Suicide is thus a sign of weakness, of relaxation of the moral fiber, and its growing prevalence indicates that there are causes at work which are slowly sapping the forces of national character.

What are some of these causes?

We must, of course, distinguish between the irrational suicide, the unconscious instrument of his own destruction, and the genuine suicide who consciously and with full knowledge of the consequences of his act violates "the canon 'gainst self-slaughter." We are not here concerned with suicide as an episode in the history of mania, melancholia, fixed ideas or psychasthenic impulse. The causation and prevention of pathological suicide belong to the province of the psychiatrist, and with the advance in the scientific comprehension of insanity we may hope for a mitigation of one of its saddest phenomena. On the other hand it ought to be noted that such an authority as Morselli traces only one third of all suicides to brain disease: the great majority are referable to causes more or less open to therapeutic treatment.

Durkheim rejects as inadequate all purely individual and particular causes and throws the whole emphasis on sociological conditions. In the first place, suicide is not hereditary. What can be inherited is a temperament or a mental disease which may predispose toward without necessitating self-killing. Repeated suicide in the same

[1] G. Stanley Hall: *Adolescence*, vol. i, pp. 376 seq.

family can be accounted for by the law of imitation, of suggestion by contagion or as the result of insanity. The remembrance or the spectacle of the tragic end of his relatives becomes in the suicide the source of an irresistible impulse. Behind the common action lies a common psychopathic taint. Again, Morselli's theory that climate has an effect on suicides cannot be proved. Suicide is not most frequent in the hot months as is popularly supposed. The fact is, it increases regularly from the beginning of the year and reaches its maximum not in the hottest months but in the month of June, from which point it gradually decreases, reaching its minimum in December. In other words, suicide increases with the increasing length of the day because, as the day grows longer, the social life, the currents and cross-currents of human relations grow, in intensity. For the true causation of suicide we are, according to Durkheim, to look at *the connection of society with the individual*. From this point of view we discern three chief types. (1) The "egoistic" suicide. In this class voluntary death is caused by the relaxation of family, social, and religious ties. A morbid individualism throws off the restraints of the collective life of the household or the community. The statisticians say that in a million husbands with children there are 205 suicides, in the same number without children there are 470; of a million wives without children there are 157 suicides, with children 45; of a million widows without children 1004, with children 526. As the domestic ties are relaxed, suicide mounts up. So, too, with the national life. As long as the national consciousness lies dormant the crime of self-murder is frequent, but as soon as the spirit of patriotism is stirred, as in war time, men are taken out of themselves and feel themselves part of a larger whole, with the result that life is too precious to be gratuitously flung away. The same thing is true of the pressure on the individual of an institutional, dogmatic, traditional religion. Here solidarity takes the place of individualism. Take Ireland, for example, which is mainly Roman Catholic. It has the honor of having the lowest suicide roll among all civilized countries: and within its borders Protestant Ulster produces two suicides for every one in the Roman Catholic provinces. In the Protestant countries, Germany and Scandinavia, the number of suicides is far higher than in Italy or Spain, the rate in Germany being five times as great as that in Italy. A recent writer says that "this probably points to the dark and hopeless Calvinistic principles of predestination, and also to the need of guidance in mental disquietude, the divine touch of human sympathy, of which every soul at some time is in need, being met, more or less well, by the system of confession." [1] A much more probable explanation is that Catholicism is far more strongly "intergrated" than Protestantism, that in the former the collective life counts for more than in the latter, and so tends to suppress the individualism which in an unhealthy form gives birth to suicide. There is no confessional in the Jewish communion, yet the Jew is as little disposed to suicide as the Roman Catholic. The orthodox Jew also finds his life hedged round with minute legal observances and but little is left to his own judgment.

[1] *International Journal of Ethics*, vol. xvi, p. 179.

(2) The "altruistic" suicide. Here we have a phenomenon the exact reverse of that which has just been described. An excessive social consciousness as well as an insufficient sense of personality may lead to suicide. Among primitive peoples where the tribal consciousness swallowed up the individual, suicide was frequent. And to-day India is the classic land of suicide permitted through a sense of religious exaltation, an overstrained feeling of the utter nothingness of the personal as compared with the universal soul. In a similar way is to be explained the high rate of military suicide. The soldier is a member of a closely organized group; he holds his life at the service of others: he obeys without dispute: and this moral and intellectual abnegation tends to make the spirit that is the natural soil of altruistic suicide. (3) The "anomic" suicide. This type is the creation of disturbances in the social organism whereby social control gives way and individual hopes and desires overstep the limits set by circumstance and cannot be satisfied. Great individual or financial crises whether of want or of prosperity are contemporaneous with an increase in the suicide rate simply because they are crises, perturbations in the social order. Men are no longer under normal rules and so are hurried by their lawless feelings into suicide. Then again in domestic crises such as the death of husband or wife, or the fact of divorce, we find suicide increases greatly.[1]

Thus, according to Durkheim, we are to look for the origin of suicide in social causes alone. And undoubtedly there is much truth in this contention. Suicide is a social fact and is powerfully affected by social relations. Yet the

[1] Durkheim, *Le Suicide*, pp. 149-154.

theory does not explain the whole phenomenon. For the question arises, Why does one individual resist the social influence and another succumb to it? The answer must be found in personal, concrete, particular causes without which the social factors are an inadequate explanation. These causes in the main are alcoholism, worry from domestic or financial trouble, shame and fear of disgrace, boredom or weariness of life, neurasthenia and other nervous disorders, insomnia, crime, extreme poverty, incurable disease, frustrated ambition, and disappointed love. No one of these factors by itself will account for the increasing suicide rate: they act and react upon each other and form a malign complex which it is impossible to disentangle. Hence the difficult and intricate nature of the problem. It cannot be attacked from one side only: the combined forces of the social reformer, the minister of religion, the schoolmaster, and the physician must be directed with scientific aim against the evil. The true prophylactic must be at once medical, philanthropic, moral, and religious. From a sociological standpoint it is sad to reflect that with all the increase in wealth and comfort which the nineteenth century has witnessed, extreme poverty still holds millions in its merciless grip. In London, according to Mr. Charles Booth, one out of every eight persons is just above the starvation line. Without home and without friends the world has few attractions for the man who is tempted to quit it. High in the scale of causation must be placed the growing drug-habit. Men unable or unwilling to bear patiently the strains and stresses of business, and women fretful and petulant under domestic cares, become the victims of "worry." Hence the growth of a neurotic, disordered temperament with its myriad attendant mischiefs. Weakness, lack of self-control, has resort to those pretended redeemers from misery, alcohol, morphine, cocaine and other narcotics; and the last state of the sufferer is worse than the first. "The unfortunate," says Dr. Saleeby, "seeks to drown his care in drink, to stifle it with morphine, or to transmute it with cocaine. A noteworthy fact of the day is the lamentable increase of self-drugging, not only amongst men but also amongst women — the mothers of the race that is to be. Alcohol and morphine and cocaine, sulphonal, trional, and even paraldehyde, these and many other drugs are now readily — far too readily — accessible to the relief of worry and of that sleeplessness which is a symptom of worry and is a link in the chain of lamentable events to which worry leads. These are friends of the falsest, as none know better than their victims. Hence borderland cases, misery, suicide, and death incalculable."[1] And again: "year by year, worry and fear and fretting increase the percentage of deaths that are self-inflicted — surely the most appalling of all comments upon any civilization."[2] But behind these facts lies another of deeper significance, though one which does not appear in the statistical tables — the weakening of hope through loss of faith in God and in a future life. It is obvious that only the man who has convinced himself that death ends all can risk the chance, in which so many of his fellow-men believe, that it does not end all, and, rather than bear the troubles that he has, prefers those that he knows not of. The advance of science

[1] *Worry*, p. 16.   [2] *Ibid.*, p. 10.

which while diminishing our faith in God increases our fear of microbes, the practical materialism of the time which regards pleasure the greatest good and pain the worst evil, the general religious unrest created in part by modern criticism, and in part by the failure of ecclesiastical Christianity to heal the deeper sores of the age — these forces tend to sap belief in a life beyond the grave. When grief or misery or shame befall the modern man,

> "Now more than ever seems it rich to die,
> To cease upon the midnight, with no pain."

If society is, as popular writers teach, the mere product of an evolutionary process with no deeper ground of existence, it is clear that the would-be suicide cannot be answered when he asks: "What claim has society upon me? It has flung me aside as an outcast, a hopeless derelict, a victim to a blind law of Survival of the Fit and Death of the Unfit. In voluntarily laying down my life am I not really furthering the apparent order of the world?" But as long as the individual retains a living faith in God he knows that his life has a sanctity, a permanent worth quite apart from the attitude of society towards him. In the deepest ground of his being he belongs to God, and on the basis of this consciousness he realizes that be belongs to society and may not withdraw from it without its consent. As a matter of fact, however, very few suicides reason deeply about their taking off. "Philosophic suicides" are very rare in our time. Perhaps the latest is that of Weininger, the youthful genius who wrote "Sex and Character" in which he strips humanity of its last vestige of the ideal and exposes it in all its stark and naked animalism. After finishing the book he saw no reason for remaining in such a world and blew himself out of it by means of a bullet.

In view of what has been said it is clear that the current proneness to suicide can be greatly reduced, for discerning clearly some at least of its causes we can attack and modify or remove them.

1. Our age is marked by sympathy with pain and misery. But too often the spirit of compassion gives birth to a pseudo-sentimentalism which in the long run is more cruel than strict justice. In a proper reaction against the barbarous laws of an earlier time dealing with suicide, we have gone to an undue extreme of leniency. Coroner's juries repeat from day to day the charitable falsehood, "suicide during temporary insanity," and as a result the deed is regarded with sympathy rather than with horror, and others on the brink of temptation are encouraged to commit the rash act. Doubtless juries are influenced by consideration for the grief and shame of the living, but they are the spokesmen of the law and of society and owe a duty to the dead as well. They should help to build up in the public mind, and especially in the thoughts of the young, a dread and detestation of the crime which would serve well the despairing and the tempted in their hour of need. And they would do this if they abandoned the senseless formula in vogue and returned, whenever the evidence warranted them in so doing, to the older verdict of *Felo de se* with a rider expressing condemnation of this "crime against oneself." It has been recently suggested that the body of the responsible suicide should be buried at midnight in silence.

2. But legal and social penalties of themselves will not cure the evil. Suicide, as has been said, is generally a sign of moral weakness. We must start, then, with infusing into our educational system a stronger ethical tone. The notes of self-control, of duty, of self-abnegation must be struck more loudly and insistently. A young naval officer shortly before ending his life writes to his parents: "I trust I shall be forgiven for the great trouble I shall bring upon all of you; but I feel I cannot longer live. . . . When I look back on life I see, that *if I had exercised only a little self-control*, I should never have done this."[1] In the great majority of suicides a defect of moral training in youth is to be observed. Hence Morselli is right so far when he says that the cure lies in developing in man the power of well-ordered sentiments and ideas by which to reach a certain aim in life; in short, to give force and energy to the moral character. A well-balanced, reasonable character is the best safeguard against suicide. Not in the school only, but in the home also, is this to be formed. It is within the power of the humblest to train their children in habits of poise, of industry, of duty, of unselfish service, of temperance in eating and drinking, of total abstinence so far as stimulants are concerned. And this is done by example even more than by precept. The conscious education of the child is by no means the whole of his training; it is in the sub-conscious region, as modern psychology teaches, that impressions, memories, thoughts are being stored up to find resurrection at a later day. It has happened more than once that a man tempted to suicide has been

[1] Gurnhill: *Morals of Suicide*, vol. i, p. 142.

saved by the sudden flashing up from the depths of the sub-conscious of a phrase or an idea or the remembrance of a long-forgotten face eloquent of goodness and patience, and he has turned once more to take up the burden of life. We know now that the most fugitive impressions leave traces on the child's imagination. The psychic atmosphere of the home more than anything else shapes for us life and destiny.

3. Modern psychology has shown what a powerful role suggestion plays in life. Man has been defined as a "suggestible animal". And perhaps the greatest medium of suggestion is the newspaper. There are many weak individuals who take their standards of action from the popular prints: and when they read the pathetic story of some unfortunate self-destroyer with minute and sensational description of the pistol, the rope or the poison with which the tragic deed was consummated, their vanity is fired and they too would win the pity and the notoriety such a death attracts. The fixed idea, the dominant thought, often ends in a mad deed. This is a commonplace of mental pathology. Every newspaper should simply publish a suicide's obituary giving, as in the ordinary "Deaths" column, name, date of death, age and place of residence. Still further, newspaper editors who rise to the dignity of their calling as molders of public opinion should, as opportunity offers, seek to raise the tone of popular thinking in this matter by showing the anti-social character of the crime and by calling attention to those tendencies in the body politic that make for its occurrence.

4. The social reformer can do much to stem the tide

of moral and physical degeneration of which suicide is merely a symptom. All drugs, stimulating and narcotic, should be made more difficult of access. Take alcohol, for example. It is now established beyond question that there is a close relationship between drunkenness and suicide. Denmark, with the highest consumption of alcohol, has the highest death-rate from suicide. In Switzerland, from one fourth to one third of the suicides, in various provinces of France from one fifth to one third, and in Belgium one third are referred to alcoholism. The only country in Europe with a declining suicide rate is Norway, and it is significant that in the same country, owing to the operation of the Gothenburg system, there is a declining rate of consumption of alcohol per head. One of the crying social needs of the time, especially in England and America, is temperance reform. The powerful organization of the liquor trade is a menace to the well-being of the people, subordinating as it does larger national questions to its own requirements. As Lord Rosebery has said: "If the State does not soon control the liquor traffic, the liquor traffic will control the State." In America the saloon system as a whole is a moral plague. All the forces that make for suicide are entrenched behind it and appear to defy the utmost efforts of civilization and philanthropy. The weakness of temperance advocates lies in their dissension: each party cries up its own panacea and has no patience with other points of view. They must close up their ranks on some practical basis of union, however far short of the ideal such a basis may be; and they must devise some substitute for the saloon and public-house which at present act as centers of natural and necessary social intercourse. There are other social problems demanding solution. The poorer districts of our large cities give the greatest contribution to the suicidal list. Hence the need for sanitary and hygienic measures, the establishment of free gymnasiums and baths, the better housing of the poor, in a word, for the humanizing and uplifting of the masses sunken in squalor and physical wretchedness.

5. The teacher whether by pen or by voice will do well to-day to emphasize the folly of suicide. A good dinner, a few hours' sleep, an offer of employment, a few sympathetic words, will often change a man's psychological climate and raise him from the depths of despair to the heights of hope and expectation. He is indeed foolish who permits himself to be the victim of an impulse so easily vanquished. Even on a purely utilitarian view of existence the self-slayer is guilty not so much of a crime as of a colossal blunder. He throws away the whole for a part. Is life a game in which the chances have gone against him? He is, in quitting the game, committing an act which is stupid and shortsighted. For if only he keeps a stout heart and refuses to surrender to the impulse of the coward, he may turn his misfortune into a means of ultimate gain.

6. Has Christianity any message to the intending suicide? Up till now the Church, as the official exponent of Christianity, has contented herself with denouncing suicide as a crime and imposing varying ecclesiastical penalties. But we now know that there are moral and psychical causes of the crime which it is the task of the Church to help ameliorate or remove. Men are discour-

aged and fear more than they hope. In the early Christian ages it was this discouragement that found comfort and consolation in the Gospel of the Nazarene, and as Christianity gained the mastery of the Roman Empire suicide almost wholly disappeared. Has religion any power to hold back the hand of the suicide to-day?

In many instances the real root of the mischief lies in the moral region. Perhaps it is an enslaving vice, a cowardly fear, a lost faith, a nervous collapse and fruit of shame or worry or disgrace. Such suffering should find sympathy and consolation at the hands of the Christian minister. He ought to be able to soothe the harassed spirit, to bring peace to the conscience, to kindle hope, to create faith, to dispel all that is evil, injurious, and inharmonious in the sufferer's life and mind. Equipped with the deeper insight into the nature of the soul and its relations to the nervous system which psychology has given him, it is his to dissipate the clouds of distress and discouragement with the breath of a vital faith and a boundless optimism. The Founder of Christianity was not only the greatest of teachers: He was also an ever-successful physician. Unhappily His followers not knowing what to make of his healing ministry for the most part ignored it. With the recovery of this new thing which Christ brought with him into the world, the moral misery that makes suicide possible cannot live. Never was the world more ready than to-day to hear the word of a religion that has power, and, hearing, to obey. For men dimly surmise that in the spiritual realm there are healing and reconciling forces, and in blind enough ways are earnestly trying to grasp and utilize them. There are deep instincts in man which rebel against a Gospel of despair. We see them at work in the creations of new religions such as Christian Science, New Thought, Spiritualism and so forth, in the widespread revolt against materialism in philosophy and in medical science, and in the strange fascination which oriental theosophic speculations are exercising over the practical-minded Englishman and American. It is not the fault of Christianity but of its popular exponents and interpreters that so many are turning away from the historic creed of Christendom to the latest quasi-metaphysical systems — arms that are shortened and cannot save. The need of the hour is the advent of prophetic spirits who will unveil to the eyes of their contemporaries the hidden resources of the Christian Gospel and will show this faith to be the one impregnable barrier against the inroads of pessimism and despair. In the light of modern science and more especially of psychological science, the great truths of Christ — a God truly personal and able to hold fellowship with the creatures of his hand, the imperishable worth of the soul, the organization of human life into a veritable Divine Kingdom on earth, — take on new and profounder meaning, and yet await practical application to the actual needs and the standing discouragements of humanity. Around these great ideas lie the perspective of the infinite. Because of them human life is seen to have issues that pass beyond time and place. Faith in God and in His purposes, a healthy reverence for what unimagined mysteries and experiences may lie behind the veil, are the forces that will stand a man in good stead when overcome by misfortune or tempted by cowardice.

"Brutus and Cato might discharge their souls
And give them furlough for another world,
But we like sentries are obliged to stand
In starless nights, and wait the appointed hour."[1]

[1] Should the reader be tempted to think that the suggestions in this chapter are visionary and unpractical, he is asked to study the Report for 1907 of the Salvation Army Antisuicide Bureau, from which he will see that some of these ideas have been applied with singular success. During 1907 about 2,250 men applied to the bureau: of these "it would be safe to say that 75 per cent. have been diverted from the commission of the rash act they had contemplated, and been helped either out of, or through, or on to the top of their circumstances. A few persons have set our counsels at naught and have perished. The remainder are possibly contemplating the act of self-destruction to-day." Among the applicants to the bureau were clergymen, physicians, military officers, lawyers, journalists, architects, company promoters, schoolmasters, actors, chemists, hotel proprietors, and general tradesmen. Very few of the most degraded and outcast classes applied for help.

CHAPTER XIX

THE HEALING WONDERS OF CHRIST

IN the history of the Founder of Christianity as recorded in the Gospels, we find attributed to Him certain wonderful or miraculous deeds. From the second century to the present time these achievements have excited in some grave scepticism, whereas in the case of others they have met with enthusiastic acceptance. Their appearance in the Gospel narrative have led rationalistic writers to doubt the veracity of the Gospel story, and the enlightened Christian of to-day often feels them rather a burden than a help to faith. Nevertheless the general historical trustworthiness of the first three Gospels is one of the most assured results of modern criticism. Although secondary elements are not wholly absent from these narratives, and although echoes of the Old Testament are not infrequently audible in them, yet to resolve the whole history into a series of mythical recitals modeled on Old Testament originals after the manner of Strauss is far from the thought of serious-minded scholars to-day. Though the threefold cord sometimes shrinks to a single strand, though St. Luke in particular has incorporated narratives as to whose origin at present we can only conjecture, yet the glad conviction has gained ground that in these exquisite and unstudied narratives we have a generally faithful picture of the life and the death of the Son of Man. The judgment of Harnack may be taken as embodying the conclusions of the best New Testament scholarship of our time. "The unique character of the Gospels," he says, "is universally recognized by criticism to-day.... The Greek language lies only like a transparent veil upon these writings, the contents of which can with a slight effort be translated back into Hebrew or Aramaic. That we have here in the main a first-hand tradition is indisputable."[1] Now embodied in the substance of these Gospels is the record of Christ's deeds. The deep impression He produced upon His contemporaries is consistently represented as effected by His mighty works as well as by His words, and these miracles are not like the trifling and immaterial acts ascribed to Him in the Apocryphal gospels, but are worthy expressions of the gracious character of their Author. So closely are most of these stories interwoven with the most probable incidents of His life, so supported are they by His authentic words, so sustained by direct and indirect evidence of every sort, that to tear them from the Evangelical narratives would be to renounce definitively and forever the hope of any real knowledge of the life of Jesus. In view of the impossibility of creating in simplicity and propriety such situations as frequently confront us in the miracles recorded in these Gospels, we may even boldly take up David Hume's challenge and affirm that the invention would be more miraculous than the miracle. Not only His friends but also His enemies

[1] *Das Wesen des Christentums*, pp. 14, 15. We do not use the Gospel of St. John as a source because it stands by itself and offers so many unsolved problems.

admitted His power to work wonders. As He hung upon the cross, the taunt flung at Him was also an unconscious tribute: "He saved others, Himself He cannot save."[1] His power was maliciously ascribed to Beelzebub, though later opponents supposed that He gained it through some occult knowledge acquired in Egypt. As to Christ's own claim there can be no mistake. His message to Herod is plain, "Behold, I cast out devils and I do cures."[2] There were two classes that lay close to the heart of Christ — the poor and the sick. In the great Judgment scene[3] He identifies Himself for all time with these classes. "I was hungry and ye gave me to eat. . . . I was sick and ye visited Me." He conceives of His mission as that of a physician, a Healer of the souls and bodies of men. "They that are whole have no need of a physician but they that are sick."[4] And the judgment which He pronounces upon the cities by the lakeside implies His wonder working activity: "Woe unto thee Chorazin! Woe unto thee Bethsaida! For if the mighty works had been done in Tyre and Sidon which were done in you, they would have repented long ago in sackcloth and ashes."[5] And yet He never proposed His ability to work miracles as a proof of His divine mission, but invariably declined such a challenge, stigmatizing it as a solicitation of an evil and adulterous generation and enjoining silence on those whom He had restored. He recognized that others could cast out demons and He admitted that false Messiahs could perform wonderful works, declaring that a

[1] Mark xv. 31.
[2] Matthew xxv. 31–46.
[3] Luke xiii. 32.
[4] Mark ii. 17.
[5] Matthew xi. 20–21.

tree is known by its fruit, not by these showy blossoms, and that character is the only proof that one is sent by God. In short, His miracles, though frequent, were with Him a secondary matter. As a rule, they were almost forced from Him by man's distress. His business on earth was to reveal God and to found His kingdom. The sign he offered to His contemporaries was the old sign of the prophet Jonah whose preaching was believed by the Ninevites.

The miracles of Jesus are usually grouped under four heads: (1) Ordinary acts of healing. (2) The expulsion of demons. (3) The raising of the dead. (4) The so-called nature miracles. We here concern ourselves only with the first two of these groups. In doing this we are not to be understood as throwing doubt upon the other types of miracle, much less rejecting them. For the present we set them aside because as yet we are unable to find in our experience a point of contact with them. A miracle, if it is to meet with acceptance at the hands of modern men, must be shown to have some analogy with facts and phenomena within their knowledge. Those of which this cannot be shown are by no means to be rejected. They are simply to be reserved to the day of fuller light. It would be rash to suppose that all the light possible in this matter has been vouchsafed us. The rationalistic criticism of fifty years ago rejected the healing wonders of Christ. Fuller knowledge enables us to smile at the sceptical dogmatism of this criticism. Why may it not be that the knowledge of fifty years hence will be able to make intelligible some of the narratives on which faith stumbles to-day?

Confining our attention then to the healing aspect of our Lord's ministry, what light has modern medical science to throw upon it? Every one has learned to recognize the reality of spiritual phenomena, the interdependence of soul and body, the effect of psychical states on physical states. There exists now in the archives of medicine, as Professor Osler in his review of the progress of medicine during the nineteenth century admits, a vast mass of trustworthy material testifying to the reality of cures effected or facilitated by other than physical means. Many persons discouraged by the difficulty of establishing a rational theory to account for these cases, or shocked by the absurd pretensions of those who claim to possess power to effect such cures, decline to enter this obscure border land of science, and prefer to ignore the whole subject. Yet that domain exists and to it presumably belong the miracles of healing ascribed to Christ and to His apostles. In this region personality counts for much, as every psychologically trained physician is aware. From time to time through the centuries men have arisen endowed with a peculiar power to dispel the moral and physical maladies of their fellowmen. Among these, "the First among many brethren," stands the Lord Jesus, the Great Physician. Of Him it was said that He taught and healed. Co-ordinating His cures with others that have been wrought in ancient and modern times, we obtain a new sense of the nature and reality of His mighty works that removes them from the stifling atmosphere of the old supernatural vacuum and gives them a place under the starry heavens and among the mysterious forces of God's universe.

In approaching a closer examination of Christ's therapeutic work, we must bear in mind that much uncertainty must attend our effort. The sources from which we get our information are admittedly fragmentary. They were written by simple and prosaically-minded men. They have no pretensions to be scientific biographies, but are rather broken and somewhat disjointed memoirs. And still more important for our purpose is the reflection that the diagnoses of the troubles cured are popular in character and are therefore vague and ambiguous. On the other hand, bearing in mind the uniqueness of Christ's personality and our own ignorance of the limits to the influence of mind over body, we will do well to avoid all hasty dogmatism as to what would be possible or not possible to such a one as Christ. Schmiedel regards as historical "only those of the class which even at the present day physicians are able to affect by psychological methods."[1] But the best physicians to-day admit that their studies are only at the beginning, that the dark border land of body and soul is still for the most part unexplored, and that when it is explored sufficiently startling discoveries will be made.

In order that we may understand the significance of Christ's healing ministry, a few words must be said as to the state of medical science in the Palestine of His day. That there was no lack of physicians at that time and place we learn from the story of the woman with an issue of blood. "She," we are told, "had suffered many things of many physicians and had spent all she had and was nothing better but rather grew worse." Luke,

[1] Article *Gospels* in Encyclopædia Biblica.

being a physician, could not tolerate this reflection of Mark's on the medical profession and so he quietly drops this remark about the clumsy ignorance of the doctors.[1] Greek medical knowledge had scarcely, if at all, affected the rabbinical views of disease. In spite of the teaching of the Book of Job, the orthodox opinion was that every sickness argued some sin, secret or open, on the part of the sick person.[2] Such a feeling of course only deepened the misery of the sufferer. In addition to this, the doctrines of demons had been elaborately developed and these evil spirits were supposed to be at work behind all forms of illness, but more especially in that particular form which went by the name of demon possession.[3] Even St. Paul could not shake himself free from this Jewish notion, for he speaks of his thorn in the flesh as a messenger of Satan.[4] With such ideas it was no wonder that, as Bousset says, the physician pursued his craft with all manner of remedies possible and impossible, good and bad, sometimes by proper means, more often with all the devices of quackery, faith healing and magic, with utterings of the mysterious name of God and even of the religious method of prayer."[5] And yet occasionally some of these crude doctors advocated methods that curiously foreshadow the therapeutics of to-day. In the Talmud, for example, a woman suffering from an issue of blood is told to seat herself at the crossroads and to cry aloud, "Let thine issue of blood be stopped" — an ancient example of the modern theory of auto-suggestion.

[1] Cp. Mark v. 26 and Luke viii. 23.   [2] Cp. John ix. 1.
[3] Cp. Mark ix. 17, Luke ix. 38, Luke xiii. 11.
[4] II Corinthians xii. 7.   [5] *Jesus*, p. 47.

The scope and range of Christ's therapeutic activity is worth noting. In the triple tradition — the material common to the first three Evangelists — we have the record of eleven miraculous deeds and of these nine are acts of healing. The diseases cured are as follows: (1) fever; (2) leprosy; (3) paralysis; (4) a withered hand; (5) demoniacal possession; (6) uterine hemorrhage; (7) reanimation at the point of death; (8) epilepsy; (9) blindness. In addition to specific cures we have a number of summarizing notices of Christ's healing ministry. For example, we are told that when He was in Capernaum, "they brought unto Him all that were sick and them that were possessed with demons, and He healed many that were sick with diverse diseases and cast out many demons."[1] And again we are told that "a great multitude from Galilee followed and from Judæa and from Jerusalem and from Idumæa and beyond Jordan and about Tyre and Sidon. . . for He had healed many in so much that as many as had plagues pressed upon Him that they might touch Him."[2] It may be inferred that the diseases named are typical of those with which He was accustomed to deal throughout His career. There is no mention in the records of His healing such diseases as tuberculosis, typhus, diphtheria and the like. He is reported to have cured leprosy, which in the view of modern medical science is incurable. But here we must remember that in the ancient world two types of leprosy were recognized, the one curable, the other incurable.[3] And from the vague description given in the Gospels we are unable to decide which type is referred to. An analogy to the heal-

---

[1] Mark i. 32–34.   [2] Mark iii. 8–10.   [3] See Lev., chap. xiii.

ing of the milder type may perhaps be found in the well-known fact that certain forms of eczema are recognized to be largely of nervous origin and are amenable to the influence of suggestion. "Eruptions on the skin," says a distinguished medical writer, "will follow excessive mental strain."[1] If we assume, for example, that this was the type of leprosy mentioned by all the first three Evangelists as having been cured at Capernaum, we can understand why the leper was permitted to come up close to Jesus and to mix with other people.

As space will not permit a detailed examination of all Christ's healing miracles, it will be convenient to select one for close study in order that we may the better understand His attitude toward disease and the methods which He employed to combat it. The incident which we have chosen for examination is that of the healing of the paralytic.[2] This story is the more readily selected because it offers certain difficulties which have excited considerable scepticism. For our part, the more we study it, especially in the light of the analogies of modern medical knowledge, the more are we convinced of its historicity. The story can be briefly told.

At some undefined point in His ministry we find Christ "preaching the Word" of the Kingdom in a house at Capernaum. The house is one-storied, as most village houses in Palestine are to-day, built but a few feet above the ground, consisting of one or at most two rooms, with a rough outside stairway leading to the flat roof. Within, all

[1] Sir B. W. Richardson, *Field of Disease*, p. 618, quoted by Schofield, *The Unconscious Mind*, p. 359.
[2] Mark ii. 1–12, and parallel passages.

the available space is crowded and even the entrance is choked by an interested audience. Suddenly, there appear four men bearing a rude pallet or quilt on which lies a young man paralyzed on one side of his body. They would force a way into the presence of Jesus, whose reputation as a healer is spreading far and wide. But the crowd will not yield. Nevertheless the friends of the sick man are determined not to be balked of their purpose. They make their way to the roof of the dwelling by the outer stairway, and, as St. Mark graphically says, "unroof the roof" by "digging up" the tiles or slabs of dried clay, and through the hole thus made they lower the pallet with the sufferer to the feet of Jesus. The faith of friends and patient fill Him with admiration. He cannot refuse such a challenge. In some way or other His inspired insight detects beneath the physical a moral paralysis, a disease of conscience, the sense of guilt, the pressure of some sin, which has led to this bodily distress. The deepest need of the sufferer is not to be cured of his physical disorder; it is to be healed of his spiritual misery that lies behind the bodily disturbance, and so Jesus turns to him with the word of comfort, "Child, your sins are forgiven." At once certain critical theologians present who have come from a distance take offense. "The man is speaking blasphemy," they say. "God alone has power to forgive sins." Jesus, with a touch of irony, turns on them with the question, "Why do you think such thoughts? Is it easier to say to the paralytic 'Your sins are forgiven,' or to say, 'Arise, and take your bed and go?'" Doubtless the critics would reply, "It is easier to assure a man of forgiveness than to cure him of paralysis, and the man therefore who can do the greater may be assumed to be able to do the less." Jesus feels within himself that He has power to forgive sins, that is, to offer such an assurance of forgiveness as is valid before God and as actually removes the guilt of sin. He is also conscious of the power of the Saviour to innervate afresh the physical life of the man before Him with a flood of physical energy. Strong in the consciousness of this double power, He addresses Himself to the sufferer, summons him to put forth His will by commanding him to rise and take up his bed and go unto his house. The sick man obeys the command to the amazement of all who are present.

This simple and artless story has been subjected by Strauss [1] to a searching criticism, with the result that he rejects it as a mere legend without the slightest foundation in fact, and accounts for its appearance by the Messianic obsession of the time working on such a prophecy as that of Isaiah: "Then shall the lame man leap as a hart." [2] Strauss's criticism is based partly on critical grounds and partly on supposed improbabilities in the details of the narrative. Matthew gives the original form of the story, and Luke in turn is outdone by Mark in wealth of detail. Matthew simply says that a paralytic was brought to Jesus stretched on a bed. Luke describes how Jesus surrounded by a multitude taught and healed in a certain house, and how the bearers, unable to get near Him for the press, let the sick man down through the roof; Mark goes beyond Luke in stating the number of the bearers and in describing how they tore up the roof

---

[1] xxxv. 6.   [2] *Life of Jesus*, pp. 455-7, English translation.

so as to let the sick man through. Thus do legends grow. But modern criticism cuts the ground from under this sceptical theory by showing that not Matthew but Mark is our earliest Gospel and that Matthew and Luke depend on it for much of their material. Thus the Gospel of Mark with its supposed difficulties stands nearest the facts. Moreover, according to Papias, a very early authority, Mark depended for his information on an eye-witness, Peter, whose recollections he wrote down. This sufficiently accounts for the lifelike detail and dramatic action of the story as it is told in the second Gospel. As to the improbabilities which Strauss finds in connection with the getting on the roof and of digging it up, they are based upon a misunderstanding of the structure of peasant dwellings in Palestine. Modern travelers make it quite clear that the action of the patient's friends was very natural and easy of accomplishment.[1]

Even Keim, misled by western conceptions of house structure, and by a wrong critical theory, agrees with Strauss in regarding the realistic touches of St. Mark as spurious.[2] On the other hand he accepts the kernel of the story — the healing of a case of paralysis, and accounts for the deed by a reference to the power of strong emotions, whether of joy or of terror, upon the physical organism. Keim is here looking in the right direction. Nevertheless he does not do justice to all the facts.

Let us, with the second Evangelist as our guide, try

---

[1] See Thomson, *The Land and the Book*, p. 358; Grant, *The Peasantry of Palestine*, p. 75; Stapfer, *Palestine in the Time of Christ*, p. 177; Edersheim, *History of the Jewish Nation*, p. 253.

[2] *Jesus of Nazara* (English Translation), vol. iii, pp. 213-218.

to understand the meaning of the story, to make it intelligible by co-ordinating it with known facts and to deduce from it our Lord's relation to sickness and His method of dealing with it. This will at the same time be the best apologetic for its historical worth.

1. We note that here Jesus recognizes the moral causes which in certain instances lie behind the physical disease. The friends of the sick man want Jesus to heal him, as it were, by a wave of the hand, but Jesus is no magician, and He knows that the moral malady is at the root of the trouble. He is very far indeed from sharing the prevailing theological notion of His time that every sickness in itself was evidence of sin, open or unconfessed. No! Rather for Him disease and sin are parts of a complex order — the kingdom of evil — to overcome which He felt himself sent by God. His Gospel or good news was in essence this: that God must be no longer conceived as the author of the misery and torture that make of human life a hell. On the contrary, He is Love, and as Love He is ever seeking to express Himself in joy. He is against disorder, weakness, pain, lack of self-control; these forces weaken life, and He is the God of the living. Nevertheless, Jesus recognizes, as every close observer of human life must recognize, that there are reciprocal relations between sin and disease just as there are reciprocal relations between the soul and the body.[1] "Medical science," says Matthew Arnold, "has never gaged — never perhaps enough set itself to gage — the intimate connection between moral fault and disease. To what extent or in how many cases what is

[1] Cp. John v. 14.

called illness is due to moral springs having been used amiss, whether by being over used or by not being used sufficiently, we hardly at all know, and we too little inquire. Certainly it is due to this very much more than we commonly think, and the more it is due to this, the more do moral therapeutics rise in possibility and importance. The bringer of light and happiness, the calmer and pacifier or invigorator and stimulator is one of the chiefest of doctors. Such a doctor is Jesus." [1]

We know to-day that many nervous disorders have their main root in the moral region. Selfishness, making undue claims on the world, leads to worry, and worry is one of the most prolific causes of neurasthenia and allied troubles. Or the sense of some moral fault unpurged by penitence creates a dissociation of consciousness which in turn may lead to hysteria, and hysteria, as we know, can simulate almost any disease and turn life into a prolonged wretchedness. Or again, wrong conceptions of God and of His relations to his creatures depress the soul, sink it into melancholy delusions and thereby set up all sorts of functional nervous disturbances. The alienist assures us that sixty per cent. of insanity may be traced to absence of self-control in one shape or another. If then the representatives of Christ to-day are to speak the healing and reconciling word, they must first understand more of the relations between abnormal states of mind or soul and the reflections of these states in the physical organism.

2. Christ's healing power required as a psychological medium and spiritual condition faith on the part of the

[1] *Literature and Dogma* (Osgood's Edition), pp. 135–136.

healed or of his friends or of both. This is the rule to which there is but one clear and necessary exception. In the cases of demon possession the mental organism was itself so disorganized that faith or any other rational and motived act was impossible. Jesus in these instances began by soothing the mind and distracting it from its obsession, and then with the naked force of his own personality, revealing itself in look, gesture, and word of command, He broke down the structure of hallucination and delusion which the morbid action of mind had built up and thereby He set the sufferer free from his disorder. But wherever a measure of self-control was left, He demanded faith. And we may assume the existence of faith even in those cases in connection with which it is not expressly named. Wherever there is a *detailed* account of a healing wonder, the presence of faith is indicated. For example, to the woman with the issue of blood Christ's word is, "Thy faith hath made thee whole."[1] The blind beggar at Jericho, whose cry of expectant trust could not be silenced, hears from the lips of Christ the same benediction. At Nazareth His hands were tied because of the unbelief of His fellow townsmen. "He was not able to do any mighty work there."[2] Only a few unimportant cases He treated because in these a little faith sufficed. This faith Jesus Himself sought to encourage. The blind man brought to Him at Bethsaida[3] He isolates from the crowd and uses the simple therapeutic remedies then in vogue and with which doubtless the man was familiar. The restoration of sight was gradual. Jesus encouraged him to try to see, but at first

[1] Mark v. 34. [2] Mark vi. 5–6. [3] Mark viii. 22.

the effort is only partially successful. Jesus repeated the operation of touching the eyes with spittle and then, as Mark says, "he took a steady look and was restored and saw everything clearly."[1] In the story before us it is said that Jesus seeing their faith proceeded to pronounce His absolution.[2] First and mainly, perhaps, our attention is called to the faith of the sick man's friends. The patient, then, has been for some time living in an atmosphere of faith. The reports of Christ's healing work have reached His companions and have stirred them to hope and trust. This very hope and trust have created a psychological atmosphere favorable to the sufferer's eventual recovery. Moreover, it has tended to awaken faith in the patient himself. As in the case of the daughter of Jairus, Christ feels Himself mighty in an atmosphere free from doubt and fear. We can see, too, how a strong faith on the part of this unhappy man was developed. The very fact that he allowed his friends to carry him to Christ showed that faith had already germinated in his heart. Every element in the strange and never to be forgotten scene in which he is to be for the moment the central figure was calculated to develop this germ, to affect powerfully his imagination and to arouse all his slumbering moral forces. First of all, there is the contagion of the crowd eager to hear the Great Teacher, and the powerful impression made upon them. Then there is the inability to find access to Him, causing momentary disappointment to be followed by a reaction of hope. Then there is the climbing of the roof and the

---

[1] Cp. Mark vii. 31–37 for a similar treatment of the deaf and dumb man.   [2] Mark ii. 5.

unusual mode of access to the Healer's presence. Nor can we forget the powerful nature of the *indirect* suggestion conveyed by his listening to the controversy between Christ and His critics and by marking the victory which Christ easily achieved. Above all, there is the tender and gracious Personality shining out in all its winsomeness and sympathy by way of contrast against the frowning and ungenial background of scribe and Pharisee. All this must have tended to create expectant attention, faith, confidence, hope, — the psychical conditions of a cure. We conclude then that the miraculousness of Christ's healing power did not consist in His refusal to use secondary causes, but rather in the Divine love and grace which moved Him to His cures and which His cures symbolized to the spiritually susceptible mind.

3. What was the secret of Christ's healing power?[1] The answer is, His sense of filial dependence upon God expressed in faith and prayer. The failure of the disciples to heal the epileptic boy at the foot of the Mount of Transfiguration Christ explains as due to their want of faith,[2] and this want is explained because of their weakness in prayer, in the strong desire which sets in motion the Divine Will. Christ's consciousness of oneness with His father is implied in His saying to His critics, "But that ye may know that the Son of Man hath authority on earth to forgive sins." This authority is delegated to Him by his Father. He is the appointed Redeemer of

[1] Some of Christ's contemporaries, such as the woman with an issue of blood, attributed His healing power to a kind of animal magnetism residing in His person and in His garments, and which could be drawn upon without any exercise of His will. Cp. Mark v. 30, vi. 10.

[2] Matthew xvii. 19.

mankind, the Founder of God's Kingdom upon earth, and therefore He was equipped with the power necessary to oppose and overcome the whole order of evil, to destroy it not in its outward manifestations only but in its ultimate causes. His power to heal is therefore only the visible manifestation of another power, His power to annul the guilt and activity of sin. This power was not something given Him once and for all, a magical endowment; rather was it an ethical quality to be sustained through communion with God. It is significant that after a day's healing and preaching activity at Capernaum He rose the following morning a great while before day and departed into a solitary place and there prayed.[1] It is here that we touch the inmost secret of Christ's power. It is the mystery of His personality, something which sets Him apart from humanity, something which lifts Him into a category by Himself. In healing as in teaching the best of men can follow Him only at a long interval.

The conditions, psychical and spiritual, of the healing wonder are now clearly manifest. The sick man, from a variety of circumstances co-operating, with his own longing to be free from misery, lies at the feet of Jesus full of expectant and of hopeful confidence. He feels a sense of security. Anything, even what seems impossible, is possible in the presence of this Divine Man. Had the poor paralytic been asked by some one later, "How did you know that Christ was able to heal you?" he might have replied in the words of Iole concerning Hercules: "Because I was content the moment my eyes fell on Him — He conquered whether He stood or walked or

[1] Mark i. 35.

sat." Moreover the man's deepest need had been met, the moral burden that had been weighing him down was removed; the various inhibitions caused by it no longer existed; in a word, all that is necessary is for the Healer to utter His word of command and the deed is done, the cure is wrought. Jesus, with a look of compassion linked with power, challenges the man to stand up. The man hears and obeys.

The records of any great psychological clinic of to-day should suffice to banish the last lingering doubt as to the genuineness of the narrative we have just discussed. One typical illustration may be given. From 1866 until 1875 a young woman was confined in the Saltperière Hospital at Paris suffering from hysteria. Her left arm and her left leg were paralzyed and by the contraction of the leg a kind of club-foot had been formed. The muscles of the tongue were so affected that she lost her speech. There was also a contraction of the œsophagus which hindered swallowing. The left eye was almost wholly blind. All the resources of medical science were tried for her relief, but in vain. Charcot, the noted expert in abnormal psychology, publicly explained that only some unforeseen and powerful impression could cure her. Three years after this statement was made, the patient was convinced that she would become well if on a certain Church festival the sacred Host should be placed upon her head. She waited in suspense for the day. As the procession approached, she began to tremble, lost consciousness, and fell into convulsions. In a few moments she was cured and was able to go into the chapel to return thanks to God.[1]

[1] See Traub *Die Wunder im Neuen Testament*, p. 37.

If any medical fact can be relied upon, it is that for certain nervous disorders suggestion has a healing power. This is brought forward here not as an adequate explanation, for suggestion is itself a mystery, but as an analogy that may well render credible the extraordinary and in some respects unparalleled cures in the ministry of Christ.

There is one type of disorder which stands in a category by itself and over which Jesus exercised especial power. It is that which goes by the name of "demon possession." There are six cases of this disorder reported, three of them with some detail and three more briefly.[1] Besides these we have a reference to another case, that of Mary Magdalene, out of whom it is said seven demons were cast.[2] Then we have casual notices of the cure of those possessed with demons.[3] Not only so, but the Twelve and the Seventy reported to Jesus that they had had power over demons.[4] This power, however, though apparently enhanced in Jesus and His disciples, was not peculiar to them, for we find a reference to an unknown man who was seen by the disciples casting out demons,[5] and Jesus himself admits that the pupils of the Pharisees were able to cast them out.[6] One receives the impression that however demoniacal possession is to be explained, it was a disease very widespread in Palestine in the time of Christ. Doubtless there were special social and religious conditions favorable to the growth of the distemper. The deep poverty of the people, crushed as they were be-

[1] Mark, v. 1–20 and parallel passages; Mark i. 23–26; Mark ix. 14–29; Mark vii. 24–30; Matthew ix. 32–33; Matthew xii. 12–22.
[2] Luke viii. 2.
[3] Mark i. 34–39; iii. 11.
[4] Mark vi. 13; Luke x. 17.
[5] Mark ix. 38.
[6] Matthew ix. 27.

neath the intolerable burden of the Roman taxation; the consequent physical and moral degradation; the overstrained Messianic expectation, leading to all sorts of fantastic and apocalyptic beliefs; the firmly-rooted and prevailing belief in the existence and activity of malignant spirits, a belief which the Jew shared with the rest of the world — all these elements formed a kind of forcing bed for abnormal mental phenomena. The consensus of Biblical scholarship is tending toward interpreting this strange disorder in the light of modern psychological medicine. From this point of view the essential element in it was the presence of some psychical nervous or mental disease of which the demoniacal obsession was an accidental symptom. Before the birth of psychological science and while the changes produced by a morbid nervous state in our conscious life were unknown, the strange phenomena of insanity were likely to be attributed to demons. When people perceived the marked and unaccountable alteration that the moral and mental state of their friends had undergone, when they heard strange words fall from their lips and witnessed all the melancholy manifestations of what would be called in our time double or multiple personality, they could hardly avoid the supposition that this profound transformation, these unreasonable fears and inhuman actions, were due to the presence of a foreign or malign spirit. They perceived that it was not the spirit of their friend that manifested itself. Hence they could only suppose it was some other spirit that had entered their friend's body and that spoke through his lips. To this psychological motive must be added the religious motive already referred to, which was at hand in the form of an elaborate doctrine of demons developed by the Jews largely out of foreign elements after the close of the Old Testament Canon, and to which the Apocryphal books bear abundant witness. The belief itself is pathological and except kept in check by the healthier elements in the individual and social life would tend to act as a powerful suggestion and would simulate a sort of pseudo-reality. Moreover, modern travelers and missionaries tell us that very similar phenomena may be observed at the present time in India, China, Japan, and other Oriental countries where belief in evil spirits is prevalent.[1] The missionaries exorcise demons to-day mainly by prayer and exhortation. The supposed demons speak through the organs of the possessed; they hate and seek to injure those who would exorcise them; they produce all manner of physical contortions and various nervous diseases; and they endow those over whom they tyrannize with apparently superhuman strength. It is clear that the demon possession of the Gospels does not stand by itself, but is to be viewed in connection with similar phenomena that were common in early Christianity, in Judaism and in many other religions. In general we may say that the Gospels distinguish between ordinary diseases and possession by demons, which latter they limit to a distinct class of nervous and mental maladies. We know to-day that it is persons afflicted with these ail-

[1] See Nevius, *Demon Possession and Allied Themes.* Tylor, *Primitive Culture*, vol. ii, pp. 108–246. Two valuable articles in *Bibliotheca Sacra*, pp. 300–324; 460–486. *Popular Science Monthly*, xxxv, p. 150. Articles by F. C. Conybeare in *Jewish Quarterly Review*, 1896–1897. Alexander, *Demonic Possession in the New Testament.*—Art. Dämonische in Herzog's *Realencyk.*

ments who are most susceptible to suggestion. In the three typical cases to which reference has already been made we may recognize some well-known form of nervous or mental disease. The boy at the foot of the Mount of Transfiguration with his falls, his convulsions, his gnashing teeth, his foaming lips, the sudden onset of the attacks in which he flings himself into fire and water, the sudden cessation of the seizure,[1] all these painful manifestations the father of the boy and the narrator ascribe, in accordance with the belief of their time, to the malignant energy of a demon. As a matter of fact, however, a modern physician would content himself with diagnosing the case as epilepsy, a disease of the highest nerve centers and appearing in different forms. The demoniac in the synagogue of Capernaum appears to have been afflicted with some type of hysteria. Luke says that though the demon threw the sufferer down yet he received no harm,[2] — a clear case of anæsthesia or loss of sensation which is one of the stigmata of hysteria. "Of all nervous afflictions," say Charcot and Richet, "hysteria is the one which in the case of possession appears to have played almost always the most considerable rôle."[3] The demoniac of Gerasa with his wild cry, his self-inflicted injuries, his frantic gestures, his ferocious onslaught on passers-by, is plainly the victim of some type of mania. In the cases of the blind and dumb demoniac and the dumb demoniac recorded by the first Evangelist,[4]

---

[1] See Matthew xvii. 15. (R. V.)
[2] Chap. iv. 35.
[3] Quoted by Soltau, *Hat Jesus Wunder Getan?*, p. 69.
[4] Chap. ix. 32; xii. 22.

the dumbness and blindness are probably the accompaniments of a hysterical neurosis. With the healing of the hysteria these symptoms would naturally disappear. Our view of the reality or unreality of these evil agencies will depend upon our general view of the universe. It is significant that as education spreads, belief in demoniacal possession dies out and that the greatest strongholds of the belief to-day are in non-Christian countries. It is hard to resist the impression that Christ Himself shared the common idea, yet we must remember that the narratives of the disorder were written by men prepossessed with the theory of demoniacal action, and even the words of Jesus Himself come to us through the minds of such men. If the evidence warrants us in believing that Jesus did share the contemporary belief, we must maintain that in no way does this fact invalidate His spiritual authority as the Founder of the Kingdom of God. His ignorance of psychology and physiology is one of the limitations of His human knowledge. In any event, He did not stop to speculate as to the psychical or physical causes of these afflictions. He proceeded to heal them and the glorious fact remains that His word, His will, His personality were sufficient for this task. Nothing impressed the early Church so much as His power to exorcise the demons *with a word!* [1] Armed alone with the spiritual power of faith in God and love to humanity, He stands over against the exorcists of His time with their fumigations, their sacramental acts, their mysterious signs, their terrible formulas. With Him all is simple and sublime. Not without significance as to the impression

---
[1] Cp. Matt. viii. 16.

Jesus made upon early generations of Christians is the legend that Abgarus, King of Edessa, afflicted with a grievous disease, sent a letter to Christ by the hands of a courier to beg Him to come and heal him. He writes, "I have heard the reports of Thee and of Thy cures, that they are performed without medicines and without herbs."[1] Jesus Himself says that it is by the Spirit or Finger of God that He casts out demons. Even at a distance, as in the case of the Syro-Phœnician woman's daughter, He is able to affect a cure, — a feat not unexampled in modern times and certainly not to be set aside when we take into consideration the results of psychical research. As a rule, it is His word of command carrying a definite forth-putting of will that restores self-control to the sufferer. "It fell," as Traub says, "on the nerves." The interposition of a mighty will, the tranquilizing contact with a calm and elevated nature, the touch of sympathy, the word of hope, were the means He employed in effecting His wonderful restorations. When He meets the raving demoniac of Gerasa [2] who could not be bound by iron fetters and had taken up his abode in the vaults of the dead, He enters into quiet soothing conversation with him so as to draw off the diseased mind from its obsession. So profound an impression did Jesus make upon the unhappy man that after the cure he entreated Jesus that he might be allowed to become one of His stated followers and to stay constantly with Him, but Jesus sent him as a preacher of the Gospel to his own kinsfolk. How a healthy personality affects an unhealthy personality, how will touches will, what it is that passes from the sane

[1] Eusebius, *Eccles. Hist.*, Book I, 13, 6.   [2] Mark v. 1-20.

and ordered mind to the unsound and disordered, it is impossible to tell, but every psychological clinic to-day is a witness to the reality of such facts. As we know nothing of the after history of those that were healed, we are unable to affirm that there were no relapses. That some of the cures failed to be permanent would appear from the little parable in which Jesus speaks of the demon who has gone out of a man passing through desert places and unable to find rest turning back to the soul from which he had been cast forth and, along with seven other spirits more evil than himself, entering into the man once more to make his last state worse than his first.[1] The relapses must have been very exceptional; otherwise we could not account for the splendor of His fame, as the Physician both of soul and body.[2]

Some readers may perhaps be willing to acknowledge the truth of everything stated so far, but they will object: "Were not the healing deeds of Christ extraordinary events, a parallel to which is never to be expected? What evidence," they will say, "is there in favor of thinking that Christ meant His healing ministry as well as his teaching ministry to be represented in His Church in all coming time?" To begin with, Christ in sending forth His disciples on their Galilean tour "gave them authority over the unclean spirits,"[3] and we are told that they carried out His commission, for they cast out many

[1] Luke xi. 24.
[2] The earliest apology for Christianity, outside the New Testament, written by one Quadratus about 125 A.D., but no longer extant, contained a statement preserved by Eusebius (*Hist. Eccles.* iv. 3) to the effect that some of those healed by Christ lived till the writer's time.
[3] Mark vi. 7.

demons and anointed with oil many that were sick and healed them. And we know from another source that the practice of anointing the sick man with oil and praying over him, both for physical and moral health, prevailed in the Apostolic Church.[1] The success of this early mission does not seem to have been great. Christ, however, repeats the experiment on a larger scale. He sends out seventy and empowers them to heal the sick that are in any city into which they may enter.[2] On the return of these Evangelists they reported that even the demons were subject unto them.[3]

Again, the greatest man in the Apostolic Church was St. Paul, and his attitude toward this question is valuable not only for its own sake but for the light it throws upon his conception of Christ's intention. In the list of spiritual gifts with which the Church was endowed, he mentions gifts of healing,[4] and he claims for himself wonder-working power.[5] We know that the power he claimed he freely exercised. If it were possible for us to accept as historical the Book of the Acts as it stands, we could point to such a narrative as that which relates how handkerchiefs or aprons that had touched the Apostle's body were carried to the sick, and "the diseases departed from them and the evil spirits went out."[6] But a great number of modern critics refuse to accept the whole of the Acts as genuine history. Nevertheless even free critics like Weizsäcker, McGiffert, and Schmiedel accept

[1] James v. 14, 15.
[2] Luke x. 8.
[3] Luke x. 17.
[4] I Cor. xii. 10, 28–30.
[5] II Cor. xii. 11–12; Rom. xv. 18–19.
[6] xix 11–12.

as genuine history the "We-passages," that is, those passages in the later portion of the book in which the writer speaks in the first person plural as though he were an eye-witness of the events he is narrating.[1] This eye-witness it is now generally agreed was Luke, "the beloved physician." Now it so happens that in this portion of the Acts we have recorded two remarkable curative acts on the part of the Apostle; the one an exorcism of a demon, the other a cure of dysentery. At Philippi a girl "having a spirit of divination" (which means that in all probability she was a ventriloquist and therefore was supposed to be under supernatural influence), followed Paul and his companions crying the while that they were the servants of the Most High God. But the Apostle, following the example of Christ, refused to accept commendation from such a dubious quarter and, turning round, charged the demon in the name of Jesus Christ to come out of her. That Paul believed in the reality of demons we know from other sources.[2] The other incident happened at Malta where he was shipwrecked on his way to Rome.[3] "The miraculous cures at Malta," says Weizsäcker, "are an historically inseparable portion of the Apostolic life." We are told that the father of Publius, the Governor of Malta, lay sick of fever and dysentery, unto whom Paul entered in and prayed and, "laying his hands on him, healed him." Then follows a notable statement: "And when this was done, the rest also that had diseases on the Island came and were cured; who also honored *us* with many honors." Now Harnack's

---

[1] Cp. xvi. 10; xx. 5; xxvii. 1.
[2] I Cor. x. 20, 21.
[3] Acts xxviii. 8-10.

keen-sightedness has seen that the Greek word rendered "were cured" would be more aptly translated "received medical attendance." The persons thus cured showed their appreciation by loading Paul and his companions with rich presents. Here then embedded in a section of the most primitive history, a section which has stood the tests of the most stringent criticism and is admitted by all scholars as genuine, we find the fundamental principle for which we have been contending throughout this book. — *Paul the Theologian, and Luke the Physician, the one with his spiritual power and his commanding personality, and the other with his training in the medical schools, join hands for the alleviation of human suffering.* From all this, it is clear that while the great Apostle of the Gentiles felt himself primarily called to preach, he knew that Christ had also empowered him to heal.

Finally, the spurious conclusion of St. Mark's Gospel,[1] which probably dates from an early part of the second century, does not indeed give us genuine words of Christ, but does enable us to see how the third generation of Christians conceived Christ's purpose as to the exercise of the healing gift. "And these signs shall accompany them that believe; in my Name shall they cast out demons; . . . they shall lay hands on the sick and they shall recover." In spite of the belief in thaumaturgy reflected in the claim to be able to take up serpents and drink any deadly thing without the slightest hurt, we have in this passage a genuine witness to the traditional belief of the early Church. For centuries, as we have seen,[2] this

---

[1] This conclusion is separated from the genuine text in the Revised Version by a space. [2] See pp. 296–299.

belief had the most powerful influence on Church life and custom, and was an influential factor in the Christian propaganda. Nor has it ever wholly died out of the consciousness of the Church. A great succession of eminent men has kept it alive through the ages in spite of the unbelief and indifference of the great mass of Christians. Paul, Origen, Augustine, Francis of Assisi, Luther, Swedenborg, John Wesley, Irving — that noble friend of Carlyle in whose meteoric ministry all London rejoiced for a season — Bengel, Erskine of Linlathen, Bushnell — these men believed that the Church was never nearer the realization of the mind of Christ than when engaged in healing the sick; nor must it be forgotten that the honored and historical Church of the Waldenses has preserved this, among other primitive traditions, till our own time. Professor Du Bose, whose sane and conservative temper gives weight to his words, suggestively remarks: "Assuredly there is more to be accomplished than our religion or our science have accomplished for the spiritual and the natural ills of mankind through the mind and through the faith of men. On the part of religion, may it not be from a lack of mental and spiritual susceptibility on our part, the absence of a due response of mind and heart, that the truth and the love of God do not work greater wonders in our lives, not only spiritual and moral, but physical also? May it not be one more of the many reproaches of our Christianity as it is that many have to go outside, if not of it, yet of its organized fellowship, to find that power of God unto salvation of soul and body which was its promise to us."[1] And

[1] *The Gospel in the Gospels*, pp. 81, 82.

again: "They (those who were healed) were the subjects and not merely the objects of His power. He carried *them* along with Himself in their healing. On their part it was mind or heart or faith healing. He told them to be well, to arise and walk, to look up and see. And they did it. Could not we in many ways do it too, if only we would believe and know?"[1] We do not plead for any return to the mere accidents of the life of the primitive Church, but we do plead for a return to her spirit and, so far as modern conditions will permit, to the manifestation of that spirit. Armed with the resources of modern science, and more especially of modern psychological science, inspired with the enthusiasm of humanity which is the grand legacy bequeathed her by the Founder of our faith, the Church of to-day should be able to outdo the wonders of the Apostolic and the post-Apostolic Age, and in a new and a grander sense to win the world for Him Who came to take its infirmities and to bear its sicknesses.

[1] *Ibid.*, p. 83. We owe these references to the Rev. Lyman Powell, of Northampton, Mass. The entire chapter on "The Authority of Jesus" will repay attentive reading.

CHAPTER XX

THE OUTLOOK OF THE CHURCH

THE religious world to-day is confronted by a very curious condition. We discern a general quickening of faith and a renewal of interest in religion on the one side, and a diminution of the influence of the Church on the other. Both these statements may be denied by persons who are not on intimate terms with the thought and tendencies of their own times. The men who are really doing the work of the Church will allow their truth. We are moreover obliged to admit this new and deplorable fact, that many of those who have withdrawn from the Church and who refuse to tread her courts are not the frivolous or the immoral, but men and women as much in love with the person and the purposes of Jesus Christ as we are, and who no longer associate themselves with the Church because they believe they can realize His ideals outside the Church better than through its instrumentality. We are far from affirming that this is always the case with these recusants. Many doubtless are led away, as Jesus foretold, by love of this present world, and because they are so engrossed in material things and sensual pleasures that they no longer care for anything that is great. As Goethe said, "When we have attained the good things of this world, it is so easy to regard those of the next as a delusion and snare." Many are deterred from entering the Church by honest intellectual scruples and difficulties, and for these the Church has a heavy responsibility. But it is safe to say that if the Church, which is the natural home of the Christian religion, declines, while humanity itself progresses, such a decline can have but one cause, namely, that the Church is not doing her whole duty. A large and ever-increasing number of intelligent persons feels that the Church has outgrown or is outgrowing her usefulness. Why do they feel thus? Because the Church is no longer indispensable to men. Unquestionably, as we have said more than once, one of the great motives of all human belief is the Practical Motive, — believing because it is good and useful to believe. The good religion has done the world and still is doing is one of the chief reasons why man believes in religion; and the more good any particular religion or church is able to do, the more men will believe in it, and the less visible good the Church does, the less men will believe in it.

The reason why men were swept into the Church by nations and races during the first glorious centuries of its existence was because they found in the Church something which they could find nowhere else, an ardent love, a living faith, the source of innumerable moral regenerations. The Christian religion began its mission to the world with an enormous sense of spiritual power. With the image of Jesus constantly before it, and taking its stand at the very center of the universe, the soul of man, the Church had gifts to bestow, gifts for all. In those days no one touched the religion without being transformed by it. "The Lord added unto the Church daily such as should be saved." He that was in Christ felt himself a new creature. The watchword was, "Let every one who nameth the name of Christ depart from iniquity." It is true, the Church of late, especially the Episcopal Church, has done much to postpone the evil day by a perfectly sincere sympathy with the sorrows and the hardships of mankind, and by an earnest and successful effort to improve the lot of those to whom life has been severe. Although we are thinking of other matters at this moment, we must pause to call attention to the great importance of this social movement. Those religions which have conquered for themselves a following and which have deeply touched the heart of mankind have done so by attacking social evils rather than theological problems. This is as true of the early triumphs of Buddhism as it is true of Christianity. Both religions found themselves confronted with a colossal task in the reclamation of the sunken and in consoling the griefs of mankind, and the love which they elicited and shed abroad has gained for them the undying gratitude of humanity. Persons who prophesy the downfall of the Church would do well to reflect on this fact. So long as the Church is animated by the divine charity of Jesus Christ, it can never fall, for the reason that in this cold and selfish world there is nothing else to take its place. No detective work, no sullen muttering about altruism, can supplant divine love. Yet we affirm that the Church of Christ cannot permanently uphold and propagate itself by anything less spiritual, less comprehensive and tremendous than the Christian religion, and the plain truth is that the Church is not bringing the whole force of the Christian religion to bear upon the lives of the people. Like other men who have seriously labored in the field of social endeavor, we feel its limitations. The people are very willing to accept what we have to give them in the way of fine parish buildings, libraries, gymnasia, music, trade-schools, art classes, and even baths. But the best that the Christian Church has to offer men is the new life in Christ Jesus, and this all our social endeavors do not seem to make people especially anxious to receive at our hands. We have heard many of the ablest and most conscientious clergymen of our Church confess with sorrow that they are doing this work with a sense of humiliation and despondency because they do not feel that they are giving their people the best they have to give. Of one thing we may be very sure: unless we soon find a way to unite faith to charity, that is, to infuse our social work with a more religious spirit, it will be taken from us and given to others. This has happened again and again with the Church's creations and it will take place once more. The Social Settlement and the People's Institute can do this work in many respects better than we can, and unless we possess some prerogative which they do not possess, it will pass to them. The great defect of the social movement in the Church is that it is not sufficiently personal, spiritual, and ethical. It can change the environment, but as yet it seems to have no means of changing the heart. It can help men in the bulk, but it has no direct access to the depth of the individual conscience. We therefore venture to believe that the social movement will soon be supplemented by a psychical movement which speaks in the name of Christ to the soul.

Another very significant sign of the times is our weariness of a continued sectarian existence. There remain, of course, stalwart partisans in all churches, but the better men of all denominations have ceased to glory in the things which separate us, and they are fixing their eyes on the great essentials of religion which unite us. Most of the Protestant churches set out with exclusive claims of enlightenment and excellence. This, however, was the result of passion or of logic and it forms no part of the Christian consciousness which refuses to accept a definition of the true Christian Church that excludes true Christians. Time has cooled our passions, and to-day logic, not to say self-preservation, points us toward unity, not toward division. During the past two years the writer has met perhaps a larger number of clergymen of all denominations than during the preceding fifteen years of his ministry. He has asked a great many of these gentlemen, "Do you look forward to any great future for your church in this country?" and with few exceptions the answer has been: "I can see no future for my church, but I believe that there is a future for Christianity." What is keeping us apart to-day is neither reason nor utility; it is only the tenacious grip of the expiring Traditional Motive which acts in religion precisely as the law of heredity acts in the domain of nature, *i.e.*, it transmits existing types. Since engaging in our new work, we have been gratified to observe what a powerful solvent this new interest has proved and in what pleasant ties of fellowship it has united Christians formerly estranged. Not only do members of all Protestant churches worship with us freely and constantly, but Roman

Catholics and Israelites also take part in our services with the approval of their priests and ministers. This small object lesson indicates how quickly the superficial differences which separate Protestant Christianity will disappear so soon as a new and powerful motive in religion which affects us all equally shall begin to make itself felt. The chief cause of our present condition is not discord and hatred; it is mere apathy due to the general deadness of the churches. When the light and warmth of a new day begin to animate us, then this coating of ice will melt and the waters will flow and mingle.

One cause of our present enfeebled condition is the fact that the Church through timidity, through sloth, through lack of enterprise, through inability to adjust herself to new conditions, has allowed herself to be sidetracked and relegated to a small and secondary rôle in human affairs. When we look back to the so-called ages of faith, to the days when the Church was everything, what amazes us most is the skill and wisdom with which she spread herself over the whole sphere of human life, entering every domain of human activity, leading every great movement of the human spirit. In those days all religion, knowledge, science, art, philosophy, and even the chief pleasures of life were in her keeping. When people went to the theater it was to witness the mysteries of the Christian religion. When they traveled, it was to go on a pilgrimage to Christ's tomb. From the cradle to the grave, on week-days and Sundays, the Church surrounded human life. Nothing of importance went on outside her borders. Therefore people believed with a devotion and an intensity of faith of which we have no comprehension; and if the Church did much evil in those days, let us also remember that she did much good. In those centuries she brought the noblest races of the new world to maturity. Nor ought the abuses of the Church ever to be mentioned without recognition of the savage and barbarous condition of the society in which she was planted.

The Protestant Churches, however, beginning with but small experience in the great practical art of subduing and subjugating man which the old Church knew so well, and fearful of the corruptions of the past, attempted to cut themselves off from all these things and to establish themselves on dogmas and doctrines. They were all more or less puritanical. They withdrew more and more from the world. They broke with science, art, literature. They created an impossible theory of Scripture, and having struck the manacles of human tradition from their hands they proceeded at once to forge new fetters. Believers regarded themselves as a peculiar people and before long the world regarded them as very peculiar people in which it took but little interest. For awhile the old dogmas, and especially bitter hatred for Rome, united them, and gave them an issue, but as interest in these subsided, the Protestant churches were hard pressed for an issue, and for many years they have been like spirits seeking a body.

In reality what has happened to us is what has happened to other historical religions behind which stands a single great person. As time has passed, the splendor of that personality has been dimmed. His ideals have been forgotten, the gold of his words buried beneath the dust of tradition. And with the obscuring of the person and ideals of the founder, the mighty moral impulse communicated by him to the world has lost itself. A religion so beset has but one chance to re-establish itself, that is, by a return to its founder. If it can find him, and salvation in him, it may yet live. Now in both these respects we are better off than any generation of Christians has been since the Apostolic Age. The greatest discovery of the nineteenth century was the discovery of Jesus Christ. We possess a knowledge of the character and purpose of Jesus which no previous age has enjoyed, and the impression made on us by His amazing image is hardly less than that which it once produced on a certain Saul of Tarsus. It would seem as if all the intervening centuries of growing knowledge, of doubt, of longing for God's face had only increased our desire to see once more the days of the Son of Man. Apparently He possessed and He offered to the world no repellent, difficult dogmas, but He revealed God to man, and man to himself. He united men in the only two points of view in which they can be united — in love and trust of a good God — and in affection to one another. That no one had done before Him; that no one could do after Him, for He had done it. And there is no other way; there is no peace for our souls except the peace of God. No Kingdom of Heaven is possible except the Kingdom of good hearts united by love. In Him Heaven and earth were united in friendship.

When we attempt to ascertain how Jesus expected to realize His sublime dream of the Kingdom of God, we are confronted by this fact: if He gave his heart wholly to God, He gave His life wholly to man. So with the new heaven came a new earth. He did not anticipate that the great ideal could be made actual merely by announcing it. With Immanuel Kant He declared the problem of the universe insoluble to speculative reason, but soluble to practical reason. From morning to night He was surrounded by human beings with human needs, and He shrank from none, not even from the poor prostitute who wished to kiss His feet. Herein is a wonderful thing, a key to the religion of Christ which we have lost. Here was this Being, call Him Son of God or Son of Man as you choose, with His infinite mission to the world and with the haunting sense of impending doom. Here were these few fleeting years which were all He had at his disposal to make the eternal revelation of God, to found His Church, to gather His congregation and to educate His Apostles that they might be able to continue His work. How will He spend them? In lonely retirement from the world, in rapt meditation, in long thought? In looking at His actual life, one would suppose that He had no thought except for the passing day, no care except for the sick, the sinful, the sorrowful, the seeker who claimed His every hour. But this was no accident. It was first the natural, unavoidable expression of the disposition of Jesus Christ, and secondly, such a religion as His could have come into being in no other way. The genius of Christianity is its fidelity to the permanent needs of human nature. Shakespeare, Goethe, Balzac have marvelously exploited human life. Jesus went deeper. Thanks to the peculiar simplicity of His mind, the delicate clairvoyance of His perception and the all-comprehending sympathy of His heart, He has shown us not only what man is, but what under God's fostering care he may become. With more justice than Terence He might have said: "Homo sum; humani nihil a me alienum puto"; and such knowledge as He possessed could have been gained in no other way than by the life He led. We are in a position to testify to the effect His consoling, healing utterances have on diseased and distracted minds on which Christ's words fall like dew from Heaven. The reason of this is that Jesus was ever in association with such persons and had them constantly on His mind.

Those who know Jesus know that there is salvation in Him and no salvation without Him. He is the Being, as even David Strauss affirmed, without Whose presence in the heart true piety is impossible. Now one of the proofs of the divine origin of our religion is its indestructible vitality. No sooner does the world dispose of one of the claims of Jesus Christ than Christ presents a new claim of which hitherto the world had not thought, and the disposal of the several claims of the Lord Jesus constitutes the moral education of humanity. The Christianity the world has outgrown is a Christianity which Christ had outgrown long before, rather it is a garment which never fitted Him. The truths of reason, far from obscuring His truths, only make them shine with new luster because they make us better able to appreciate the truth as it is in Jesus. During the past generation the best thinkers of the world have been coming to a new conclusion in regard to man. The substance of this thought is its recognition of the essential unity of human nature. It does not sacrifice the soul to the body like the older materialism. It does not seek to dissipate this compact and marvelous human frame into a mere idea, like Christian Science, nor to represent it as a garment of the soul as does the so-called New Thought. But it regards body and soul together as essential to the integrity of human nature, and it points out the innumerable correspondences and points of contact between the two. While ignoring no fact of biology, chemistry, physics, or sociology, it passes through them and behind them to the eternal and spiritual in man. It recognizes the truth that for every event in the mind there is an event in the body, that the simplest emotion or thought is accompanied by an expenditure of nervous energy, and that no good or evil can come to man which does not affect the whole man, body, soul, and spirit. In short, it proves in a thousand ways not merely how the body affects the mind, but how the mind reacts on the body.

What interests the Christian in these conceptions is their appropriation of the habitual thought of Christ. We remember that Jesus recognized human nature in its entirety, that in His solicitude for the soul He did not forget the body and that in giving peace to the conscience He also gave health to the whole man. This noble truth has long been allowed to drop from the Church's conception of its mission, but it will not be ignored much longer. Everywhere men and women are seeking for this lost truth and hence, as in the days of the Son of Man, we see the same feverish anxiety, the same willingness to follow almost any false Messiah who promises to restore it to them. Everywhere men and women are feeling and apprehending, however dimly, that the religion taught and practised by the churches is not the whole religion of Christ; hence we see, on one side, a wholesale defection to strange cults and institutions which, with all their aberrations, hold up the promise of immediate help to the whole man, and on the other hand we observe a growing apathy and indifference toward the Church. In short, it is plain to the unprejudiced student of religion that one cause of the Church's present weakness is that the Church has mutilated the Christian religion, retaining with some degree of faith Christ's message to the soul, but rejecting with unbelief His ministry to the body. But, as a student of the New Testament, I affirm that if any portion of the Gospel is true and authentic, it is that part of the Synoptic Gospels which describes Christ's healing ministry, His commission to His disciples to heal the sick and to cast out devils, and which portrays His general manner of life. These stories are in themselves so natural, so exquisitely probable, so supported by internal and external evidence and by authentic sayings, that if we surrender them we must surrender with them all real knowledge of Jesus, His life and His teachings. But when to-day, with our own eyes, we see so many of these scenes re-enacted, so many of the same diseases cured by means of faith and the authoritative word, such a spirit of scepticism and incredulity becomes doubly and trebly absurd. The writer ventures to say that within five years contemporary evidence will be offered which will change the attitude of the educated world on the subject of Christ's acts of healing. St. John, or the author of the Fourth Gospel, habitually called these healing wonders "signs" (semeia), that is to say, proofs of a living faith and of a present spiritual power, and it is precisely in this light that we regard them. We do not consider restoration to health as in itself the end and aim of religion, but we do affirm that the face of the Lord is ever set in the direction of the health and happiness of His children, that God does not take pleasure in sickness and suffering, but has means to remove our anguish, that faith and trust in God bring peace to the heart, that the moral life powerfully affects the physical life, and that if these blessings are really contained in our religion it is a pity that we should not enjoy them.

Perhaps a greater evil than that to which allusion has been made is the weakening and conventionalizing of all our religious conceptions. For this the Church is not particularly to blame. It is the fate of all noble ideas to lose their nobility and to be shorn of their glory when they are generally accepted by common minds. Yet how many conscientious and faithful ministers are doing their work to-day with a sense of depression and of failure because their people will not accept at their hands the best and highest they have to give? How many able and religious young men are deterred from entering the ministry because they perceive that they can serve God better and find freer employment of their higher faculties in some other profession? Many persons like to go to church and they are glad to cultivate pleasant social relations with their clergymen, but the idea that there is any power in the Church to save them, or in the minister as the representative of Christ, does not occur to them. If they are ill, they send for their physician, if they desire advice on important matters, they consult their lawyer; but the clergyman is as a rule excluded from the serious and great events of life which require special knowledge, higher wisdom or peculiar ability to help, and this through no discourtesy, but through a tacit assumption that there is no help in him. He has even been banished very largely from the sick-room which used to be his peculiar domain, because he is associated in the minds of the sick with the thought of death, not of life. "So 'a cried out *God, God, God,* three or four times. Now I to comfort him bid him 'a should not think of God; I hoped there was no need to trouble himself with any such thoughts yet." The chief satisfaction we have found in the work which we are attempting to describe is that it has indefinitely increased our usefulness. Instead of sustaining merely conventional relations with people, our relations have been sacred and delightful. For we have been called upon to help and permitted to help in the real and serious business of life. We have passed through the deep waters with hundreds upon hundreds of men and women. We have stood between them and temptation, between them and despair, between them and death. We have had the supreme satisfaction of using constantly our highest faculties and of exerting our utmost power in behalf of our people in their hour of need. The response to our invitation has been overwhelming, altogether beyond our expectation or merit. The mere knowledge that disinterested clergymen and physicians are willing to be consulted in regard to the conduct of life and as to life as a whole has brought persons to us in such numbers that although our staff numbers eight men, we are unable to see one person in four who wishes to come to us, even for a single conversation. If there is so great a demand for spiritual guidance and moral help, it would seem as if there ought to be clergymen at least in every large city who are able and willing to bestow it, that we should not be overwhelmed, and that people ought not to be obliged to travel hundreds of miles to attend the simplest of services and to obtain the aid they might just as well receive at home. To be sure clergymen are busy, but after all, in what can a clergyman occupy his time to greater advantage than in reproducing the life of His Master and in saving not merely souls, but men and women and also children? Ill-informed persons have expressed apprehension that the work we are doing may obscure the purely spiritual ideal of the Gospel, but what has charmed us in it is that it has enabled us to communicate spiritual life and a living faith in God and Christ to hundreds of persons who had remained untouched by religion and whom we could have reached in no other way.

Perhaps I can express what I mean by our conventional attitude toward religion by an old Oriental legend I once read in regard to Alexander the Great. A barbaric king once made Alexander a present of three great dogs of ancient family and of priceless merit. One day Alexander was amusing himself in his park and, wishing to test the mettle of these animals, he set one of them in pursuit of a stag. To the king's great disgust, the noble dog looked at it, yawned, and lay down to sleep again. Alexander, being angry, had him killed. He then tried the second and the third dog which behaved in exactly the same manner and accordingly they, too, were put to death. After a few days the barbarian chieftain came to inquire after the welfare of his favorites and Alexander told him what he had done, and the chieftain, moved to tears, cried out: "Oh! Alexander, you have done a great wrong. You set free a stag and a deer, and they paid no heed, but if you had let loose a lion and a tiger you would have seen what dogs I had given you." The Christian religion is a great social institution. It despises no undertaking, no matter how humble, that is intended to benefit man, but its quarry is the soul, it concerns itself only with great things. Like Lao Tze, the Founder of Christianity might have said: "My religion is to think the unthinkable thought, to speak the ineffable word, to do the impossible deed, to walk the impassable way." His religion is not less than when He delivered it. Spiritual truth cannot die. It is our faith that has failed, our apprehension of the power of our religion that has grown weak. If we should bring our deepest wounds to Christ to be healed, our most inveterate habits to be corrected, our saddest griefs to be consoled and our worst sins to be forgiven, we should soon learn what a religion we have. What the world craves to-day is a salvation that really saves and that begins now. What men desire is a creed that does justice to soul and body. What men are looking for is a faith which lifts them not merely above sin but above temptation. We are tired of renunciation, we are tired of sheltering evil impulses and of resisting them after they have emerged into consciousness, and we desire a heart that is free from evil, a will that is one with God. If we can attain this we shall find in it new life for the

Church and for the world, a practical reconciliation between jarring sects, between real religion and genuine science, peace for the soul and health for the body. To simplify religion is not to destroy it; almost always it is to strengthen it. The question is, can we find this in Christ?

One hundred and eight years ago Friederich Daniel Ernst Schleiermacher addressed his celebrated Discourses on the Christian Religion to the Educated among its Contemners. Without presuming for an instant to compare myself with that illustrious man, I venture to address this appeal to the educated, to the scholarly among the friends of Christ who see and deplore the present condition of His Church. Again and again in the course of the long history of our religion the Church has wandered from the living way, the way her Founder not merely commanded but which He declared Himself to be. She has been encrusted by superstition, seduced by worldly and carnal policy, corrupted by sensuality, withered by rationalism, and at times she has borne few of the lineaments of her heavenly origin. But she has revived and has taken up again her divine mission, and this revival has invariably come in a return to her divine Master. In the person of her incomparable Founder, the Church has a treasure which the world did not give her and which it cannot take away. But within that Personality are contained the germs of ten million moral regenerations and renewed life for the world. From time to time men have arisen like Augustine, Dominic, Francis of Assisi, Wycliffe, Savonarola, Martin Luther, Boehme, Tauler, Fox and his Friends, Wesley, Schleiermacher, Newman,

Keble, Fechner, Harnack, who, as the author of John Inglesant, says, "have shaken the earth to its foundations and have drawn thousands into the ranks of Christ," and they have done so by returning to Jesus, by revealing Him anew to their contemporaries and by interpreting His mighty purposes in terms of modern life. For Christianity, and I believe for the world, there is no other way, for it would be impossible for any man now living to draw the faint imaginary outline of the third religious teacher who should be able to follow Moses and Jesus.

For nearly a generation the cry has been raised, "Back to Jesus." The difficulty is that no one has yet appeared who can show us the way. Yet we may be sure the way to Jesus is a living way, the way He declared Himself to be. By this I mean Christ can be found, Christ can be given again to the world, not by antiquarian study, but only by visibly reproducing His actual life in our midst and by the fulfilment of the purpose He set Himself in the sense in which He undertook it. For this the strength of no single man would suffice. But is there not a sufficient number of friends of Christ now living to attempt this task by united effort? I ask this question of the Christian community with the utmost seriousness. Never perhaps since the first century have the opportunities for such an undertaking been so favorable as they are to-day. We are confronted with these two conditions — a general dissatisfaction with our present religious state and a knowledge and appreciation of the past greatness of our religion such as no previous generation has possessed. For more than a century the necessary preliminary studies have been prosecuted by the greatest scholars of the world. Shall we make no practical use of the splendid material which they have bequeathed to us? Is it likely that the results of the great critical movement, one of the noblest achievements of the human mind, shall serve no other purpose than to satisfy the curiosity of the inquisitive? May we not hope that here as elsewhere, the facts and principles having been discovered, the practical application will follow? In any case, such an attempt to reproduce the character, purposes, and methods of the Divine Redeemer, if it were seriously and honorably made, could be productive only of incalculable good. In saying this I do not of course dream of attempting to restore the temporal conditions of Jesus' life or of reviving a past that is forever passed away. Such an attempt would be childish; the hand of the heavenly clock cannot be turned backward. Since the time of Christ the world has advanced not merely in worldly knowledge and in all the arts of life, but in the sanity of thought which springs from a rational interpretation of the phenomena of the universe. All these things we thankfully retain. There is, however, in Christ something which we have lost and for which all our worldly knowledge is no compensation, an eternal truth which is as applicable to this age as to any other, a knowledge of God, a life in God for which we thirst and hunger, a single-hearted desire to serve God and man with the necessary strength to do it, the simplicity of a life which is satisfied with the one thing needful, an abyss of saving love which is able to take away the sin of the world. This timeless element in the Gospel is what we might recover if a sufficient number of fearless and good minds would lend themselves to the task. But whether or not any general movement shall be made to reproduce the life of Jesus, this I know, that no human being can come into His presence, or act in His Spirit, without a blessing. We have shown what can be done in one single direction in our own humble venture. We have proved that this small attempt to follow Him more closely and to obey His command has made life and religion a different thing to ourselves and to others. One such practical demonstration as this is worth a library of argument and discussion. What then might be done if a sufficient number of abler and better men should be willing to consecrate their lives to this purpose, if they would take up the infinite problem of Jesus Christ and show the way?

APPENDIX I

SOME PHYSICAL DISORDERS HAVING MENTAL ORIGIN

"All good things are ours, nor soul helps flesh more than flesh helps soul." — BROWNING.

THE mind is the capital city where the consumers dwell, those law-makers and manufacturers of thought and nervous impulses. The body is the outlying country. If the country parts are well tilled and cared for by the farmers or makers of healthy physical conditions dwelling in this outlying country, the consumers in the capital city are able to secure what they need to satisfy the wear and tear incident to mental effort or nervous stress of whatever sort. A sound body waits on a sound mind, and the material for repair of the nervous system is furnished by the digestive tract. The converse of this statement has long been known to be almost equally true. The mind, acting through the sympathetic and vaso-motor nerves, affects the secretions of the internal organs, especially of the stomach and bowels, it acts on the kidneys and the heart, on respiration and perspiration, and influences the amount of blood flowing through the arteries. Digestion may be retarded or hastened by the condition of the mind; and the assimilation of food and the elimination of waste products may be disturbed, to the extent, that if a state of unrest or unhappiness obtains, such as may be occasioned by worry, sorrow, anger, or depression, from whatever cause, a loss of balance between the mind and the body follows, even though the body is sound. All this results in unnatural and unhealthy conditions for both. In a word, an unhealthy mind reacts deleteriously upon an otherwise healthy body.

It has been the practice to regard the body as the part mainly at fault in chronic disorders, with the exception of a few classified diseases, and treatment for relief has been instituted usually from the standpoints of the physical. A great many people are unhealthy nevertheless because of their disturbed attitude mentally toward life and living. That these mental states have existed right along no one questions, but that they have not been fully appreciated, and treated with intelligence by those presumably qualified to do that work, is also equally true. The majority of all ailments are doubtless due to physical causes, and many to inheritance; but there have been an ever-increasing number of people whom physical measures have failed to relieve or have only partially restored. The physical and mental balance both must be cultivated and maintained if life is to go on well, and end happily. The head as well as the body parts must be considered, in cases of illness, for the chances are that both need patching up and not one end at a time. The physical and organic ailments of the body have been and are still the province of the physician and surgeon, and these ailments arise from physical causes, we will assume, for the greater part. Spiritual and ideal conditions have been and are still within the province of the clergy, broadly speaking. But we have a mental-habit field, below the spiritual and above the physical, —

an open field for both clergy and physicians. The mental attitude of people toward life and living is quite as susceptible of treatment, and is quite as important a subject, as the care of the body. How to deal successfully with this mental-habit field, is a question that is being threshed out industriously at the present time.

Young people are generally healthy, if born of healthy stock; and youth is optimistic. The bodily machine being new, it stands the wear and tear it is put to, as well as the abuse; and we hear little complaint from beginners who have but recently entered the world's arena; — at least for a term of years, unless circumstances have been such that the young life has had to shoulder the burdens of older years from the start and has been undone mentally and physically in consequence.

Although this statement is true in the main, we sometimes see the worry habit in children, developed in connection with their lessons at school, or other tasks. Every child is an individual, and what one child can do in a given time should not be made the measure of ability for another child. Mental aptitude and physical endurance differ as much in children as in grown people. A highly organized child with over-sensitive nerve centers will soon acquire the habit of worry, if urged or criticised in regard to work. A child should be led to do as well as he is able in a given time, but he should never be nagged or allowed to worry because he works with less aptitude than another. The thing to measure is the effort on a child's part, and not the result attained.

Nervousness is essentially a mental state. But all nervousness has a cause that possibly may be understood and controlled. The temperament of children can be successfully influenced by training and example. A child abnormally sensitive, who is regarded as excitable or nervous, can be brought to exercise mental control, but it takes time and patience to do it, — to educate any mind into control of abnormally sensitive nerve cells, — not much longer, however, than it does to perfect any other attitude or mental attainment that is worthy of cultivation. The temperament of a nervous child becomes amiable and lovable if the child is handled rightly; and grown to manhood, this child is loved quite as much for his temperament as for his intellectual attainments. In fact, temperament in its influence upon people, as an element of success, is worth quite as much as a merely well-trained brain. More than one man in active life has come to realize that it is his defect in temperament and not his lack of ability or education that costs him the success of his life.

A child should be made especially happy at meal-times, because happy nervous impulses influence digestion favorably. This is accomplished by a good story, if it starts a laugh which ends in a blush or a nerve thrill that tingles in the toes. Laughter sets the digestive juices flowing as its effect upon the appetite goes to show, while the parent's look that blanches a child's cheeks stunts both his moral and physical growth. The laugh that causes a blush of pleasure has in it constructive physical and constructive nervous force. The growing nerve centers in a child should be fed on emotions that tone up and not upon those that depress, and upon influences that stimulate its entire being. It is a good plan to begin the day with a laugh started at the breakfast table. Nutrition, as well as tonic nervous impulses, — both constructive forces, — are carried in greater volume to every cell in the body under happy or stimulating atmospheres, and the whole system rings with applause as a result, just as a theatre is heard to ring, when a vast audience, raised to the point of enthusiasm over something well and beautifully done, clap their hands in approval.

A lad twelve years of age, a sensitive boy, because of his delicate inherited organization, was found to lie awake after he was put to bed. No cause could be found for this. He was given only a light supper and was sent to bed early, as all growing children should be. His mind evidently worked far into the first half of the night. One day his uncle, a physician, said to him, "When the sun goes down the day is done, and the night is yours in which to sleep. Don't carry to bed with you the thought of anything you may not have said or done well during the day. You are to get up every morning and make a fresh start. I love you all the more because you are imperfect. If you were perfect in the beginning you would have nothing to work for except money, and that does not always make happiness, and it is happiness, lad, you are after, — the distinctive qualities and mental poise that make happiness for you *now*, and especially as you grow older. Fire your sunset gun as the government does, when the day is done, and haul your flag. Next morning set it again. Go to bed to sleep." Some time afterwards, this boy said to his aunt, in an appreciative way: "Tante May, Tante May, since uncle said the day was over when the sun set, I can sleep like anything." This lad had evidently been reviewing the result of each day's work, and perhaps worrying over some part of what he had said or done or failed to do. When told that the day ended with the going down of the sun, and that each succeeding day he was to begin anew, and that he was loved all the more because of his present imperfections, which he would some day conquer, he quietly rested his head upon the pillow and fell asleep.

This life is man's school, — conditions, his tools. In his aim after perfectness he often fails from shortness of vision, from unripeness, and from weakness, which can only become strength by the exercise of just such faculties as are now his modes of expression. If those who "miss the mark," which is the most intelligent understanding of "sin" (another name for imperfection), would so construe it, and count instances of missing the mark as "target practice" which will result finally in a perfect aim, all that demoralization resultant upon an accusing conscience would disappear.

A mother having four children wore a heavy black dress and veil because of the loss of one of the children. She forgot that the living children were equally dear to her. One day her children begged her to wear bright colors, saying her "clothes hurt them," but she did not realize how much they meant by what they said, until on a later day one of them took a pink bow from a doll's dress, a poor faded affair, and pinned it quietly to her waist. Those who wear black because of the loss of dear ones forget the effect the black may have on others living, who are equally dear. Grief is only intensified by this custom, and the attention of thousands is drawn in this way to a person whose face and manner can but act depressingly upon all. A crape veil often works serious mischief to both the spirit and the body. People have been known to grow faint at the sight of the thing. "Why should we wear black for the guests of God"? The wearing of mourning may be a mark of respect or love for those who have departed, but it serves also to intensify grief, and draws the attention of others to our sorrow, to no good end; while it may cause suffering to many. It would certainly help the happiness of the world if this fashion of wearing black could be put aside. If it is worn for self-protection, as some assert, a more hopeful color might be selected and that would do quite as well, perhaps. The change that a funeral represents should be looked upon as the end of a beautiful life, and the beginning of another life even more beautiful. Since every one has to move on, wouldn't it be better, if we cannot rejoice, because of personal loss, to avoid intensifying, at least, a result that cannot be helped. Children are very susceptible to external impressions or influences. It is possible for habits of introspection, or worry, or fault-finding even, to be acquired in youth, by some children at least, if left to their own way of thinking, or because of what they see or hear their elders say or do. If the mother's voice is low-pitched the child's will become so. If the father is nervous and excitable and goes storming about the house because of disturbing trifles, his children are likely to become something more than disturbing trifles in time, and have their father to thank for it. Children are great imitators, as some of us know to our sorrow or amusement as the case may be. A child with a stick in her hand stood before her sawdust doll. She was heard to say, "If you don't mind you will get a damn-darn beating." I wonder which one of her parents this child was quoting or imitating.

Some of the causes for mental unrest and wretchedness among maturer minds are apparent to the average observer. Altogether too rapidly people are losing sight of their capacity to enjoy little things. As the writer has said, "The south side of a red apple gave pleasure in childhood, now it takes the echoes of a Krupp gun to create an impression, such is the spirit of unrest and sensationalism." As children we play with toys, — the tin horse, the tin cart, the tin soldier, and the paper tent. As "grown-ups" we play with a real horse, a real cart, and live in a real house. Pray tell us why this change in the *size* of the toys should make so many of us miserable. This world was given us to work in and play in, it is a pretty place, but thousands of people under existing conditions seem to make a nightmare out of ordinary life and living. People find fault with the weather and make themselves miserable by doing so. Of what use is such fault-finding? Why not learn to like a rainy day? We have them. The flower by the roadside blooms a thing of beauty; perhaps it has just as hard a time as any of us getting along there in the dust and dirt where the soil is poor, the rocks are bare, and moisture scant. The poor horse gets only his board for his toil, and yet he never complains. Too many people are afraid they are going to be measured by the size of the roof they are under. The plane of life upon which people find themselves should be dignified by their attitude toward it. Imitation instead of emulation is the habit of too many people. The luxuries of life have become the necessities of life. False pride and vanity are too often in evidence while real pride seldom shows its head. With six days in the week devoted to competition and a little more than an hour in the one day that is left devoted to spirituality, delivered at arm's length, usually, is it any wonder that many lose sight of the great purpose for which life is worked out and lived through.

Under the stress of modern competition one-half of mankind overpowers the other half, and then has them to take care of as invalids. Women compete with men under the laws made for men, although women are rated but half as strong, physically, as men. Laborers will some day be classified, and every life will be preserved for whatever there is in it; every one, no matter what his limitations, can do something useful.

When men worked in the fields and women in the homes there was mutual dependence, and life went on more simply and steadily than it does now. The frugal, abstemious ways of living that obtained in earlier days were certainly more natural than is now the case, and the minds of the people were generally more at ease. Wealth was more evenly distributed then. With potatoes in the cellar and corn in the barn there was no such vital question as to where the next meal was coming from. A day's indisposition was not necessarily a nightmare. People are crowding into the cities, where there is rent to pay and where food costs money, instead of the labor necessary to plant it and get it out of the ground. If more beginners had the experience that world winnowing affords, they would stay on the land. Wages have advanced, but the cost of living has advanced, and existence, for those who have no resources except what their daily toil affords them, is much more exacting than it has ever been before. The man who happens to have a business mind, or has been trained in a business way, has by far the best chance at the "loaves and fishes" as the world of money is distributed to-day.

Aside from this question of daily necessity among the weak, and the working people generally, which is responsible for much of the unhappiness experienced, a lack of mental poise exists, quite as serious, though not as frequently met with, among the well-to-do and the rich.

It is not stress of life then, or actual want, that causes all the mental misery seen and felt, and so some of it must be accounted for on other grounds. The poor man's wolf is an ugly customer, but we see poor men at every turn in the road who are not afraid to face that customer. Perhaps, after all, lives lived through have much in common, whether they be lives of the rich or of the poor. There may be the same amount of character, or lack of it, to contend with, the same weariness attending endless festivities, that might be expected to follow years of toil, the same amount of care or sorrow, and finally the same amount of pain. Who knows? Or the causes may lie deeper still, for happiness must come from within. We get back what we give out. Browning says, "Man is not yet; he is becoming." In the evolution of the world, the work is done both by those who are struggling at the bottom of all creation, and by those who fall on the firing-line, — who are pushed on from behind. Man is on the up-trend all along the line the world over.

Much of the old orthodox religions no longer satisfies the modern mind or supplies the mental needs of the present. There are rare preachers whose sermons are messages of uplift; whose statements are hopeful and helpful spiritually and through them the perplexing and rough places in daily life are smoothed and blessed. Scaring a man to death, as the ministers used to do forty years ago, doesn't work to-day. The writer distinctly remembers the effect Thursday evening prayer-meeting had on him. It resulted in a hole, big enough to get into, back of his father's barn. When the Angel Gabriel blew that trumpet of "hisen," he and his brother knew where they could be found.

The depression concerning "sin," depression amounting often to anguish, calls for treatment; either through enlightened views concerning the moral government of God, or through psycho-therapeutical treatment, that will displace the hobgoblins of a crude theology, — a theology which forgot to include the Fatherhood of God and His absolutely benevolent plan concerning the rise (not fall) of man. The church conducted as an ethical culture society cannot altogether fulfil its mission. The church must be brought to the people through the power which it demonstrates, and this will also bring the people to the church.

Certain mental habits are among the mental causes for physical disturbance, in maturer minds especially. Worry stands first, and then follow, fear, anger, oversensitiveness, introspection, retrospection, looking forward (fear of the future), irritability, pessimism, depression, melancholia, hysteria, epilepsy, and many others depending upon the individual, and the circumstances that promote these disorders. These harpies of the mind play havoc with the mental machine, they interfere with rational thinking, and in extreme cases have been known to jar and fret the brain cells until they become worn out with their own friction. This is what is meant by the expression "Worried to death." Nerve cells are over-sensitive or stable in proportion to the size of their nucleus or center. The excitability or inhibition of a nerve depends upon the power it has of responding to a stimulus or withstanding a shock. This varies with the individual. Two boys are born of the same father and mother. They go through a railroad accident; one comes out whole, the other comes out nervously unstable, because of mental shock. His nerve centers, the storehouses of energy, spill their force on the slightest provocation, instead of discharging it only as needed and in the amount required, as when one moves an arm. Both boys saw the same sights, and neither one was physically hurt. Both have the same "ingrediences" in their make-up; they are two-thirds of what has been and are one-third of what is, but no one can tell just how the "cake" is coming out in the baking. The vaso-motor spasm due to "shock" produced but little change in one of them, while for the other, the unstable condition resulting, is prolonged, and if not strengthened by mental-moral training, may prove constant. Physical courage, or a stable nervous system, is a great invigorator, while timidity tends to destroy the energy of the nervous sytem. Shocks may be either mental or physical. Both mental and physical shock produce the same results which differ only in degree and duration. A blow on the head produces a vaso-motor spasm, or a contraction of the nerves that regulate the flow of blood through the arteries. This is how the physiologists explain shock. If the blow is severe enough, we get concussion of the brain or even contusion of the brain, and unconsciousness. Mental shocks produce vaso-motor spasm in the same way, the degree and duration depending upon the cause. Fear and worry acting through the vaso-motor nerves affect the caliber of the blood-vessels. Under fear, the person afflicted turns pale, as those nerves contract, and if the depressing influence persists, as for example a sense of guilt, the irritated nerves continue to hold their grip. And that grip may never let go until the shock that produced it is released. Under the stimulation of hope and expectation or praise, the vaso-motor nerves relax, the color returns, and the blood and lymph flow freely. The same result follows play, laughter, music, or the sight of color such as the sunset affords, when the sun, with a blush of pleasure, bids us "good night," because of what he has seen the good people of the world accomplish, while the earth is turning around once. Worry and fear, acting through the sympathetic nervous system, affect the secretions of the mouth, stomach, liver, pancreas, and intestines. So the digestive secretions are diminished, the appetite fails, and the stomach nerves, because of the indigestion induced, become irritated. A sore feeling stomach results with nausea, or vomiting even may cap the climax. The appetite will frequently improve if meals are eaten under congenial conditions, when every one is having a good time. Worry and fear are banished for that hour because of our enjoyment and the sight of generous hospitality. Bilious attacks, which evidence irritation of the stomach mucosa, may follow mental disturbances, or it may be that the secretion of bile becomes affected. Constipation, either spastic, — due to spasm of the intestines, — or due to diminished intestinal secretion, is often a concomitant of mental disorder. A faulty assimilation of food and a deficient elimination of waste products are factors in ill health. Chronic rheumatism, a result of these two disturbances in part, at least, is nothing more or less than an exhibition of waste material floating in the blood current; something that dieting and a decent frame of mind will cure. By dieting I do not mean starvation, but thorough munching and the adaptation of food to fit the physical condition and occupation of the patient. If the normal capillaries (smallest blood-vessels above one-fiftieth of an inch in diameter under normal mental and physical conditions) cannot pass along morbid material floating in the blood current, they certainly cannot do so when the vaso-motor nerves, under negative mental influences, contract the blood-vessels. Things get into our bodies in but two ways, either through our minds or our mouths. There are but five ways by which they get out, — by the bowels, kidneys, breath, sweat, or through mental processes that liberate. The pessimist is generally sallow-skinned and constipated. He is under constant negative mental influences, because he allows himself to imagine that nothing in this world is quite as it should be. He probably thinks everything is going to the devil, but happily for the rest of us there are some who doubt this.

> "The difference betwixt the optimist
> And pessimist is droll,
> The optimist sees the doughnut
> The pessimist the hole."

Cold, damp hands and feet are often due to mental depression, which causes a relaxation of the vaso-motor nerves. Anger frequently brings on headaches. Anger floods the brain with blood, and if the arteries are brittle, as they often are in old age, — for a man is just as old as his arteries are old, — the rise in the arterial tension may result in rupture of the vessel, when apoplexy follows, due to hemorrhage. Attacks of anger hasten the deterioration of the arteries. Anger brings on attacks of hysteria and epilepsy. In this way anger, discharging the pent-up nervous force, has been known to cause death. Outbreaks of anger are comparable to a severe thunderstorm, with destructive, blinding flashes of lightning. The shock resulting from an attack of anger may last two or three weeks.

There is a cyclical recurrence in many forms of mental disturbance, showing that the nervous system is periodically aroused by some unseen cause. The exciting cause of a nerve storm may be either physical or mental. The "blues," so-called, are the outcome of periodical poisoning, due to indigestion probably, and the indigestion may have sprung from over-excitement, or other morbid mental condition, such, for instance, as worrying over fancied sins. Epilepsy in some cases can be controlled by mental training, especially when mental disturbances precede the attacks. Hysteria is essentially a mental state, and in its effect upon the body, acting through the sympathetic nervous system, has been known to produce a condition closely simulating tuberculosis. A woman, a teacher by profession, had been vomiting almost daily for a year. She had lost twenty pounds in weight, and she coughed throughout much of each night. She had a daily rise in temperature, but *no* increase in the pulse rate. She resigned her position and returned home to enter a hospital. The vomiting had begun when she was given an order by her superior officer with which she did not wish to comply. The case was diagnosticated as one of chronic hysteria. Hysterical persons see the world through irrational lenses — their point of view is wrong. The best and most effectual treatment is by direct suggestion. After receiving some wholesome advice, that was neither coddling nor criticising, this woman regained her health and strength, and has worked regularly.

During the recent financial crisis a prominent financier lost twenty pounds in weight, although eating regularly but with perhaps less zest than formerly. He was examined by his physician and pronounced physically sound. The week following this examination he gained three pounds in weight and has since improved rapidly. His was an instance of loss of weight due to depression, resulting from anxiety connected with money matters. The depression was maintained by solicitude because of his rapid loss in weight without assignable physical cause. When told by his physician that he was sound, his depression was relieved, and his digestion improved. The vasomotor spasm, due to mental shock, no longer checked the flow of his gastric secretions, or blood current. His case illustrates the effect of negative auto-suggestion, followed by the beneficial effect of a direct statement, optimistic in character. But auto-suggestion works affirmatively as well as negatively. A well-known American general, whose arm had been shot away below the shoulder years ago, appealed to his physician for relief from nervous irritation and discomfort in the stump of the amputated limb. It had become irritated by the jostling of people at receptions. The general was known to believe in God. He was told that whenever any one hit his arm, he was to say to himself, and mean it in good faith, — "God bless you." His adviser was convinced that the stimulating effect of praise passing over the nerves to the point of irritation would have a soothing, healing influence upon the nerve tissues. The general was told to direct his thoughts toward the injured member whenever he made his affirmation. He did so, and in less than four months' time he is reported to have said he wished some one would knock against that arm, he wanted to bless him.

A woman afflicted with constipation consulted her physician. She was one of the over-sensitive kind. Her father desired her to attend church with him but she did not enjoy doing so. Every Sunday morning the church question was an issue. She always became nauseated at these times. Later, when advised by her physician to attend the church of her choice, and to keep out of the room where her father was accustomed to sit, whenever the "injured innocence" atmosphere he created there by his mental attitude depressed her, she promptly recovered from her constipation. This was a case of spastic constipation (?) brought on by the young woman's mental state under certain circumstances. While still afflicted she had been treated for a year by a physician who did not understand the cause of her trouble. His failure was not to his discredit, for she made no statement to him in regard to her home life. Another young woman, a doctor's daughter in good health, and physically well except for constipation, was referred to a specialist in stomach and intestinal disorders. He treated her without success. She did not tell him that she had lost her lover. Finally she espoused the idea of harmony as taught by the church, when promptly she recovered from her constipation. Mental disturbance had been the cause of it. We must not infer from these citations that constipation can be cured ordinarily by mental treatment alone, but it is fair to conclude that the mind as well as the body must be considered when one is dealing with chronic disorders. Incompatibility of persons is nothing but inharmony. A person who has mental poise can soon strike the note that harmonizes with the note of another person, and it does not matter whether or not the effort is a conscious one on the part of both. When both parties are aware of a difference between them, and are willing to make the effort to get in tune, they can quickly succeed. A party of five traveling together were found to have inharmonious relations. It was agreed they should not speak of anything that disturbed them at the time it happened, but wait for twenty-four hours. At first they all covered sheets of paper filing exceptions and making notes. Inside of five days they were all laughing at each other, the exceptions were never argued, and from that time on they got along famously.

Worry belongs to the mental-habit field. It is neither

a physical condition to be treated with drugs, nor one to be relieved by spiritual teachings, unless the person afflicted can overcome the habit by faith and prayer. Worry is a form of nervousness, and nervousness is a mental state. A person may have attained the spiritual level and yet be a worrier to the extent that renders life miserable, not alone for the person afflicted but for all intimately associated with him.

A railroad conductor consulted a physician. He had been discharged from the railroad on account of nervousness. On the physician's examination he was found to be physically sound. When asked what he was "fussing" over, he replied, — "I suppose I have been worrying for fear some one getting on or off my train would get hurt." When asked if any one ever had been injured in this way, in connection with any train he had charge of, he replied in the negative. He was told that his nervousness was due to worry, that worry was a mental condition and not a physical state, and that there were no drugs for nervousness of this kind. He was told he must learn to dismiss worry from his mind, as he would stop any other habit, mental or physical, that detracted from his usefulness or happiness. He was given one hundred yellow-eyed beans, and was told to put one, every morning, in a little box in the corner of his bed-room, and then say, "Worry is in the bean and the bean is in the box." He was not to forget where he left the worry, in the bean, any more than he would be expected to forget where he left his hat. He was to walk away with the feeling that the worry was not in his head, but out of it. Before the hundred beans were exhausted he was free from his nervousness or worry and had been restored to his place on the road. Another good way to eliminate these habits from the mind is to have a regular place where they can be left. An old chair bottom in the corner of the room will serve the purpose. The person afflicted is to go to that place and deliberately deposit his worries there as he would boxes or bundles. This practice persisted in becomes a useful resource. The funny side to the procedure helps solve the trouble.

It may not be necessary to cultivate a substitute-habit in the strong man, for dismissal will suffice. In others, it is only by patient practice that the mind can be freed from worry; and the attempt must be kept up until the brain recognizes and yields to the newer impulse. One does not learn to play the piano by sitting down before it once. We go down, to be sure, before new shocks, and for a limited time we are more or less influenced by them, but if our powers of resistance have been strengthened by training, we promptly rally, when the better impulses and better feelings hold sway. It is possible to train the mind to a point at which one's inside nature simply refuses to get "on edge," or if it does, like a stove cover it can be turned down, no matter what the provocation. The mind can be discharged from the consideration of any vexatious subject, and the attention given to the enjoyment of any other. Mind cure is simply the acquiring of control over impulses, emotions, or habits that demoralize. It substitutes other habits, if necessary. The person gains mental poise, and leans towards optimism. The mind liberates the nervous mechanism and vital fluids of the body so that all the functions, both physical and mental, are performed normally. Whether the condition recognized as a chronic disorder or disease is due to mental or physical causes, one cannot always easily determine. If the person suffering is willing to cultivate one or two new habits for the old ones he suspects, although he may not be able to see that they are the cause of his trouble, he will often be surprised at the outcome. He may find that this is all that is required to cure him of the chronic ailment from which he has been seeking relief by the usual methods, in vain. It is useless to expect permanent results from one habit taken up with, if the old bad habit is still indulged. The first essential of cure in cases of bad mental habits is a willing mind.

The best time for training the mind to control itself is in childhood, but few of the middle-aged people of to-day were fortunate enough to have had mental discipline of this sort; most of us were not trained at all, but were left to battle with our habits, or with the "old adversary" as Deacon White used to say. He is reported to have taken a fall out of this old wrestler more than once when out in the pasture with his oxen, hauling wood. Confronting a bad habit often intensifies it. It is better perhaps to turn away and leave the adversary behind, in spite of Deacon White's experience. A good way to banish habits that detract from happiness is to discuss with our neighbors and friends the questions of conquering them, and the best way to do it. By such discussion one strengthens his own powers of resistance and at the same time helps his friend. Even if one does not believe in all his friend may say, or in all one hears, it pays to preach and listen, if the preaching points to something better than the thing one is doing. They who keep themselves occupied with wholesome mental and physical activities keep their spirits steady, — only empty vessels rattle.

Many people live to mature life without any earnest spiritual effort, or any expectation of developing the spirit. They lay claim to belief in eternal life, and look for the gradual development of the divine spark in themselves, but they so crowd their daily lives with superficialities that they have little time or room for the consideration of spiritual truths. They depend entirely for happiness upon what they can get out of material things, and upon the purchasing power of money. The man who makes material things the end of life, instead of a means to an end, makes a miss of it.

Every man is the gardener of his own life. In the first years youth untrained rushes on and on, leaving half his fields untilled. These waste fields grow up to weeds, — worry, fear, anger, over-sensitiveness, hysteria, introspection, depression. Later, if he is wise, he turns back and ploughs and plants again, that all life's garden may be seen a thing of beauty, — a completed garden in full bloom when life draws near to its close. Appreciation, responsiveness, good temper, mental poise, optimism, frugality, dignity, faith, — these are the virtues he forgot in the first planting of the garden. When our fields have been reclaimed, the men and women who come to us or care for us, those who pass through our garden, can always gather a buttonhole bouquet, at least, and the memory of the meeting and the passing will always remain delightful, as the memory of some beautiful landscape, viewed in the fall of the year when the trees are full of color.

As we grow older, it becomes us to grow graceful in spirit, and this can be done by bringing our minds to the point at which the inner self must not become irritated. One who learns the art of self-control, or mental poise, remains calm and lovable under all conditions. His presence and his influence are desired by all during his declining years. To grow old with a distressed spirit that creates an atmosphere of unrest in one's life, which is in turn imparted to those about us, is to make a failure of the last years of life.

J. WARREN ACHORN, M.D.

APPENDIX II

AN ARTIST'S EXPERIMENTS IN AUTO-SUGGESTION

"My work, as you know, brings me constantly before the public, and consequently my most essential need is self-possession and self-confidence. These qualities I lacked to such a degree that I was never able to do myself justice. A few days after I began the study of suggestion I had an important duty to perform. About two hours before going on to the platform I made some suggestions to myself according to your instructions, such as that I should feel no fear or nervousness, and that I should be able to throw myself into my work, etc. I then dismissed the matter from my mind. The result was truly remarkable. When the time came I had a sense of ease and power and self-possession such as I had never experienced before, either in public or private, and I held my audience from the beginning to the end. Not only that, but it was a perfect joy to me to be able to do it. I have had several successes since that time, and can now take an entirely different attitude toward my art and my public work. Instead of the helpless nervousness which used to possess me, I have a feeling of confidence and power, so marked that those who know me have commented upon the change without knowing the reason. I have gone steadily on, and I not only hope, but I know that it is within my power to reach the full expression of my talent — a thing which seemed utterly impossible before. I have used auto-suggestion in many other ways and with surprising success. I find that it is quite possible to put out of my mind little annoying vexatious things, which are not worth a thought, but which destroy peace of mind as effectually as large troubles. I can banish the 'blues' as with a magic wand. On one occasion I had a piece of business to transact, requiring the utmost tact and delicacy. It was a matter of vital importance to me. On going to sleep the night before and on awakening in the morning I suggested to myself that when the time came I should know how to say the right thing in the right way. When the eventful hour came my mind was clear and alert, and I seemed to have a deeper insight into the matter. I said just what came into my mind to say, and I could scarcely believe the evidence of my senses when the thing so much desired was accomplished. I could give other instances, but do not wish to weary you. It has made life over for me. It seems truly as if the crooked things are made straight and the rough places plain."

A CLERGYMAN ON AUTO-SUGGESTION

'In writing this letter, I hope, in as simple a way as possible, to give several reasons why I believe in auto-suggestion. These reasons will take the form of illustrations of the good which has been accomplished in my own case. I am a minister. For some time I have been engaged in literary work. Before and during that time I had been troubled with nervousness, sleeplessness, imaginary worries, dismal forebodings. I heard of the work being done in Emmanuel Church, a work which was and is designed precisely for such a case as mine. Yet I did not put much faith in it at first. It seemed too simple. I examined further. I found that it was simple, but also that there are profound pyschological laws which may be put into operation for the healing of mind and of body. The method alone is simple. I came to discover reservoirs of stored-up forces lying in the depths of the subconscious self of which I had never dreamt. I determined to give the new "cure" a trial. My first weakness was a great tendency to worry, to anticipate troubles that never came to pass. All this, of course, reacted upon the nervous system. My nerves became demoralized. I determined to check these miseries. In the morning and evening I "suggested" to myself not negative but positive qualities, *e.g.*, courage, self-confidence, cheerfulness. At first, it all seemed a delusion and a snare; but in two weeks or so things looked brighter, the world took on a more roseate hue and life appeared a different and better thing altogether. To-day, while not wholly delivered from the bondage, I am on the way to complete and permanent conquest. I may add such a thing looked impossible three months ago. Again, to any one who knows what insomnia is, it is scarcely necessary for me to speak. In the morning I arose unrested, at night I went to bed tired and sleepless. Again I "suggested" sleep, a good night's sleep. At first it failed. The fault was mine. I did not treat the method seriously enough. Again I tried more suggestion, say fifteen minutes. That night, the third or fourth, I slept the sleep of the just for five hours. I kept the "suggestion" up until to-day I sleep from six to six hours and a half.

Finally, nervousness in the pulpit troubled me a great deal. I wanted to get rid of it. Well, on the Wednesday or Thursday previous to the Sunday on which I was to preach I began to "suggest" to myself "self-confidence," "courage," "faith." If I had these I knew I had won half the battle. That first Sunday it worked like magic. I felt like a new man. I was a new man. I had more power, more energy, consequent upon more courage and self-confidence. I was more at my ease, which meant that the people were more at theirs. A message I tried to give was no longer so formless, not quite so dead.

This letter, I fear, is becoming long. Yet I cannot close without saying that in other directions I have been wonderfully helped. Ministers, like other persons, have a temper. I think I was especially human in that respect. That, at least, is a frank confession. Perhaps I can afford now to be frank when I say that the "old man" is being put off continually and the "new man" of deeper faith, of more buoyant hope, of larger sympathies, is being put on day by day.

I find auto-suggestion is also good in my studies. If I wish for more concentration in my thinking, more ease in grasping ideas, more fluency in writing, with the will comes the strength or capacity for execution. At first, the results may seem, like the blind man, who, when his sight was restored, saw men as trees walking. Things are blurred — distorted — then they become clearer, until, at last, they stand out in distinctest outline. At the beginning we do not seem to get results. The bad temper, or worry, or nervousness seem to be still master. It may be so: but another trial, and still another, and the first victory is won.

After that it becomes easier. At the moment of worry or nervousness it seems as if the suggestions I made during the day came back to me like an old friend to remind me of my good resolutions, and I am certain they will, after a time, become a second nature.'

INDEX OF AUTHORS

	PAGE
Abgarus	362
Achorn, Dr. J. W.	163, 411
Alexander the Great	383
Ambrose, Archbishop	316
Aristotle	269
Arnold, Matthew	350
Assisi, St. Francis of	95, 299, 367, 385
Athanasius	299
Augustine, St.	316, 367, 385
Bacon	275
Balzac	25, 29, 377
Barker, Dr. L. F.	5, 264
Beard, G. M.	133, 170, 177, 278
Bechterew, W.	228
Bengel, J. A.	367
Bernheim, H.	40, 41, 71, 78, 229
Bleuler, E.	81
Boehme	385
Booth, Charles	327
Bousset	344
Brahman	94
Braid, J.	71, 222
Bramwell, J. Milne	33, 34, 40, 70, 71, 75, 76, 78, 82, 87, 89, 222, 287
Bridgman, Laura	196
Büchner, P.	136
Bunyan	282
Bushnell, Horace	367

	PAGE
Cadmus, J.	264
Calkins, Miss	83
Catherine of Siena	95
Celsus	10, 296
Charcot	41, 70, 77, 91, 113, 222, 229, 356, 360
Claparède, E.	198
Coleridge, M. E.	270
Coleridge	22, 86, 319
Conybeare, F. C.	359
Coriat, Dr. I. H.	15, 213, 217, 243, 263
Crapsey, Rev. A. S.	26
Cuvier	193
Cyprian	299
Darwin	9, 266
Dawson, W. J.	302
de Lagrave, Dr. C.	100
Delbœuf	88, 91
Dominic	385
Doutrebente, Dr. G.	129
Dubois, P.	40, 56, 60, 98, 264
Du Bose	367
Durkheim	323, 326
Eddy, Mrs. M. B.	10
Edwards, Jonathan	308
Emerson, R. W.	103
Erskine of Linlathen	313, 367
Esquirol	131
Eulenberg	321
Eusebius	362, 363

INDEX OF AUTHORS

	PAGE
Falconi	318
Fechner, Theodor	11, 14, 151, 386
Feuchtersleben	293
Fiske, John	21
Flournoy, T.	211
Forel, A.	25, 40, 41, 71, 76, 81, 84, 222, 242, 228, 229
Fox, George	299, 385
Franklin	220
Freud, S.	206, 281
Galvani	220
Gibbon	297
Gilbert, Dr. J. A.	241
Gilles de la Tourette, G.	222
Goethe	25, 377
Grant, E.	349
Gull, Sir William	20
Gurnhill	331
Hall, G. Stanley	269, 271, 321, 323
Hansson, Ola	29
Harnack, A.	296, 297, 339, 365, 386
Hart, Ernest	71, 77
Harvey, W.	191
Heidenhain, M.	77, 82
Hermann	314
Herzog, F.	359
Hirsch	80
Hodge	198
Hudson, T. J.	28
Hume	339
Huxley	179, 308
Hyslop	211
Irenæus	298

	PAGE
Irving	367
James, Prof.	14, 104, 213, 222, 262, 280, 309
Janet	15, 41, 42, 203, 207, 210, 234, 281, 282, 287
Jastrow, J., Prof.	199
Johnson, Dr. Samuel	102, 273
Jowett	303
Juvenal	10, 273
Kant	152, 377
Keble	386
Keim, Theodor	349
Keller, Helen	196
Kingsley, Charles	173
Kircher, Father	219
Kraepelin, E.	242
Krafft-Ebing, R.	222, 237, 246
Kurz, E.	242
Lange, C.	62
Lao-Tze	384
Lateau, Louise	95
Lecky	276, 304
Lefevre, A.	97
Leibner	82
Liébeault	41, 105, 222
Lloyd	41, 71
Lodge, Sir Oliver	305
Luke, St.	365, 366
Luther	299, 310, 367, 385
Mantegazza	169
Marlowe	25
Martyr, Justin	298
Maudsley, H.	58, 136, 150
Maurice, F. D.	294
Maury	82

INDEX OF AUTHORS

McGiffert, A. C. 364
Melanchthon 310
Mesmer................... 221
Metaphysical School........ 134
Mill, John Stuart 11
Mitchell, S. Weir 49, 50
   75, 111, 112, 159, 161, 175, 282
Möbius, P. J. 47, 109,
   111, 121, 127, 128, 129, 135,
   143, 151, 160, 163
Mohammed,............... 308
Moll, A..... 41, 71, 83, 222
Monica, St. 316
Moreau 126
Morel 128
Morselli 323, 324, 331
Mosso 267, 271
Mumford, Dr. J. G. 80
Myers, Fred 87, 89, 90
   91, 92, 95, 112, 113

Nancy 41
Nevins................... 359
Newman, J. H. 385
Niebuhr 131

Osler, Prof. 276, 342
Origen............... 299, 367

Pagniez, P................. 264
Papias 349
Pascal.................... 278
Patrick, Prof. G. T. W. 241
Paul, St. 365, 367
Paulsen, F................. 8
Philip of Hesse 310
Pierce, Prof............... 21
Powell, Rev. Lyman 368
Pratt, Dr. Jos. H............ 1

Preyer, W................. 82
Prince, Dr. Morton 25,
   199, 200, 203, 207, 217
   222, 263
Proal, M.................. 321
Putnam, Dr. James J. 2

Quadratus 363
Quatrefrages 131

Renan 8, 10
Reymond, Emil Dubois 61
Richard................... 311
Richardson, Sir. B. W...... 346
Richet 360
Roosevelt, President........ 155
Rosebery, Lord 333
Royce, Prof............... 290

Saleeby, Dr. 277, 280, 328
Savonarola 385
Schleiermacher, F. D. E. ... 385
Schmidkunz, Hans 31
Schmiedel 343
Schrenck-Notzing 237
Schofield, A. T..... 18, 19
   50, 58, 346
Schönberg................. 83
Schopenhauer 36, 37,
   92, 131, 161
Seckendorf................ 311
Shakespeare 29, 377
Shelley 278
Sidis, Boris....25, 87, 213,
   217, 222, 262
Smith, Dr. A. H. 164
Smith, Dr. Geo. Carroll 127
Spinoza 15
Spurzheim 131

INDEX OF AUTHORS

	PAGE
Stapfer	349
Starbuck	269
Strahan	321
Strauss, D. F.	338, 348, 349, 378
Sully	82, 83
Swedenborg	94, 367
Tacitus	10
Tauler	385
Taylor, Isaac	299
Tennyson	307, 315
Terence	378
Tertullian	296, 303
Thomson, I.	305
Thomson, W. H.	92, 140
Thomson, W. M.	349
Traub	356
Tuckey, Lloyd	41, 71
Tylor	359
Tyndall	21, 61
Verrall, Mrs. A. W.	211
Verworn, Max	218, 219
Virchow	179
Voltaire	86
Von Bunge	134
Von Hartmann, Edouard	16
Von Jhering	161
Von Lilienthal	73
Wagner	145
Weber	14
Webster, Daniel	193
Weininger	329
Weissmann	134
Weizsäcker	364, 365
Wesley, John	299, 367
Wilde, Oscar	139
Winslow, Forbes	96
Wundt	109
Wycliffe	385

INDEX OF SUBJECTS

	PAGE
Absent-mindedness	203
Affinity	37
Agitation	68
Agnosticism	295
Agoraphobia	214, 283
Agraphia	196
Alcoholism	36, 128, 134, 136, 184, 243
Amnesia	80, 202, 207, 212, 216, 236
Amulet	94, 302
Anemia	163
Anesthesia	230, 236
Anger, effect of	61, 403
Animal, capacity for the inhibition of pain	92
Animal organism	17
Anti-toxic substances	19
Aphonia	207, 236
Apostolic phenomena	94
Ataxia	257
Athletics	156
Auto-hypnosis	95, 224
Auto-intoxication	252
Automatic action	17
Automatic writing	202, 210, 211
Automatism	231
Auto-suggestion	93, 99, 100
Auto-suggestion, method of treatment	106
Auto-suggestion, experiments	412, 413
Auto-suggestion, aid in literary composition	101
Baldness	171
Beauchamp, Miss, case of	25, 205, 215
Bed-wetting	244
Blindness, hysterical	208, 209
Blood poisoning	279
Blues	403, 413
Brain	140, 182
Brain fag	157
Brain lesion	193, 194
Brain tumor	197
Brain-worker	177
Buddhism	11, 280
Catalepsy	230
Cell	179, 180
Character	55
Charm	94
Child suicide	321
Children, overworked	140, 143
Cholera	121
Chorea	122, 264
Christ's law of prayer	311
Christian Science	10, 12, 58, 103, 273, 293, 379
Christianity	150, 280, 377
Church, healing work of	6, 297, 301, 371
Civilization, effects of	133

INDEX OF SUBJECTS

	PAGE
Claustrophobia	283
Clergyman, duties of	157
Climate, affecting nervousness	173, 175, 176
Cocainism	241
Coffee	174
Cold hands	403
Compensation for services	6
Competition	397
Complex	252
Confession	248, 325
Consciousness	20, 22, 200
Constipation	45, 406
Control of children	43
Conventional religion	381
Co-operation necessary between physician and patient	56
Co-ordinate muscular movement	256, 257
Coughing	46
Counter-suggestion	64
Creed	384
Crime by hypnosis	72
Criminal cases of hypnosis	73
Crystal-gazing	202
Cures made by suggestion	53, 54
Death	274
Degeneration, organic	46
Delirium of fever	22
Delusion	121
Demoniacal activity	296, 297
Diagnosis	5, 54
Dictator in hypnosis	224
Dipsomania	243, 244
Disease	18
Disease, transmission of	129
Dissociation	24, 87, 204, 205
Divorce	139

	PAGE
Dogma of modern psychology	309
Dormant powers evoked by suggestion	70
Double personality	202, 203
Dream	78, 79, 82, 85, 228
Drowning, mental activity when	22
Drugs	52, 174, 232
Dysmorphobia	284
Ecstasy	94
Ecstatic state of Hindu Mystics	225
Egotism	55
Electrical machine	64
Electricity	5, 49
Eloquence, fostered by auto-suggestion	101
Emmanuel Church movement, religious and scientific principles of	1, 7, 9, 12, 13, 57, 108, 383, 414
Emotion	38, 62
Epilepsy	214
Ereutophobia	284
Ether	17, 228
Etherization, suggestion in surgery	47
Evidence of unconscious mental action	16
Evolution, spiritual	39
Excitement	63
Exorcism	299
Exorcist	361
Eye-strain	3
Faith, as a therapeutic agent	44, 53, 54, 65, 288, 289, 293
Faith-healing	103

INDEX OF SUBJECTS

Fanatic	98
Fatigue	197, 198
Fatigue, hypnotism for	78
Fault-finding	396
Fear	63, 266, 271, 281
Fetichism	306
Fever	163
Finger-nails, biting of	69
Fish, change of color	92
Food	172
Friendship distinguished from love	36
Functional nervous diseases	2, 4, 48, 108, 126
Gastric disorders	264
Genius, works of	28
God cures by many means	3, 4
Gospel, resources of	336
Habit	145
Habit neurosis	252
Habit spasm	254, 250
Hallucination	230
Happiness	148, 160
Healing power of God's Spirit	67, 68, 355
Healing in early Church	295
Healing ministry of the Church	380
Healing wonders of Christ	338
Health and happiness the portion of God's children	292, 381
Health of soul and body through the religious life	300
Health class supported by voluntary offerings	6
Heredity	125
Hydrophobia	121
Hypnagogic state	227
Hypnosis	41, 42, 65, 81, 207, 219, 220, 222
Hypnosis in animals	218, 219
Hypnosis, elevating to the moral faculties	73, 85, 89
Hypnosis, experiments in	74, 75, 83
Hypnosis, limited power in insanity	246
Hypnosis, three transitions	229
Hypnotism, public exhibitions denounced	273
Hypochondria	96, 120
Hypochondriasis	238
Hysteria	42, 112, 207, 208, 236
Imitation, law of	324
Incompatibility	131
Infinite Spirit	38
Insanity	201, 351
Insomnia	48, 66, 240, 312
Inspiration	27
Instinct	16
Intercessory prayer	315
Intermarriage	131
Intoxication	165, 166
Isolation	262, 264
Jew	125, 154
Joy	294
Key to religion of Christ	377
Kindergarten	141
Kingdom of God	376
Knee jerk	187
Laughter	392
Leprosy	345

INDEX OF SUBJECTS

	PAGE
Library, Emmanuel	54
Literary composition	25, 26
Lockjaw	184
Locomotor ataxia	184, 250, 255
Longevity	155, 177
Love	34, 36
Luxury	146
Magnetism	221
Mania	122
Mannerism	98
Marriage, subconscious basis	37
Massage	49
Masturbation	69, 143
Materialism	8, 153
Mechanical theory of the world	153
Medicine, see also *drug*	2
Meditation	152
Melancholia	118, 321
Memory	21, 212
Memory, conscious and subconscious memories distinct	25
Mental disturbance followed by disease	402
Mental healing, see *psychotherapy*.	
Mentality	92
Mesmerism	77, 221
Metaphysical healing	103
Microbe	18
Mind, power of	2, 46, 62
Mind, blindness	196
Miracle	311, 341
Monomania	121
Monophobia	283
Monotony	158
Moral education of children	144
Moral malady	5, 49
Moral obliquity caused by drugs	241
Moral regeneration	57
Morbid conditions created by fear	121
Morphia	168
Morphinism	241
Motor aphasia	196
Motor exercises	258
Mountain climbing	35
Mourning	395
Movements, normal and abnormal	255
Multiple personality	203, 205, 214
Muscular movement	254
Muse, the	27
Mysophobia	214
Mystery in religion	38
Nature, healing power of	292
Nausea	47
Neo-platonic ecstasy	94
Nerves	185, 187, 188
Nervous disorders indications of organic disease	5
Nervous disorders and moral origin	351
Nervousness	48, 111, 133, 177
Neurasthenia	98, 111, 157, 206, 237, 238
Neurologist	65
Neurosis	110, 123
New religion	378, 379
New Thought	336, 379
Nirvana	280
Nocturnal paralysis	264
Noise	161

INDEX OF SUBJECTS

	PAGE
Nomenclature of nervous diseases	108
Oil, anointing with	364
Opium	168
Pain	19
Paralysis	45, 68, 236
Paranoia	263
Paresis	46
Passive prayer	317
Patent medicines	51
Peace	376
Personality of physician	5, 342
Personality, diseases of	5
Personality, see *double multiple*	25
Persuasion — suggestion, Dubois	60
Phagocyte	19
Phantom tumor	115, 208, 209
Phenomena, psychological	27
Phobias	281
Physician's responsibility	156
Physician, moral relations with patients	50
Physician of the soul	20
Physiological psychology	49
Placebo	64
Poise	411
Post-hypnotic suggestions	226, 230
Poverty	273
Powers for good	15
Prairie insanity	160
Prayer	302, 309, 312, 317
Prayer, marked characteristic of movement	8
Psychasthenia	115, 116, 122, 206, 213, 239
Psychical influences in combating disease	52
Psycho-epileptic attacks	248
Psychology	6, 14
Psychopathy	237
Psychotherapeutic procedures	247
Psychotherapy	4, 248, 260
Ptosis	252
Raja-Yoga	103
Rationalizing of religion	38, 39
Record	5
Recuperative energy	19
Re-education	238, 248, 251, 254
Reflection	26
Relic	293
Religion	8, 38, 151
Religion, possesses the greatest of all therapeutic agents	58, 59
Rest cure	49
Rest on Sunday necessary	160, 161
Ricin poisoning	183
Salvation	150, 378, 384
Schools, American and German compared	142
Science	13
Séance, hypnotic	226, 229
Secret of Christ's power	354
Secret of health	150
Sedatives	48
Selfishness	351
Self-suggestion	97
Self-will	99
Senile dementia	184, 246
Sensory aphasia	196

	PAGE
Sexual aberrations	236, 237
Sexual selection	36
Sexual vice	138
Shock	47
Sickness no evidence of sin	350
Silent suggestion	64
Sin	67, 351, 394
Sleep defined	227
Sleep, hypnotic and natural	77, 78, 81, 225, 227, 228
Sleep, interpretation of	198
Sleep, mental activity in	86
Sleep, narcotic	17
Sleep, perception of time in	32
Sleep, tendency of injured animals to sleep	92
Sleeping on a problem	27
Sleep-walking	69
Social movement in Church	372
Spasm	244
Specialist	3
Spectacular cures not desired	54
Speech, rapidity of	175
Spirit, Universal	28
Spiritual energy	67, 68
Spiritual life	7
Spiritualism	293, 336
Stage-fright	99, 101
Stammering	69
Stigmata	95
Stimulant	173
Stimulation of music, color, praise	401
St. Vitus' dance, see *chorea*.	
Subconscious mind	15, 19, 22
Subconscious mind, activity of	29, 91
Subconscious mind consists of	201

	PAGE
Subconscious mind, diseases of	199
Subconscious mind, functions of	20, 28, 29, 34, 38, 42, 43
Subconscious memory, examples of	22, 24
Suggestion	40, 44, 47, 52, 65, 66, 69, 70
Suicide	320
Suicide, effect of climate on cannot be proved	324
Suicide, legal and social penalties for	331, 334
Suicide, statistics of	324, 325
Superstition	297
Summer favorable to crime	161
Sunstroke	162
Surgery, suggestion in	47
Swearing	99
Tea	174
Teeth	171
Telepathic	65
Telepathy	315
Temperament	392
Temperance	135, 333
Threshold of consciousness	201
Thought	55
Time, perception of the lapse of	31, 33
Time sense	32
Tobacco	174
Tongues, "speaking with"	94
Tonic	49
Toothache	46
Traumatic neuroses	162, 213
Trust	295
Truth	378
Tuberculosis	1, 46

INDEX OF SUBJECTS

	PAGE		PAGE
Tuberculosis Class	1, 2	Vis medicatrix naturæ	18
Tumor, see *phantom*.		Vocabulary	197
Universal Spirit	42	Waking suggestion	64, 226
Unrest, cause of	396	Will	55, 103, 250, 255
		Work	288
Vedantist philosophy	94	Worry	277, 401
Venereal disease	137	Worship	152
Vice, secret of freedom from.	67		

BIBLIOLIFE

Old Books Deserve a New Life
www.bibliolife.com

Did you know that you can get most of our titles in our trademark **EasyScript**[TM] print format? **EasyScript**[TM] provides readers with a larger than average typeface, for a reading experience that's easier on the eyes.

Did you know that we have an ever-growing collection of books in many languages?

Order online:
www.bibliolife.com/store

Or to exclusively browse our **EasyScript**[TM] collection:
www.bibliogrande.com

At BiblioLife, we aim to make knowledge more accessible by making thousands of titles available to you – quickly and affordably.

Contact us:
BiblioLife
PO Box 21206
Charleston, SC 29413